One More Time

One More Time

A Journey of Love and Loss

Gloria Fox

Wisdom Moon Publishing
2016

ONE MORE TIME
A JOURNEY OF LOVE AND LOSS

Published by Wisdom Moon Publishing LLC

www.WisdomMoonPublishing.com

ISBN 978-1-938459-45-0 (softcover, alk. paper)
ISBN 978-1-938459-47-4 (eBook)

LCCN 2015952846

For Sylvan and Erica

Preface

I began keeping a journal in 2007, when my husband, Sylvan, died, after we had been together for sixty years. I wrote ceaselessly about the grief that consumed me and left me wondering whether there was any reason to go on living. I sought solace in trying to preserve the beauty of the life I had lived with Sylvan by encapsulating it in words. What emerged from my writing, beyond whatever cathartic benefits it produced for me, was a remarkable love story, unique in innumerable ways—a story that I thought would appeal to anyone who has ever searched for love, regardless of the outcome. It was then that I considered the possibility of publishing what I had written.

When I started writing, I thought my narrative would be limited to the years that Sylvan and I shared together; as I continued, I realized that it would be incomprehensible unless I included background on how I had become the person I was before I met Sylvan at Juilliard—a troubled teenager from an isolated mining community in northern Canada, alone in New York. Writing that part of my story would be a formidable undertaking.

Because I had forgotten and repressed so much about my early life, most of what I knew was drawn from stories told to me by my brothers in later years. Although I questioned the accuracy of their sometimes-conflicting accounts, they were my only source, other than my own few hazy recollections and some tattered photographs. I tried to combine all of these strands into an account of that early period. The process of trying to reconstruct a description of that time sometimes unexpectedly triggered a fleeting memory of an incident or simply a feeling that had previously been unavailable to me. These recollections became significant, often painful, additions to the picture.

Having experienced repeated losses during my childhood, I didn't dare imagine a future in which I would discover a world of hope and fulfillment. Yet that is what occurred when I met Sylvan and my life began to become richer than I ever could have dreamed. We always looked back at our meeting as a kind of miracle; and the development of our relationship was miraculous in its own way. We knew that few people are fortunate enough to enjoy a life together for sixty years.

Our love grew even as we both changed and matured in our own ways. We each changed our professional goals: Sylvan became a journalist, while I became a psychiatric nurse. However, our philosophy of life was a constant that always bound us together. It was based on our belief in each other's intrinsic value, unwavering in spite of what were often disheartening circumstances. We wanted to explore the world, regardless of the risks that entailed; and so we often took chances, refusing to settle for the easier route when we faced a crossroad in our lives. The choices we made took us outside the United States, to France, Israel, and Vietnam, where we discovered other cultures and experienced great pleasure and excitement.

Our lives were enriched by our daughter, Erica, who, in spite of having rather unconventional parents, emerged to become an adult for whom we could not have felt greater love and pride.

Sylvan's talents as a journalist, increasingly recognized throughout his career, led to his becoming one of the most respected members of his profession and to being awarded a Pulitzer Prize for his reporting. His success, however, came with a toll, given the exceptional commitment that was demanded of him. He learned that the prestige of being on a major newspaper does not come without a price. Not only was his work the significant theme in much of his life, but it directed the course of much of the family's personal life as well.

My own career in nursing, while rewarding and successful, traversed an arc that I hoped could bend to the demands made by Sylvan's work, and to what I believed were Erica's needs. Although I allowed for interruptions in my work life, my interest in psychiatric nursing and nursing education continues to this day.

What brought Sylvan and me together originally—studying the piano at Juilliard—evolved into a leitmotif in which music became a lifelong, shared enjoyment. Each piece of music, whether we played it or listened to it, always carried the memory of how we experienced it together. I still cannot listen to any musical work without its bittersweet association.

In 2007, my life, which began in sadness and loneliness, and reached peaks of joy as a wife and mother, seemed to return to the original bleakness from which I had escaped. Sylvan's death ended the story of the two of us, but I was still here. As I struggled to deal with the loss of Sylvan and of who I now was, I learned that loss and the way one deals with it as a child are not the same seventy years later. Not only does loss assume different shapes for each person, but it differs for the same person at different times. The outgrowth of the journal I kept was this memoir, which could not end with Sylvan's death. In the final chapter, I present my view of a fractured world in which I have yet to heal.

There were so many beautiful memories. I wish I could live them again, one more time.

There are two people without whom this story would never have been written: my daughter, Erica Fox, who has encouraged me, supported me throughout my often faltering attempts, and undertook the job of providing her skillful editing, and my therapist, Brian Mahon, who patiently accepted me, understood me even in my most troubled moments, and guided me through the difficult self-examination the book demanded.

What both Erica and Brian gave me was essential not only to my writing this book but also to rebuilding my sense of self. I can only reciprocate by offering my love and deep gratitude to both of them.

I would also like to thank my brother, Don Endleman, who died in 2015, while I was completing this book. Over many hours, he provided me with a wealth of information I would otherwise not have known about the early history of our family.

Wendy Salinger led a seminar in memoir writing that I attended at the 92nd Street Y, in New York. Her encouragement and astute criticism of the first chapters of my manuscript gave me the incentive to persevere.

Thanks are also due to the dear members of my book club, who were determined to read my manuscript in its unedited state and gave me their feedback. Their enthusiastic response was immeasurably helpful.

I am also grateful to my friend Elaine Zimbler, who suggested in the early stages of my mourning following Sylvan's death that resuming a part-time professional position might be therapeutic. She was correct. I am grateful as well to Margery Garbin, who unhesitatingly gave me the opportunity to do so. They both were instrumental in my regaining enough confidence in myself to undertake writing this book.

Finally, I would like to thank my editor at Wisdom Moon Publishing, Mitchell Ginsberg, for bringing my manuscript into the world.

Chapter 1

I entered the world in Sudbury, Ontario, a year to the day after the stock market crash of 1929. As a child, I was told that this iconic event, which heralded the Great Depression, marked the division between the good times that had existed before, within our family and the world, and the grim circumstances that followed. My father, Harry Endleman, who until then had had a profitable business in raw furs and a large investment in stocks, was destroyed financially. He lost all the money he had invested in the market, and then found his fur business just about wiped out as the demand for furs disappeared with the collapse of the economy. For a few years he tried unsuccessfully to develop the mineral resources in several properties he owned in northern Ontario, but that brought him no income and left him further in the hole. He went from being one of the more well-to-do members of the community to being unable to support his family, which consisted of my mother, my four older brothers, and me. Saul was older by ten years than I was; Victor, by eight years; Robert (Bob), by seven years; and Don, by four years.

Because I was told repeatedly as a child that everything changed for the worse when I was born, my fertile imagination led me to believe that there was a causal relationship between my birth and the beginning of the Great Depression. Comparisons were constantly being made between the times of plenty that the family enjoyed before I came on the scene and the austerity that existed afterward. "Before you were born, we were able to do. . . Before you were born, we had. . . Before you were born, we didn't have to worry about..." I began to feel responsible for every woe that ever befell us, and concluded that my birth had brought disaster upon the family, if not the entire country. Quite a burden for a little girl.

My mother, I was told, greeted my birth with delight; I was, after all, the first girl after four sons. My father, however, was disappointed because I dashed his hopes of having a family hockey team.

Sudbury, in northern Ontario, had a population of about eighteen thousand at the time, and was at the center of a number of large nickel and copper mines owned by the International Nickel Company and the Falconbridge Company. In addition to the mines, there was a smelter nearby with three huge smokestacks that were almost constantly belching sulfurous-smelling black smoke. It destroyed all the nearby vegetation, leaving the immediate area looking like a moonscape. In those years of the 1930s and 1940s, there were virtually no regulations on the emissions of industrial operations, a situation that eventually changed, but only after everyone had been exposed to years of poisonous contaminants. I still remember the acrid smell of sulfur when the wind blew in the right direction. I'm surprised that anyone emerged unscathed by that toxic environment.

Beyond the area affected by the fumes of the smelter was dense forest composed predominantly of evergreens, jagged outcroppings of rock that are characteristic of the Laurentian Shield of northern Ontario, and innumerable small lakes of pristine beauty. Tolerable during the summer, it was difficult to live in during the long winter, when the frigid air made breathing painful and no amount of heavy clothing could protect you from the piercing frostbite.

Most of Sudbury's businesses and services were in some way connected to the mines, which meant that when the mines were doing well, the town flourished. The population was a mixture of English-speaking and French-speaking Canadians. These two groups had minimal contact with each other, a situation a Canadian author at the time described as "two solitudes." The term *English Canadian*, in contrast to *French Canadian*, was something of a misnomer, since it included people of every ethnicity—Finns, Poles, Irish, Italians, Germans, and anyone else who was not French-speaking. Almost every ethnic group and religion was represented in Sudbury, including about forty Jewish families, of which we were one.

Our home was a stone bungalow that when it was first built must have been an outstanding addition to the neighborhood; by the time I was born, it was badly in need of painting and a good many repairs. I don't remember how many rooms there were or where I slept, although I do remember that my four brothers shared a bedroom. I also remember that in the center of the large living room, close to the stone fireplace, was a polar bear rug, which, according to the story I was told, my father shot in Alaska during the time he spent there as a young man. I can still feel the rough, scratchy fur of the bear's head, against which I laid mine as I stretched out on his grayish-white pelt. This was my special place, where I could dream, oblivious to the activity around me.

The room that was most intriguing to me lay behind heavy, sliding oak doors that we were not allowed to enter without my mother's permission. It housed my mother's most treasured possessions: a highly polished black upright piano; stacks of music scores; her Victrola phonograph on a heavy table; and a large collection of classical records. It was in this room that my mother introduced me to the piano at about the age of three. I was enchanted by the magic of my hands touching the ivory keys and producing delightful sounds as I tried to imitate the beautiful music that my mother drew from the instrument. It was the beginning of a love affair with the piano that continued throughout my life. Playing for others was another matter. In a picture taken when I was three or four, I am seated at the piano with my legs dangling awkwardly, looking like I'm about to break into tears. I am told that I was playing the piano before I was able to walk, although I suspect the story was somewhat exaggerated over the years.

We had a big yard in front of our house with an untended lawn and a lot of trees, mostly elms, poplars, and maples, which provided welcome shade in the summer. An even bigger yard ran the length of one side of the house. It was here that we made a skating rink every winter, where we all developed our skating proficiency and where endless hockey games were played between my brothers and their friends. I was the final recipient of the black hockey skates that had been handed down from one brother to another. They came to me in hopelessly shabby condition from years of wear, and they were so ill fitting it was a wonder I was able to skate at all. I dreamed of having a pair of beautiful white skates like those worn by female figure skaters, but the family's frugal circumstances made that impossible.

During a heavy winter snowfall, it was a favorite project of my brothers to make an igloo in the back yard. There was always enough frozen snow to make a fine structure that was just big enough to accommodate one small person—me—who had to squirm through a small opening to get inside. I loved being ensconced in this icy cocoon, away from the eyes of everyone, in complete silence. The igloo retained its architectural beauty for months until the spring thaw led to its demolition.

What I remember most clearly from that yard are the lilac bushes that grew in the springtime in untended proliferation along one side of the house. Among my most vivid memories of my early childhood is of retreating to a place under the boughs of the bushes, where, with my legs folded against me and my arms tightly wrapped around me, I could be enveloped by the lilacs' sweet fragrance, completely hidden from sight. How many hours did I spend there, dreaming dreams I don't remember? Could I possibly have imagined a future of love and excitement in cities around the world? Although it seemed a contradiction that I wanted to be unseen but also feared being left alone, the two impulses were not really in opposition to each other: I wanted a place to hide, but I also needed to know that someone would seek me out and find me.

My brothers were my closest companions, each one occupying a special place in my life. Saul was a star hockey player, fun-loving, outgoing, and happiest when he was outdoors. Yet, in addition to being the consummate athlete, he loved to play the violin. As the firstborn, and because he shared many of my father's interests, he was the golden boy of the family.

Victor, always tall for his age, was more than six feet when he was not yet sixteen. He was thin, with an exceptionally handsome, fine-boned face. Contemplative, sensitive, very intelligent, and with a lively imagination, he played the piano and the saxophone. He was the most attentive to me of all my brothers, patiently telling me stories when I was afraid to be alone in the dark at bedtime, and spending hours building me a dollhouse because he knew how thrilled I would be with this plaything, which my family could never afford to buy. While I felt loved by all my brothers, Victor occupied a special place as my favorite.

Bob distinguished himself as an outstanding student from an early age. He was extremely competitive with his classmates and especially with Victor, only a year older than he. Bob was very proud when he was able to skip a year in primary school, thus putting him in the same grade as Victor, and able to compete for being first in the class. Bob, or Bobby as he was known then, was determined to outdo all of us in school and at the piano, if not in athletics.

Donald was the mischievous one. He excelled in sports and decided that he would distinguish himself, contrary to my mother's wishes, by being the only member of the family not to play a musical instrument. He, too, was a fine student, but he had to contend with the fact that his teachers had all known the outstanding achievements of his older brothers, and thus were probably a little weary of the Endleman boys by the time Don arrived.

Then there was me, the only girl in the family. I was probably what someone today would consider precocious. With everyone around me an avid reader, it was not surprising that I began to read at a very young age, and I was interested in hearing all about what my brothers were learning in school, which they freely shared with me. By the time I started school, I was bored with the arithmetic and spelling drills that filled most of the day, and for whatever reason, I found making friends difficult.

The long winters in Sudbury forced us to be resourceful in creating indoor entertainment. I remember games like variations on blind-man's bluff displaying the imagination of whoever was the inventor and therefore the rule-maker and referee. Bob was the most imaginative in making up board games, skillfully using paper, cardboard, and pieces of odds and ends. And then there were construction projects, which usually involved the cooperation of several members of the family. The musical instruments that all of us—except Don—were studying were a continuous source of enjoyment. In impromptu recitals, we were each either a performer or part of the not-always-appreciative audience.

Don could not avoid being recruited as an audience member, until the call of a hockey game beckoned. My mother was often an enthusiastic participant in our musical ventures, happy to see the results that her endeavors had produced in her offspring.

All my brothers had paper routes when they were growing up. It was not an easy job for a youngster during the hard winters, making your way on icy streets before dawn to pick up a heavy load of papers, and then trudging from house to house to deliver them, but it brought in some much-needed income at the time. I think they had these jobs during the period when my father had completely run out of resources; thus, any amount of money, no matter how little, was welcome.

Although money was scarce, I don't remember ever thinking we were poor. There was never a time when we didn't have food on the table, always nutritious if not sumptuous. All the other families I knew seemed equally unable to afford anything but the barest necessities; after all, it was the midst of the Depression.

My brothers and I were reasonably well dressed, since my mother, an experienced seamstress, could repair and alter the clothes that were handed down from one brother to the next. When my brothers had all outgrown something, my mother adeptly salvaged the usable material and turned it into wearable skirts and jackets for me. The only time I was aware that some people had more money than we did was when a package arrived from an aunt in New York containing clothes that her daughters had outgrown or grown tired of wearing. I resented the people who had sent us the hand-me-downs and hated the idea of wearing any of their clothing.

My parents seemed a most unlikely couple, from different backgrounds and with completely different interests. My mother, Rose, whose parents had emigrated from Russia, grew up on the Lower East Side of New York. She took advantage of the cultural opportunities that were available in the city, managed to study piano and voice, and as a young woman began a career giving private piano lessons. She went to the theater, was an ardent reader, and, from what I could gather later, led quite an independent life, considering that this was during the First World War.

My mother's brother Nathan, who knew my father—I think through some connection in the fur trade—introduced them to each other when my father was in New York on a business trip. This attractive, vivacious young woman made enough of an impression on my father that he quickly invited her to visit

Sudbury to see the wonders of northern Ontario—in the summer, of course. The prospect of such an adventure must have been appealing, because she accepted his invitation, and, accompanied by her sister-in-law as chaperone and loaded with all the necessary clothing for hiking in the bush, made the long and arduous train trip.

I don't know how long she stayed in Sudbury or how long afterward my father proposed to her, but she accepted, in spite of the great differences in their interests and personalities. I can only imagine that the idea of starting a new life in a faraway place, with a young man who could provide her with luxuries that she hadn't known before, must have seemed very romantic, even though it meant giving up so many of the important elements of her life: concerts, the theater, lectures, good libraries, not to mention her parents and siblings.

I have no idea how much she missed New York in later years or whether she regretted what she came to see as an ill-fated decision to start a life in such an alien environment. I remember that when I was very young, as a way of maintaining contact with New York City, she subscribed to *The New Yorker* magazine and listened every Saturday afternoon to the Metropolitan Opera broadcasts that were transmitted over the local radio station. And, of course, she had her piano and her Victrola.

My father, Harry, had immigrated alone as a teenager from Lithuania to Canada. I know that he had been orphaned, but I never learned the circumstances or how he managed to get to Canada by himself. Like so many immigrants, he seemed unwilling to reveal details about his past. When he arrived in Canada, a relative provided him with a place to live and a year or two of additional education. Then, he was off on his own to find adventure, a search that took him as far as Alaska to join the legions of miners panning for gold, a pursuit that brought him little success.

There were other exploits in Alaska, including working briefly for an uncle who, according to the tangled tales I heard from my brothers, operated a saloon/brothel in one of the mining towns. At some point during those years, he shot the polar bear that ended up as a rug in our living room. He never spoke about how he did that. Eventually, he made his way to northern Ontario, where he was introduced to the business of buying furs from trappers to be sold to the wholesalers in Canadian cities. He had finally found a way of making a comfortable living.

My father was always most comfortable in the wilderness—the uninhabited stretches of bush and forests and endless lakes of the far north. His enjoyment of creature comforts, whether in his own home or during the trips he had to make on business, did not extend beyond a few days at a time; he wanted to spend as little time as possible in cities.

He was away from the house most of the time. I never knew why he was absent so much, where he was, or what he was doing. When he did appear, his presence was usually accompanied by muffled arguments with my mother behind closed doors. If my brothers had any knowledge of what was going on, they didn't share it with me. I remember that we had to be on our best behavior while he was there—stop giggling, be quiet; and the atmosphere was always thick with tension until he left. I came to dread his unexpected appearances. No one talked about what occurred, and I could never understand why after his visits my mother always looked as though she'd been crying. What I remember most clearly is that I developed an intense fear of my father and wished that he would stay away and not disrupt the relative calm of the family. While a photograph showing him standing formally with his four sons, his arms around the two oldest, portrays a man with great pride in his offspring, I learned from my brothers that he had great difficulty expressing warmth or affection to any of them.

When I was older, I learned that during this period my father was trying to make some money by developing the mineral rights on some property that he still owned. When that project became fruitless, he managed to get a loan that allowed him to lease a small general store in Levack, one of the mining towns north of Sudbury. It would be several years, however, before the store turned into a minimally profitable business. Throughout that time, the lack of money must have been a great source of conflict in my parents' marriage, the topic of the arguments that occurred behind closed doors.

The first of several family catastrophes struck in the summer of 1938, when my mother took Victor to Montreal for a routine operation. She made what was probably the correct decision to go there because she believed that he would receive better care in Montreal than in Sudbury. I knew that Victor had been suffering from some kind of nasal condition for which he had already had one operation, that he had not been well, and that he'd looked pale and thinner than usual for some time. I was told nothing more, neither about the nature of his illness nor about what was planned at the hospital.

They had been gone only a few days when my mother returned alone. All I could grasp was that something disastrous had happened. A black void enveloped the house, as the sounds of sobbing came from the bedroom where my mother had closeted herself. My father maintained a grim silence, and my brothers, clustered together, spoke only in hushed whispers. What had happened to Victor? Where was he? I was afraid to ask, as I sensed that it was forbidden. I heard fragments of conversations, the words "burial" and "funeral," but I was told nothing.

I have no recollection of the events that followed: how long my father remained in the house, what my mother did until she finally resumed her place in the household, or how my brothers began to return to something resembling a normal life. I remember only the aching realization that Victor was gone and I missed him terribly. I suppose at some point I figured out that this is what death meant.

Many years later, when I asked my brothers what had actually happened to Victor, they gave me the few meager details they had been told at the time. The doctors had never agreed on a definite diagnosis; there was talk of nasal polyps, or an infection, about a tumor either in the nasal passages or in the brain, and the possibility that something had gone wrong while he was under the anesthesia. Nothing was ever confirmed. All we knew was that Victor had died during surgery and the cause was not known, or, at least, not revealed to the family. His death was a searing blow to all of us, yet we each bore our pain alone. Lost somewhere in the fog of silence were implications of blame and guilt. On whom? For what? These questions, which were beyond my comprehension and remained unanswered, left me with a lingering sense of unease whenever I looked back on them.

Our lives continued, with the remaining cloud of sadness and the pinch of living frugally on the small amount of money that my father managed to earn from the store. The arguments between my parents when my father visited, which were supposed to be hidden from our view, became more heated and harder to ignore. My mother's great concern, that the family's financial situation would prevent her children from attending university, a goal that was of the utmost importance to her, was, I am sure, a major factor in their arguments. We could only imagine what occurred behind the closed doors and were left with the tension that remained after these confrontations.

Not long after Victor died, I went into the local hospital, a Catholic institution staffed by the Sisters of St. Joseph, to have my tonsils removed. The minor surgical procedure was carried out without complications except for my fighting strenuously against having the ether mask placed over my face by white-robed nuns. I'm told that I managed to land a few punches before finally being anesthetized.

A few weeks after apparently recovering from my surgery, I became ill with what was eventually diagnosed as rheumatic fever, a result of a strep infection following my tonsillectomy. I remember feeling weak and feverish and having such severe pains in my joints that I was unable to do anything but lie in bed.

Rheumatic fever is now rarely seen in developed countries because antibiotics can easily destroy the streptococcus bacterium that is responsible for the ensuing immune reaction of the illness. At that time, antibiotics were not yet available, and the only treatment was bed rest and aspirin, not always with a successful outcome.

While I had to endure the physical discomfort of the illness, I knew nothing about the most serious risk it carried: permanent damage to the heart that in some instances could lead to death. Nor could I imagine what my mother was going through: after losing one child, she now had to deal with a second child with a serious illness with potentially permanent consequences, while in a dire financial situation and with little support from her husband. I was unaware of the stress she was under as I lay bedridden, gradually getting some relief from my acute symptoms as they were replaced with a general feeling of malaise and the boredom of being confined to bed. I knew only that she was there almost constantly, supplying me with library books, drawing materials, and occasionally paper dolls, which were such a treat for me, and plying me with food that I had little interest in eating. My brothers willingly played endless games of Chinese checkers and other board games with me to pass the time and cheer me up.

As for not going to school, I was quite delighted that I would be out for some time, since I had never felt comfortable there since I first started. My formal education was put on indefinite hold, although I'm sure I was learning something from my reading and conversations with my brothers and mother.

The monotony of bed rest was broken up by the visits of Dr. Jones, our family doctor, who came to see me twice a week. He was a tall, courtly man who stood out from the other men in town, as he was always dressed in a fine wool suit and had the bearing of someone who had been an officer in the army, although he spoke in a very soft voice. When he came into the house, he brought an air of calm assurance as well as his little black bag. I can still smell the alcohol that he used to clean everything he touched.

When he drew up a chair to sit next to my bed and ask how I was feeling, he listened carefully to my responses, unlike most adults.

"I still feel so tired. My arms and legs still hurt and sometimes I have a headache."

"Are you following the rules about staying in bed?"

"Yes, but it gets boring."

"I'm sure it does. It's hard not being able to do the things you usually do. Are you drinking the milkshakes your mother makes for you? They'll put a little weight on you."

"I try to."

"And taking the aspirin as you're supposed to? If you keep up the good work, then before long you should be able to get out of bed and move around a little."

As he was taking out his stethoscope, he often commented on the books that I had next to my bed. "You like to read, eh? Like your brothers," he would say with a smile. Then it was the feel of the cold bell of the stethoscope as he placed it on my chest, first in one spot, then another, and another, listening somberly without saying anything. I always wondered what mysterious sounds he was hearing. When he finished examining my knees and wrists, pressing gently to feel for swelling, he took out a little leather notebook in which he entered his observations. He patted me on the head as he said goodbye, then left to confer with my mother in the living room. Muffled voices, then the sound of the door closing and a car pulling away. I would see him again later in the week.

After about three months of bed rest, I progressed to being allowed limited physical activity in the house if I took a nap every afternoon. Things seemed to be going well, until I experienced symptoms indicating a recurrence of the illness, a not-uncommon event when the original strep infection has not been eliminated. So I was back on total bed rest, a blow to both my mother and me. I wondered if I would ever be free of rheumatic fever.

The months that followed were a tangle of events. I gradually recovered, with minimal damage to my heart, but was still not allowed to return to school, and the family's money problems became more pressing and eventually resulted in our losing our house to debtors. In no order that I remember, my brother Saul went off to Queen's University in Kingston, Ontario; Bob graduated from high school, first in his class; Don was still in high school; and my father was still struggling to make a living from the store in Levack.

Then, in September 1939, World War II broke out and Canada joined Britain in the fight against Germany. I was frightened by the news I heard on the radio because I assumed bombs would soon be dropped on us by the Germans. Needless to say, we were not bombed, but we were hit by the impact on the family when my brother Saul, after finishing a year of college, enlisted in the Royal Canadian Air Force. I learned from Don long afterward that when Saul was about to resume his studies at Queen's University my father told him that he couldn't afford the cost of tuition and that Saul would have to go to work for him in the store. Saul chose instead to enlist in the air force. In addition to the other problems that our family was facing, we were surrounded by the insecurity and fear that every family felt during the war when a loved one was subjected to danger.

I have no clear memory of what occurred during the months that followed, only that it was a period of dark uncertainty, anxiety, and the constant presence of something threatening.

***

The early winter of 1940, when I was ten years old, is a scrambled jigsaw puzzle whose pieces—fragments of memory—I still can't put together. My mother and I were living alone in a rented house in Sudbury, because our family had been forced to move out of the home where I had lived since I was born. I knew that the move had something to do with my father not having enough money. I didn't understand what that meant, but I could sense that something terrible had happened.

My father was living in Levack, about thirty miles away, running the general store that he had opened several years before. Occasionally he would appear unexpectedly, stay for a few hours, and then disappear as mysteriously as he had arrived. I never found out what transpired during those visits, but I remember feeling relieved when he left.

My brothers were living in various places: Saul was stationed in Quebec with the air force; Bob was a student at the University of Toronto; and Donald had interrupted his high school studies to help my father in his store. We were all without the familiar home base that had previously provided us with some stability.

Because I was still restricted in my physical activity after my bouts with rheumatic fever, I wasn't in school during this time. My mother, I suspect, was overly cautious about my health after my brother Victor's death. I don't know how I occupied myself while I was at home all day, probably by reading, drawing, and playing the piano. Certainly, I had few friends, so that I had little contact with people other than my mother during those long days. All that seemed of little importance as I began to notice that my mother had become sadder than ever. I saw other changes in her behavior too, appearing slowly, almost imperceptibly. In the past she had always worn a stylish outfit when she went out; her hair was carefully arranged, and a touch of makeup finished off her perfect grooming. Now she had become unkempt, wearing the same rumpled housedress every day, and rarely left the house. A wariness that had crept over her, first of little, unimportant things, then of everything, was visible in her facial expressions and words. She said someone was coming to take her away because she'd done something for which she'd be punished. I didn't understand what she meant and couldn't find a way to ask her to explain what she was talking about, which I doubt she would have been able to do anyway. I became more and more disturbed by her behavior and by not having any sense of what was happening.

As her fearfulness increased, she grew agitated, moving from room to room in constant motion, with little purpose or apparent meaning. She gave up trying to prepare meals or take care of the household. My world, and hers, had fallen into total disarray.

I became terrified as I saw her transformed into someone I could no longer understand and no longer recognize as my mother. I was even more alarmed when one day she told me, "I have arranged with my friend Mrs. Benjamin to take care of you when they come to take me away." I could only think: how could she be planning on leaving me with someone who I always felt disliked me and would make my life miserable? There was no one I could turn to for answers as I struggled to comprehend what was happening. All I knew was that I was going to be abandoned.

Finally, one night, my mother became totally out of control. Dressed in a nightgown, she ran into the street in the snow and bitter cold. She was convinced that the police had come to get her. I can't remember who brought her back into the house or who was informed of the incident, but somehow my brother Bob came home and made phone calls to arrange for her to be hospitalized in Toronto. More confused than ever, I was still not told what was happening. I felt overwhelming panic and horror. The next image I have is of my mother, in a car, staring straight ahead, her face like that of a hunted animal. Bob is sitting next to her, as they are driven to the train station from which they would leave for Toronto. I didn't know if I would ever see my mother again, having learned from past experience when Victor died that someone could go to a hospital and never return.

There was more activity: talk of where I would live; accusations from some of my mother's friends, led by Mrs. Benjamin, that I was the cause of my mother's "nervous breakdown." I didn't know what the term meant or why she had to go to a hospital because of it, but I quickly absorbed all the blame and guilt that was heaped on me. I was convinced that what awaited me was the punishment I deserved for my transgressions. My sentence was to live in Levack with my father, a man I hardly knew and whose mere presence had always terrified me. All I could grasp was that my mother was being sent to a hospital, for some unknown reason, and I was being sent to live with my father, for whatever I had done.

Chapter 2

My worst nightmares could not have prepared me for the dismay I felt when I arrived in Levack—I don't know how—to live with my father. It looked to me like the end of the world. Not really a town, it was more of a mining camp that had been built to house the workers in the huge nickel mine. Reached by only one road that came to a dead end, it would be hard to imagine a more desolate, bleak place, a dead end by every definition. The town consisted of little more than a cluster of buildings that during the winter were barely visible above the mountains of snow, in which I thought I would be buried alive. Two unpaved roads formed an intersection at the center of town; one road led to the mine and the other to some small houses where most of the engineers, who oversaw the operation of the mine, lived. A two-room schoolhouse that served the engineers' children was a short distance away.

My father's store, a plain two-story frame building close to the intersection of the two roads, was flanked on one side by a second general store, owned by a French Canadian man, that was frequented by the French Canadian workers. The sharp division of customers in the two general stores epitomized the cultural separation between the English-speaking and French-speaking people of Canada at that time. If you shopped in one place, you did not shop in the other. Both stores carried groceries, household supplies, hardware, men's clothing, and just about everything else the workmen needed.

On the other side of my father's store was a drugstore that also served as the local post office. The newspapers from Sudbury and Toronto, as well as the mail, were brought there from Sudbury by bus each weekday, if snow didn't make the road impassable.

The largest building in town was a sprawling, ugly wooden structure referred to as the bunkhouse. It housed several hundred men, a mix of French and English Canadians, who worked in the mine. Most of them worked there as a way to get draft deferment during the war, while filling the need for labor in an essential industry. Many people, including my father, viewed the workers with considerable disdain, because they had chosen not to serve in the military. I saw the bunkhouse only from a distance, because one of the first things my father said to me was never to go near it. I imagined, at first, that it was a place of some mysterious danger, so I dutifully heeded his admonition. Only later did I discover that the men were simply miners, admittedly a grimy, not very attractive lot.

On the second floor of my father's store was the place where I was destined to live for about three years. It was meant originally to accommodate one man and consisted of only a small living room, bedroom, kitchen, and dining area. A spartan apartment with bare white walls, bare linoleum floors, and bare windows, it was totally devoid of any embellishment or suggestion of a desire to make it more comfortable. My father had lived alone here for several years when I knew him only from his infrequent and frightening visits to Sudbury. In anticipation of my coming to live with him, he had had a second bedroom constructed in what had been unused space. It was a huge room with little furnishing other than a new bedroom suite and linens for the bed. It seemed so empty, with no hint that someone could live there; but it was clean, freshly painted, and I discovered that it afforded me the privacy to do whatever I chose. A mirror over the dresser caught my reflection as I walked by: a thin, sad-faced little girl, with hair hanging down around her shoulders, dressed in worn clothes that she had already started to outgrow.

To my relief, I discovered that the piano, the sheet music, the phonograph, the records, and the bookcases with their books had been moved into the apartment from Sudbury. At least I had some remnants of what had previously constituted my life, though that did little to help me deal with the loss of my mother, the loneliness of being without anyone to console me, and the fear of being in my father's presence.

My father was a stocky man, of medium height, with steely-blue eyes, a thick shock of white hair, and what seemed to me to be a perpetually stern facial expression. Whenever he had been in the house in Sudbury, I was acutely aware of the tension and distress that his presence had caused my mother, and we had all been careful not to do anything to trigger his anger, though I never did understand exactly what my brothers and I had to do to avoid getting him angry or what would happen to us if his anger erupted. Would he strike us? As far as I knew, he never did.

In any case, I remember feeling a great sense of relief when he finally left Sudbury and we could return to our normal routines. In the magical thinking of my early childhood, I had willed him to disappear and never return.

Now, here I was living with him. Because, initially, I wondered if somehow he knew what I had hoped would happen to him, I tried to keep my distance. Yet he gave no indication of being aware of my evil thoughts, and silently went about showing me what I could do to be useful by making breakfast, washing dishes, and generally tidying up. At least it was something to occupy my time.

Since my father was in the store all day, I was alone, with interminable hours to fill by myself. I was still not receiving formal education, so I didn't have school to occupy me. I played the piano with the little music I could handle, but without instruction or supervision, I made mistakes that even at the time I knew were proof of how badly I played. When I could find no more music to tackle, or more correctly mangle, I resorted to making up tunes that defied all rules of composition. When I found paper and drawing materials, I drew pictures that in some way expressed my feelings of pain.

As much as I wanted to read, there were only a few books on the bookshelves that caught my attention, and there was no library in Levack. The *Toronto Star* and the *Sudbury Star*, to which my father subscribed, as well as *Liberty* magazine and the Canadian magazine *Maclean's* provided some additional reading material. At some point my father started giving me an allowance, most of which I spent on magazines that I could buy in the drugstore.

My father soon allowed me to venture downstairs into the store to observe the activity there, as long as I remained quiet behind the counter. It provided some brief diversion, although I never talked to anyone. I was a silent little mouse watching the customers as they did their shopping, some quickly making their purchases, others asking questions and closely examining each article before making a decision. It was the beginning of my fascination with observing the limitless variation in the behavior of people engaged in the simple activities of daily life.

There was little for me to do outside either. Taking a walk in the subzero cold, in snow that usually was more than ankle deep, was not an option. There was a skating rink in town, to which I was allowed to go for brief periods, as long as I didn't converse with anyone. I can't remember whether my father imposed these limitations or I imposed them on myself.

When my father had shut the store for the night, he came upstairs and cooked dinner for the two of us. There were usually steaks, or thick lamb chops or roast beef—always the choicest cuts, since the store included a meat department from which, of course, we could select the best of what was available. I got used to eating a diet rich in animal protein but without much in the way of fruits or vegetables, other than what came from cans. There was no conversation, except for the few words of instruction he gave me about helping to prepare the meal. The rest of the evening was spent in silence as we sat in the living room, my father with a pipe in his mouth, usually dressed in a dark flannel shirt, woolen trousers, and sturdy leather boots, reading the paper while the radio broadcast the news from the CBC and American comedy programs picked up by the local station. His silence was a frightening steel wall that kept me from saying anything to him.

Even now, I don't know what terrified me so much. I don't know what I was afraid he would do if I spoke to him. His dour expression was broken only occasionally by a faint smile in response to a particularly funny line in something like the *Jack Benny Program*.

He never said a word about my mother. It was as though she had vanished. There was no one to answer any of my questions: What had happened to her? What was happening to her now? Would I ever see her again? I didn't dare ask.

Yet he was not unkind to me. I think he was struggling with the question of what to do with me, or for me, since up until then he had had such limited contact with me; and it was the first time that he had to deal with a daughter, after being a father to four sons. In a gesture of some concern, he told me that if I ever wanted a snack, I could go down to the store and take whatever I wanted. I soon got in the habit of having a Cadbury's chocolate bar and a Coke every afternoon. I shudder to think of what all that sugar did to me nutritionally, though it did nothing to add weight to my scrawny frame.

When I look back now, I see that the man who so frightened me was deeply depressed, trying to deal with the emotional blows of the death of a young son, the devastation of knowing that his wife was suffering from an illness that he could not understand, and the transformation of his life from a financial success into a struggle just to make a living. And, on top of all that, he had me to contend with. But of course I couldn't see any of that then.

Even with the despair I was feeling, I didn't allow myself to cry except when I was alone in bed, with the covers over my head, so that no one could hear me. I gave up even hoping that I would see my mother again. I believed that nothing was ever going to lessen my feelings of being totally abandoned, help-less, and trapped in Levack.

I don't remember having much contact with my brothers during this time. If they came home to visit, it was for very brief periods. Donald was back in Sudbury, finishing high school; Bob was still at the University of Toronto; and Saul was stationed in Lachine, Quebec. I do remember the one visit that Saul made, when he was on leave. It turned out to be the last time we would see him. He briefly brought some joy into the house, with his irrepressible sense of humor and his warm affection for me, his little sister. He looked so handsome—his blue, crisply pressed R.C.A.F. uniform matching the color of his eyes. Had he grown taller, I wondered, or was it just his new military posture? He surprised me with a gift of several records of the big bands of the day—the Dorsey brothers, Benny Goodman, Glenn Miller—and he patiently tried to teach me how to jitterbug, to the accompaniment of the scratchy sound of the records on our ancient phonograph. During the few days of his visit, I felt someone actually cared about me, enough to hug me.

At some point during this period, I was enrolled in cor-respondence courses provided by the provincial government for children who lived in remote places with no access to schools. Bob must have arranged this for me, since I'm sure my father wasn't aware of this program. Suddenly, I received textbooks and other materials that were presumably appropriate for my level of study. Somebody had decided, without ever testing me, that I belonged in seventh grade, although I had not consistently attended school for several years. To my delight, I received weekly assignments that I was told to complete and mail back to the provincial agency responsible for the program, where I was assigned a teacher who would be my personal long-distance tutor. I was excited that I would finally be able to continue my education, to go to school, albeit remotely, and even more excited when I discovered that my assignments would be returned to me with personal comments from my teacher.

The work seemed incredibly easy, and I would have liked something more challenging, but at least I was doing something constructive. I impatiently awaited the arrival of the weekly package, eagerly devoured the material, and completed the assignments in less than a day. Then came the long wait until I got back the teacher's corrections and comments and the new assignments for the coming week. My teacher always gave me lavish praise for my work, giving me a sense of pride that I hadn't felt in a long time. I now had a connection to the outside world, through this man who signed his name at the end of his comments. I never got to meet him, but I imagined him as a scholarly, elderly, Dickensian gentleman sitting at a desk in a book-lined office. How far that image must have been from the truth!

I don't remember when my mother appeared in Levack, but suddenly she was there. Bob told me that the doctors thought that she was well enough to be discharged from the hospital.

All I can remember is that she looked like a ghost of the mother I had known. She seemed distracted, still terribly depressed, and barely able to take care of herself, let alone give me any attention. I found her presence even more disturbing than her absence. I couldn't bear the idea that this was who my mother had become. Even with my limited understanding, I knew that she was not well enough to be home. She had been in Levack for only a brief time, however, when, in February 1943, we received the horrific news that my brother Saul had been killed. The plane he had been flying during a training mission had crashed in the Laurentian Mountains.

I have no memories of what happened after we got the news, other than that I was not allowed to go to the funeral in Montreal and was told almost nothing about the circumstances of the plane crash. I don't know how my mother and father tried to deal with their grief. I know only that my mother had to return to the hospital. Much later, I learned from Bob that even after several series of electroconvulsive treatments, she was still highly suicidal. How did I deal with what had happened? What did I do? What did I feel? I don't remember, but experiencing yet another devastating loss convinced me that I would always be doomed to lose anything that I loved or was important to me.

Whatever flicker of life that had remained after my mother's first episode of illness was totally extinguished by the shock of Saul's death. She was gone. She no longer existed for me. I had lost her. I felt that giving up any hope of seeing her again would at least protect me from being dealt yet another emotional blow.

Somehow, my father went back to running the store, and I was alone once more in the confines of the apartment. Again, there was the awful silence that allowed no expression of feelings, no questions, no sharing of the profound grief that we were both experiencing. When I look back at that time, my thoughts are always of pain, and loss, and silence.

The interminable winter finally gave way to spring. I was able to get out of the apartment to take walks in the woods outside town. In contrast to the ugliness of Levack, the surrounding countryside had the rugged beauty of northern Ontario, with forests dominated by pine, spruce, birch, and oak, growing so densely that they seemed impenetrable.

I enjoyed tramping alone through the dense brush, surprised by the sudden appearance of a sparkling stream, and astonished when I encountered a bear that, like me, was exploring the chilly water. The silence of the woods, broken only by the cries of birds or the crackle of a bush disturbed by a small animal, was in sharp contrast to the stifling silence I was used to; this brought me a sense of peace. My walks became more extended as I became familiar with the surrounding area. I found comfort in the thought that the endless expanse of growing, living things around me could continue forever, untouched by humans, and without their fleeting existence. At the time, the trees offered me a more solid, reliable, undemanding presence than I found in any person. In adulthood, they became some of my favorite subjects for drawing and sketching.

Sometimes I wondered whether my father ever got any pleasure from having me there with him, getting to know me a little for the first time. Did he see me finally as his fifth child, even though I was not a boy? Or was I just another unnecessary burden when he had so many other problems to deal with?

What still stands out in my memory is one of the few pleasant experiences I had with my father during those years. I'm not sure exactly when it occurred, but one day he informed me that he was taking me on an overnight fishing trip. He said simply that he had made all the plans, and we were to leave the next day. I was so surprised by his announcement that all I could do was nod in agreement. The following morning, he stowed everything for the outing into the back of his pickup truck: food, cooking utensils, camping equipment, and two sets of fishing gear, which he probably hadn't used in years. My job was to prepare sandwiches for the day.

We drove for a couple of hours on unpaved roads, going farther and farther into the bush, until we finally arrived at a beautiful, crystal-clear lake. The only sign of human habitation was a little shack whose owner rented small rowboats and sold worms for bait. After getting a boat and bait, we set off on the lake. My father showed me how to put bait on the hook, how to cast the line into the water, and how to reel in a fish, if I should get a bite. He looked on approvingly when I skewered the worms on the hook without flinching. I had passed the first test. Nor was it difficult for me to sit quietly, as instructed, so as not to disturb the fish, since I was a master at remaining silent.

I was awed by the beauty of the lake: the sun, glinting on clear, blue water whose stillness was broken only occasionally by the movement of a passing fish, and the dark trees in the distance, making the shoreline almost invisible. And then, I had the exhilaration of having a fish tug on my line, and of successfully reeling him in. And this was soon repeated! My father's equally good luck made it an afternoon of excellent fishing. He seemed familiar with the lake and its surroundings; I wondered if this had been one of the properties he had owned years ago for its mining potential. I never found out.

For the first time, I saw my father not as the threatening ogre he had always appeared to me but as a man enjoying the outdoors and patiently teaching me how to fish. He looked particularly pleased when I landed a good-sized pike without assistance. Once or twice, while talking to me, he accidentally addressed me as "son," but he didn't seem to notice his error and I didn't correct him.

That evening, we made a campfire and I learned how to clean the fish and fry them over the fire. Potatoes were added to the pan to complete the dish. It was the first time I had eaten fish that way, and it was undoubtedly the tastiest fish dish I would eat in a long time. After dinner, we cleared a place under the trees and slept, tightly wrapped in our thick blanket rolls, in the chill of the open air. In the morning, we made coffee over a fire, finished off the bread and butter we had brought with us, packed up everything, and headed home. It was a unique experience, enjoying time with my father like that; unfortunately, it was never repeated.

Back in Levack, he returned to his usual withdrawn, stern self. He never mentioned the outing, and I couldn't get up the courage to tell him how much I had enjoyed it.

The months passed with a deadening sameness. By the summer of 1943, at the age of twelve, I was through with primary school. My graduation ceremony consisted of receiving a letter from a provincial government office informing me that I had successfully completed eighth grade. Now what? Where would I attend high school?

Chapter 3

Fortunately, my brother Bob was concerned enough about me to volunteer to be my guardian so that I could go to school in Ottawa, where he was on leave from the University of Toronto, after completing two years as a modern language major. He had taken a position as a censor with the federal government, doing translations of the correspondence of German prisoners of war who were interned in Canada. Having been turned down by the army because of a heart murmur, he had decided that he could best contribute to the war effort by using his skills at languages. My father unhesitatingly agreed to Bob's suggestion that I go to school in Ottawa, and I was delighted with the idea of leaving Levack for a city.

Bob made arrangements for us to live in a family's home where we would have private bedrooms, meals, and use of a piano. We had almost no contact with the people whose house we lived in; we were boarders, nothing more. It was an uncomfortable arrangement in which I felt like an unwelcome alien inhabiting someone else's territory. I enrolled in the local high school and had similar feelings among the students, all of whom seemed to know each other. I barely had a chance to become familiar with the schedule and the routine when we moved—for a reason not explained to me—to a different house, with similar accommodations, in a different neighborhood.

Moving meant that I had to transfer to a new school and deal with yet another new situation. Again, I felt like an outsider, with no hope of altering the alien image that I must have presented to other kids. Was I speaking a foreign language that no one understood? What kind of person lived with her brother as a boarder in somebody else's house, with no parents in sight, and had never attended a regular school? Not surprisingly, no one made any effort to be a friend. My exclusion was complete; I can't recall ever having more than a brief conversation with anyone.

Although it was a relief to be out of Levack, and good to have Bob close by, I was still unable to cope with my feelings of overwhelming hopelessness, of wondering whether I would ever feel that I belonged and be able to find peace somewhere. That hadn't changed. I don't think Bob could understand why I was not making friends and why I looked perpetually gloomy. At one point he suggested that I might be interested in joining a Zionist youth group, Hashomer Hatzair. After attending a couple of meetings, I could no longer stand the pressure Hashomer Hatzair exerted on its members, most of whom were considerably older than I was, to prepare to join a kibbutz in Palestine. I was not that interested in Zionism, and I was even less interested in engaging in agricultural labor in some isolated Middle Eastern wilderness. I soon ended my affiliation with the group.

I was so absorbed in my own misery that I couldn't appreciate the sacrifices Bob was making as my surrogate parent. I could only feel the discomfort of the double bind I was in: Bob was the only person I could rely on, yet I resented being dependent on him. I resented having a brother taking care of me rather than a parent, a situation that he was hardly responsible for and was certainly beyond his control. At the same time, I couldn't risk the consequences of showing any rebelliousness toward him, since that might result in yet another abandonment. It was only much later that I gave some thought to how much his social life must have been restricted by the responsibilities of acting as my guardian. I don't remember him going out for an evening with friends, or his ever going out on a date. He was always a gregarious, outgoing person, so he must have had some social activities, but I certainly wasn't aware of them.

Bob conscientiously supervised my piano practice and homework, as well as all the other parts of my life. I have no recollection of the nameless, faceless person who was giving me piano lessons at the time. Did I get any enjoyment from playing the piano? What did I think of my teacher? I know only that I was studying the piano, and like so many other events of that time, my memory of it is clouded in fog. I think that Bob was also taking piano lessons; his interest in the piano, which had begun when my mother gave him lessons, as she did me, had continued through his adult years. Although he never played very well, he enjoyed it greatly. His approach to a piece was often like that of a lion tamer facing a ferocious beast: exert a lot of energy, show a lot of bravery, and don't be subtle.

In spite of the peculiarities of my educational background, I was getting good grades in school. The one exception was a class in aircraft recognition, which during the war years was a requirement for graduation from high school. The whole student body met in the auditorium to see silhouettes of airplanes projected on a screen at the front of the room. We were supposed to be able to recognize the planes just from seeing the silhouettes, but I could never tell a Messerschmitt from a British bomber and I couldn't understand how some students, particularly the boys, were able to do so without effort. Nor could I understand why we were expected to report the sighting of a plane flying over Ottawa. Wasn't that the duty of the air force? My flippant attitude to the contrary, I worried that this inability to distinguish one aircraft from another would prevent me from graduating.

Since I had no friends to spend time with, the only recreation easily available was skating on the Rideau Canal, which runs through a large part of central Ottawa. During the winter, the canal was turned into a long skating rink that was free to the public. I usually went skating alone, or sometimes with Bob when he wasn't working. Skating was, in effect—and I guess still is—Canada's national pastime, and fortunately I enjoyed and was quite good at it. I've often thought that most Canadian children learn how to skate before they walk, an idea that was never disputed by any Canadian I've met. At any rate, as a result of my hours of practice, my skating improved considerably, although never to the level of the Olympic skaters I had dreamed about when I was younger.

Ottawa was a pretty city, with the parliament buildings dominating the skyline, many well-tended parks, and the tidy appearance of a carefully cared-for residence. It was terribly straight-laced, however, adhered strictly to blue laws, didn't offer much in the way of diversions, and was marred by a brutally frigid winter; all in all, it held little attraction for me. As I had at other times in my life, I managed to survive, but with little joy.

At the end of the school year, I returned to Levack, with no idea of where I would go next, since Bob was preparing to leave his job in Ottawa to go back to the university in Toronto. His move meant that I would have to start in a new school in September. I could only hope that Bob would come up with something; he was the only person who was willing to look for a solution to the problem of how I was going to get an education.

At least for the summer, there was some improvement in my life in Levack: my father had bought a little cabin—a camp, as it was called—on nearby Windy Lake, and I could spend most of the time alone there during the day, with my father coming out in the evening or when the store was closed. A simple log cabin with no running water or electricity, it was surrounded by woods and a profusion of wild blueberry bushes, with a rocky incline leading down to the lake. One other camp, some distance away, was the only sign of other people.

Getting to my father's camp from Levack entailed driving on a dirt road to a dock on the other side of the lake and then riding in a motorboat for about fifteen minutes. Each morning, I took my father in our boat to the dock where he had parked his truck. He would then drive to the store in Levack and I would take the boat back to the camp. In the evening, I picked him up for the trip back. He brought the daily supply of food with him. We had a well that provided excellent cold water; an icehouse, some distance from the camp, from which we carried ice; an outhouse, kerosene lamps, and a wood stove on which to do the cooking. Bathing was done in the lake. As primitive as the camp was, we had all the necessities for a simple life. I enjoyed the solitude, swimming in the lake, roaming the woods, and reading the books that I had brought with me from Ottawa. I was even feeling less tense with my father, for reasons I couldn't identify at the time. When I look back, I think it was in part because my father seemed less formidable in a setting in which he was comfortable; and he was away from the store, which caused him so many headaches. I also like to think that maybe he was glad to see me again, after my being away at school, and pleased that I liked "the bush" as much as my brothers did. In any case, we were not as bound by silence as we had been previously.

By the time the summer was over and it was time to leave for Toronto, Bob had arranged for both of us to board with a family that had a daughter about my age. The house was in a predominantly Jewish neighborhood of the city, near the university, and we had an arrangement similar to what we had had in Ottawa—we were boarders, but in this case we ate with the family. I was enrolled in the local school and for the first time was surrounded by Jewish kids. I don't know whether Bob thought that I would have an easier time fitting in—an unlikely assumption since I didn't identify myself as being Jewish—but it turned out that I was left out as much as I had been in Ottawa. I found no way to overcome the wall of exclusivity I encountered. I was reminded again that I would always be an alien, regardless of where I was.

Bob had switched his major to sociology and was so deeply involved in his program that he didn't immediately notice that our landlord and his wife were becoming concerned that my presence in the house was interfering with their daughter's ability to concentrate on her homework; I was distracting her, it seemed, because we sometimes engaged in conversation. The parents were immigrants from Eastern Europe; their hopes for gaining acceptance into the community rested on the academic achievement of their daughter, and I was endangering it.

During this time I learned about the Toronto Royal Conservatory of Music, which had a reputation as being the best school of music in the province, and decided that was where I wanted to study the piano. My father agreed to pay for my lessons, after Bob told him about my plan. All decisions of this sort typically went through a two-step process: first Bob had to give his okay, and then my father had to agree to provide the finances.

I'm not sure how I knew about the Royal Conservatory or why I felt compelled to get the best musical training available to me, but I suspect that my interest reflected the influence my mother's aspirations had on me as a child. At any rate, I was accepted into the school, where I became a pupil of Clifford Poole. He was a perceptive, accomplished pianist with a broad knowledge of music and excellent skills as a teacher. A charming man, whose love of the piano was evident, he immediately put me at ease with his warm smile and relaxed manner. He seemed particularly adept at dealing with gloomy adolescents like me. He lost no time in identifying and starting to correct the innumerable bad habits I had developed in my playing: he demanded that I pay more careful attention to the notation and the structure of the musical score that I was studying, and he insisted that I work more diligently to improve my technique. I responded with great enthusiasm to this unaccustomed challenge. The piano had become the focus of my attention and a way I could finally express myself.

It was not long after I started my lessons with Mr. Poole that our landlord asked Bob and me to find new living accommodations. Bob could have easily moved into a student dormitory, but where would that have left me? I always look back with amazement and gratitude for his unfailing willingness to assume the responsibilities of being a surrogate parent for his difficult kid sister, although at the time I could see only the most negative aspects of being supervised by an older brother.

After consulting with some of his professors, Bob decided that the best idea was to send me to boarding school. He selected the Ontario Ladies College in Whitby, about twenty miles east of Toronto. Highly recommended, the school was willing to accept me, although the term had already started. I agreed to the idea as long as I could continue studying with Mr. Poole at the conservatory. I was assured that I would be able to travel to Toronto on Saturdays for my lessons. So I was off to O.L.C., the fourth high school I had attended.

I was in awe when I first approached O.L.C. The school, housed in a large stone building that looked almost like a castle, was surrounded by well-manicured grounds with trees resplendent in brilliant autumn colors. It certainly looked more impressive than other schools I had gone to. I was greeted at the entrance by one of the teachers, who showed me inside. I was struck by the beautiful dark-wood paneling and sweeping staircase with highly polished balustrades that led to the second floor.

After a brief tour of the common rooms and the library, I was taken upstairs to my room, where I was introduced to Charlotte, my roommate and the only other Jewish student at the school. She was from Montreal and a grade ahead of me. She was pleasant enough, though I never found much in common with her except for our religious background.

There were about seventy-five students in the school, with a few in the seventh and eighth grades and the rest in grades nine through thirteen. (Ontario at that time had a five-year high school program, which has since been shortened to four years.) The school was under the auspices of the United Church of Canada, but almost every Protestant denomination was represented, as well as the Jewish faith, by Charlotte and me.

The headmaster was an ordained minister whom we rarely saw except at the daily morning assemblies. These were conducted in a large chapel and usually began with his reading of a passage of scripture; this was followed by hymns, which we sang to the accompaniment of an organ played by one of the older students; some brief prayer recitations; and finally the announcements for the day. I became very comfortable with the hymns, especially if the music was by Bach. I was less impressed with the prayers, which always struck me as vague requests that were unlikely to be filled. Since I had virtually no attachment to the Jewish religion, of which I knew little, the presence of Protestant rituals didn't seem particularly intrusive.

I discovered that most of the students had fathers in the armed services, many of them fighting overseas, and came from families that had sustained the disruptions of war. Most of the English girls had previously been in boarding schools in England but had been sent to Canada because it was safer. The students were a much more heterogeneous group than I had previously encountered, and everyone was away from the familiarity of home, which made me feel that I was not so different from everyone else. I was asked fewer difficult questions about my family than I had been at other schools, and, ironically, the discomforts shared by all of us provided me with unexpected relief.

I thrived on the classes: a rigorous program of Latin, French, history, geography, English literature, composition, science, mathematics, and, of course, physical education, which I never liked, all with only six or seven students in each class. The school day extended well into the afternoon, with an additional two hours of supervised study hall in the evening. Somehow in that crowded schedule, I found time to practice the piano in a room provided for music students. The room was tiny and tucked into the attic of the school. Practicing there was one of the few times I could have complete privacy, a luxury in short supply in a boarding school.

I also managed to get some decent art supplies so that I could continue drawing and doing small paintings. As I recall, there were no art classes, but that didn't deter me from plowing ahead on my own, which was almost as rewarding as playing the piano.

The highlight of the week came on Saturday, when I took a bus to Toronto and headed off to the conservatory for my piano lesson. I needed special permission to travel off-grounds by myself, with the understanding that a responsible adult, Bob, would meet me. My increasing enjoyment of the piano and music provided me with a fulfillment I had never experienced before. During the time I was studying at the conservatory, I began to think that dedicating myself to music could be the lifesaver that would enable me to avoid an otherwise bleak future, and perhaps I should consider it as a career.

When I was in my second year of lessons with Clifford Poole, I hesitantly asked him if he thought I had sufficient ability to support my dream of becoming a professional musician. He assured me that my talent could lead to a successful career if I was willing to devote myself with total commitment to intensive study at a first-class conservatory. But he was quick to warn me of the sacrifices that would be required, the extended hours of practice much beyond what I had ever done, and the prospect of repeated disappointments in a highly competitive field.

He suggested that if I was serious in choosing to follow this route, I could try to get into one of the top music schools, such as Juilliard, when I completed my secondary education. I was elated by his encouragement, which became a significant influence on the choices I made in the next few years.

While I was at O.L.C., I didn't allow myself to think about my mother, and never considered visiting her, although the conservatory I attended was only a few blocks from the hospital where she was a patient. I tried to survive by denying her existence, an act that I now find unforgivable. My refusal to acknowledge that she was still alive, the defense I first adopted when I was living in Levack, was supported by Bob's rarely speaking of her and, on the few occasions he did, only to tell me that she was still very sick, not responding to ECT, and probably unable to recognize me. I don't know whether he himself visited her during that time.

Then, one day he told me that the doctors had informed him that she had made some improvement and might benefit from a visit from her children; therefore, I could go see her. I can't imagine what Bob was thinking when he allowed me to go by myself, totally unprepared for seeing the inside of a psychiatric hospital for the first time, and certainly not prepared to see my mother.

One Saturday afternoon, I went alone to the Toronto Provincial Psychiatric Hospital, a large gray building that looked more like a prison than a hospital, with stone walls, barred windows, and heavy locked doors that creaked noisily when they were opened. When I was let in, and fond the reception desk, I encountered a woman dressed in a starched white uniform who fired a series of questions at me. "Your name? The patient's name? You're a daughter? How old are you?" "Almost sixteen," I lied. She looked at me suspiciously while she searched through a thick pile of papers. She told me to follow her. We went through one locked corridor after another; and at each door: snap, unlock, snap, lock. Finally: "This is her ward. She'll be in the day room." And she left.

I found myself in a large, dismal hall where patients were moving in slow motion oblivious to time and place. All I heard was a soft, moaning voice coming from somewhere nearby. I stood frozen in fear, my eyes searching the room, until I saw a gaunt, ghostly figure dressed in a shapeless hospital smock, her hair, totally white, hanging limply, her arms clasped tightly around herself. This was my mother. This was not my mother. This could not be my mother. I couldn't see. I couldn't breathe. The gray walls spun around me. I had to get out. I started to run, and somehow the doors were unlocked for me as I ran through the corridors and reached the outside, where I was able to breathe again. I managed to find a bus that took me back to school.

The following week, I reported to my brother: "I was too upset to stay and visit with her." If he questioned me about what happened, I'm sure I had nothing more to add. That was all I could say. I was angry that Bob had been so insensitive to allow me to make the visit by myself. Thinking about the episode, or my mother, was too painful. I had lost her many years ago.

My time at O.L.C. went by with the comforting regularity and predictability of daily routines, the small pleasures of winning awards for my academic achievement, and the surprise of developing some friendships, all new experiences for me. I might even have said I was fitting in.

At times I lulled myself into seeing my life enclosed by the school for the next two years, except that my interest in the piano was still driving me to set goals beyond all that. I was particularly uncomfortable with the idea that if I stayed at O.L.C., I would have to complete a total of five years of secondary education. I came up with the idea of finishing high school outside of Ontario—somewhere where I could get good piano instruction—and then applying to Juilliard. By this time I had decided I wanted to go to Juilliard rather than any other school.

When I presented this plan to Bob, he raised a number of objections. First and foremost, he thought I was making an impetuous decision, without examining the consequences. There was the problem of finding a place to live where there'd be some supervision while I finished high school; and he thought that a liberal arts college would provide me with a broader, and thus more appropriate, education than I'd get at Juilliard. He drew up a list of good colleges in the United States that he suggested I could apply to after finishing four years of secondary school in Canada. (American universities generally accepted students who had completed four years of high school in Ontario.)

Of course, I dug in my heels and wanted no part of his recommendations. In spite of the academic success I had achieved at O.L.C., I still doubted my ability to deal with the challenges of a college program. I viewed the previous acknowledgment of my intelligence as some kind of fluke, and I was sure that it would eventually be revealed as a hoax. But more important, the pursuit of my musical education had become the focus of my thinking.

We finally arrived at a resolution, probably because Bob thought that by the time I was ready to apply to college I might have a change of heart. "Okay, you can go to high school in New York. Then we'll make further plans." Bob and my father arranged to have me live as a paying boarder in the home of my uncle, my mother's brother Nathan, and my aunt Ruth, in Brooklyn, where I would complete my fourth year of high school. They agreed to keep an eye on me in addition to providing me with lodging. It was an arrangement not much different from what I had in Ottawa and Toronto, other than that I ate with the family. This was not particularly pleasant, as the parents had two young adult daughters and a son, all of whom were in the house only occasionally but whose presence always seemed to precipitate contentious arguments among everyone.

Although my father was paying my aunt and uncle a more than adequate amount for my lodgings, they made sure that I knew they were doing me a great favor by allowing me to live with them.

I had little contact with my uncle, who was usually out of the house for one reason or another; but, unfortunately, I did have to interact with my aunt more frequently. She exhibited an attitude of condescension that I think was based on my coming from what she considered an uncivilized part of the world and a family that she thought had lost all semblance of normalcy.

My aunt and uncle lived in what had once been an attractive house, but by the time I was there, it had long since seen better days.

My room, which was shabbily furnished, had once been a sunroom and probably hadn't undergone any renovation since the house was built. I didn't know why things were in such disrepair, and I wasn't particularly interested in finding out. The one thing that made the situation tolerable was that they had a grand piano, out of tune but playable, which I was permitted to use.

I think it must have been Clifford Poole who referred me to Gordon Stanley for piano instruction in New York. My memory fails me as to how I contacted him and whether I auditioned for him before he accepted me as one of his few pupils who were not enrolled at Juilliard. Every Saturday I went to his home, in Greenwich Village, where he taught his private students. Born in Australia, he was in his fifties, slender, and had a slight limp that I assumed was from polio. He had taught at Juilliard for many years, and had a reputation as a teacher who valued musicianship more than pianistic bravura. I remember how awestruck I was when I first saw the beautiful brownstone where he lived. It had an opulent salon, housing two full-size Steinways, where he taught and hosted intimate recitals given by his students. I had never seen so many books, music scores, paintings, and works of art, all occupying one splendid room. He lived alone in the house, and I, in my adolescent romanticism, thought it a shame that he had no one to share it with until I discovered that he had a male companion who was a frequent houseguest.

Every week I took the train from Brooklyn into Manhattan and walked to Gordon Stanley's house, always stopping along the way to peer into the shops displaying books and records, which I dreamed I could buy someday. I marveled at the rows of beautiful brownstones on tree-lined streets, the bustle of activity at the little food stores and cafés, the intriguing signs outside the jazz clubs; each time I turned a corner, the street seemed to hold new wonders. I fantasized about the lives of the people upstairs in the walkups of these old buildings. What were their lives like? Could I ever live as they did? These experiences, and the hours of my lessons, which absorbed me completely and went by so quickly, were my first taste of the New York that I was now determined to become more a part of.

The time I spent with Mr. Stanley, in addition to greatly improving my playing, gave me a chance to learn more about Juilliard and to attend recitals, more like master classes, that he held periodically for his students in his home. Only the most accomplished pianists performed, but there were always interesting and informative discussions and critiques afterward. Through these events, I became familiar with a large part of the piano repertoire, and also met other music students, many of whom were already at Juilliard.

Other than the trips to my piano lessons, though, I rarely went into Manhattan. Traveling by myself outside the Village frightened me: I found the noise, the press of the crowds, and the unfamiliar geography extremely unsettling.

My life during the week was in stark contrast to my Saturdays. I had enrolled at Midwood High School, in my uncle and aunt's neighborhood, where a guidance counselor had determined that I had more than the required number of credits for graduation but needed courses in American history and civics. In addition to those classes, he added a few others to fill out my schedule that I think included literature and French.

Attending Midwood was the greatest culture shock I had ever experienced. Suddenly I was surrounded by what seemed like mobs of people speaking so rapidly that I could barely understand them, and in voices so loud that I was sure they were all consumed by rage. It took me some time to decipher the Brooklyn accents, all delivered at rapid-fire speed.

But the greatest difficulty lay in making the transition from the quiet, discreet environment of a girls' boarding school in Canada to a huge, bustling public school in Brooklyn.

The most telling event occurred at the beginning of my first class. When the teacher entered the room, I rose from my seat, as I was accustomed to do. Within a split second, every student in the room was staring at me, mouth open in disbelief, as though I had just landed from another planet. I couldn't imagine what kind of terrible faux pas I had made until I learned that standing for a teacher was not customary in American schools. Once again, I was the hopelessly feckless alien.

The next encounter with this bewildering culture came when one day, at the end of a class, I was summoned by the teacher—a woman whose rasping Brooklyn speech I could barely understand—and informed that I had to report to the school's speech therapist for remedial sessions. Stunned, and not understanding the logic of it, I nevertheless did as I was instructed. Fortunately, the man I met with, after talking with me for a few minutes, quickly realized that my "speech impediment" was the distinctive Canadian way I spoke: the slow pace, the quiet tone, and the unmistakable pronunciations and inflections of Ontario. Barely able to contain his laughter, he tossed the referral into a wastebasket and assured me that I didn't need speech therapy, and should convey that message to Miss Whatever-her name-was. Over the years, my "speech impediment" disappeared.

I felt so foreign at Midwood that I made no attempt to connect with any of the students, all of whom seemed surrounded by cliques and wrapped in post-graduation plans. By this time, my goal was to get through the year, put up with the discomforts of living with my aunt and uncle, be finished with secondary school, and somehow find a way to survive. My social life while I was at Midwood was almost nonexistent; I was befriended by one student, Peggy, who I think took pity on me, spent some time with me at school, and even invited me to her home. However, the awkwardness of my not being able to offer a reciprocal invitation prevented me from developing a close friendship, though I did remain in touch with her for a few years after she went off to Vassar.

My dating experiences were similarly limited. My cousins introduced me to a couple of their friends, with whom I went out once or twice, without being interested in any of them. Those months at Midwood were certainly not the fun-filled time that other people seemed to be having then or that I heard adults reminiscing about years later.

Chapter 4

As I approached graduation, I was faced with deciding what my next step would be. I considered three possibilities. The decision was not really a matter of careful consideration, but rather of choosing the most likely way I could survive. I briefly considered applying to art school, because I had been told that I had some talent that could be developed in a studio art program; but although that choice held certain attractions, I was unsure it was a route that I wanted to follow. There was the possibility of applying to a liberal arts college, the choice that Bob had been pressing on me, which I continued to resist, because I doubted I was intellectually capable of succeeding in a demanding academic program. And then there was the idea that for years had held the most attraction, and still did: applying to Juilliard.

I'm not sure what made me believe that I had a chance of doing well at Juilliard. Maybe it was the fantasy that I had a future as a pianist, or perhaps the self-defeating idea that my likely rejection would prove to me, once and for all, that I really was incapable of ever doing anything well. Bob eventually lost patience with me for refusing to accept his advice and washed his hands of trying to influence my future. I had to come to a decision on my own.

I applied to Juilliard in the spring, while I was finishing high school in Brooklyn. Subsequently, I received a letter giving me a date in the summer when I was to appear at the school for an audition. I was told to prepare to play three pieces: one each from the Baroque, the Classical, and the Romantic periods. I selected works that were most familiar to me and with which I felt comfortable. I don't remember exactly what they were, but there was probably a Bach prelude and fugue, a Mozart sonata, and something by Chopin.

As the date of the audition approached, my anxiety grew as I feared being rejected and realized that I had few options in that event.

Actually, by that time, the only alternative would have been to accept an offer my piano teacher, Gordon Stanley, had kindly made; since he knew the head of the music department at Furman, a small university in South Carolina, he had arranged for my acceptance there if I was not accepted at Juilliard. While the thought of going to school in South Carolina didn't appeal to me, I was unable to come up with any other possibilities, since it was too late to apply anywhere else in music, art, or liberal arts. I had boxed myself into a very tight corner.

After spending most of the summer in Levack and a few weeks in Toronto, I returned to New York. My audition was on a hot, humid day, and Juilliard at that time had no air conditioning. I arrived at the appointed hour, sweating and trembling with nervousness, barely able to focus on the massive black piano at one end of the room, behind which sat the three wise men who constituted the jury that would hear my performance and decide my fate. I started with the first piece in a fog of anxiety, but before I had gotten very far, one of the judges signaled, "Enough. Go to the next piece." After playing a brief portion, I was stopped again and told to go to the last selection. It was also cut short after a few minutes. I realized that I was finished and managed to stumble out of the room. As I left, someone said that I would receive a letter indicating the jury's decision in a week or two.

When I came back to full awareness, I was certain that I had performed miserably and that the jurors' interruption of my playing was evidence of their dissatisfaction. Only months later did I discover that this was standard procedure during Juilliard auditions. There was no one to console me in my misery, or to admonish me for not being foresighted enough to make backup plans. I felt totally alone and sure that my hopes had been shattered. I went back to Levack to await the verdict in a state of total discouragement.

About two weeks later, a letter arrived informing me that not only had I been accepted as a piano major but that I had been awarded a full scholarship to cover my tuition. I was filled with a mixture of disbelief and astonishment that someone had judged that I had some worth. As there had been no one to console me when I was certain that I had failed my entrance exam, there was no one to give me a congratulatory hug now that I had been accepted; no one to exclaim: "You made it! You were accepted!" The loneliness I felt, because there was no one with whom I could share my excitement, made it impossible for me to enjoy what should have been an impressive achievement.

Although my scholarship covered my tuition, I needed money for living expenses, which meant asking my father if he would continue to support me. Because speaking to him still filled me with fear, it was only with great difficulty, after several false starts, that I asked for his help. He readily agreed, and freely discussed with me how much I thought I would need. Looking back after all these years, I regret that I was not able to fully appreciate his willingness to help me pursue my dream and that, in spite of our lack of communication, he understood how important it was for me to go to Juilliard.

I was back in New York in September, faced with the task of finding somewhere to live. From the school's listing of places for rent, I found a tiny, dreary furnished room close to Juilliard, barely big enough to accommodate a small bed and dresser. Because I wasn't familiar with the many ways to locate rentals in New York, I assumed that this was the best I would find at the rent I could afford. I shared a bathroom with several other people and I had no piano, of course, which meant that I had to schedule practice hours in the rooms available at school. As a beginning student, I was allotted the least convenient hours, from 7:00 to 9:00 in the morning and from 7:00 to 9:00 at night. I soon began to feel the fatigue and stress of practicing during those hours, and the discomfort of my living arrangements.

After a few weeks, I knew I wouldn't survive if I didn't do something to improve my living conditions. Again, I searched the student bulletin board. With a stroke of luck, I found an offer to share an apartment with a female voice student. I quickly arranged a meeting with the young woman, Juliene, who had placed the advertisement. I met her at her apartment, in a well-maintained building on the corner of Amsterdam Avenue and 113th Street, and was impressed by how comfortable and spacious it was.

Juliene told me that she preferred to sleep in the living room and that I could have the bedroom to myself—a luxury I hadn't expected. The kitchen and dining area were also available for my use; and, miracle of miracles, there was a baby grand that I could use except when Juliene needed it for her vocal practice! It was more than I could have hoped for. After agreeing on the rent, somewhat more than what I had been paying but still affordable, it took me only a few hours to collect my belongings and move in.

We soon found that, because of our divergent schedules and strong need for privacy, we had minimal contact with each other and engaged in only the briefest conversations. As cordial as we were with each other, I think we both sensed that we could never develop a close friendship, though our relationship was ideal for sharing the apartment.

As I settled into the routine of classes and piano instruction, still with Gordon Stanley, I began having doubts about my musical talent compared to what seemed like the impressive accomplishments of so many students. A number of the other pianists, many of whom were older, had already performed professionally. Some of the most talented ones, seasoned and self-confident, had come to Juilliard from other countries, using their status as students to facilitate their immigration to the United States. Considering the competition I faced, I wondered if I had made the right decision or whether I was pursuing an unrealistic fantasy.

Nor was I dealing well with the anxieties and persistent depression I'd suffered since childhood. I still had the sense of somehow being responsible for my mother's illness, and that additional disasters would befall me in the future. I wondered whether there was any hope of ever feeling happy and in my darkest moments began to think that maybe the only way to find relief was to end my life.

This was some of the emotional baggage I was carrying when I was introduced to Sylvan by Bert Bial, a bassoon major whom I met in a class we were both taking. What the class was or how we struck up a casual conversation, I don't remember. Bert was a tall, gangling fellow with unrestrained amiability and a very prominent Brooklyn accent. One day, at the end of class, he asked me if I would like to meet some of his friends in the student lounge, among them "this guy I've known since elementary school, Sylvan Fox."

I agreed, and we headed off to join a group of students who were relaxing in the lounge between classes. My eyes were immediately drawn toward Sylvan: a striking-looking young man, lean, with an athletic build, well-chiseled features, deep-set hazel eyes, and a sensuous mouth.

He was animatedly dominating the conversation of the group around him, but he stopped to greet me when Bert introduced us. I guess I was attractive enough to draw his attention, because we immediately started talking to each other and lost awareness of the other people who were there. For some inexplicable reason, it seemed that we could understand each other beyond the superficiality of casual talk—and that we both recognized the significance of our meeting.

We continued our conversation with a rapid exchange of basic credentials: I discovered that Sylvan was in his third year at Juilliard as a piano major; he told me that he was a student of Lonnie Epstein, and I told him that I was studying with Gordon Stanley. He told me that he was born and raised in Brooklyn; I told him I was born in northern Ontario and raised in a number of places in the province. With a raised eyebrow, he asked me, "How the hell did you end up here?" Startled by his abrupt question, a conversational style to which I would eventually become accustomed, I could only respond: "That's a story you may not want to hear."

I could not have anticipated then that over the next few months I would not only share that story but more details about my life than I had ever shared with anyone. As we continued talking, we were surprised to recognize in each other the same wry humor that was an intrinsic part of how we saw the world. Sylvan's air of self-confidence and poise, and a manner that was full of a wonderful buoyancy and energy, made him extremely attractive to me, more so perhaps because these qualities contrasted so markedly with my own self-doubt. His energy and passion for things that were important to him, which I first saw then, were a hallmark throughout his life.

How long did our conversation last that day? Long enough that by the time it ended, Sylvan had asked me if I would like to go to a concert with him later that week. I was elated that he had invited me, and eagerly looked forward to seeing him again. After that first short meeting, we were both aware of our remarkably strong attraction to each other.

The concert was a piano recital at Carnegie Hall that we attended with student tickets, seated of course in the uppermost reaches of the auditorium. While I don't remember who the pianist was, he was one of the major soloists of the time, and I do remember that as much as we enjoyed an excellent performance, our enjoyment of being together was even greater.

As we talked about the concert, and our reactions to it, it was clear that we were beginning to feel comfortable with each other more quickly than we could have imagined. Years later, when we reminisced about that time, as we often did, we agreed that there was something magical about the way we knew that our meeting would significantly change our lives.

In the following weeks, we spent almost all our free time together, either just the two of us or with Sylvan's Juilliard friends, mostly woodwind players, who came from all over the country—each one extremely talented and fun to be with but with his own array of psychological problems. I grew accustomed to some of their strange habits: regardless of where they were, they were always whittling and shaping reeds, which required repeated sucking on them to test their readiness for use. I also became familiar with the terminology they used to describe the techniques, the embouchures, and the various tonal qualities that characterized individual players. As I got to know his friends—their goofiness and idiosyncrasies—I became very comfortable with them; and because I was Sylvan's partner, I was accepted with no objections. For the first time, I felt part of a social group, an entirely new experience for me.

Our little coterie often spent the evening together, having an inexpensive dinner and, later, talking endlessly at one of the local student hangouts. At that time, Juilliard was housed in one small unimpressive building on Claremont Avenue, adjacent to the Columbia University campus, in contrast to its expansive presence in the Lincoln Center complex today. Our discussions during those evenings usually ranged across the topics of current Juilliard gossip, the comparative rankings we made of faculty members, evaluations of new music that we had heard, and our preferences in the presidential contest that was beginning that fall of 1947. The strong and conflicting opinions held by the group about Henry Wallace, the progressive third-party candidate who was running for president, provided the meat for many lengthy arguments. All of this, accompanied by a lot of groan-inspiring jokes, punning, and uncontrolled laughter, would go on for hours, until someone remembered an early class he had to attend the following morning.

In the long conversations that Sylvan and I had over the following weeks, we began to reveal more of ourselves to each other. Sylvan described the complex, quirky characters in his extended family, which, in spite of their limitations, provided him with the warmth of a supportive home and a childhood of rich experiences. I, in turn, was able to talk to Sylvan about the losses and traumas of my early years, and feelings that until then I had been unable to express to anyone. For the first time, I was able to tell someone about the circumstances of my mother's removal from my life. Until then, whenever questions arose about families, I referred to having lost my mother at the age of ten, and did not correct the inevitable assumption people made that she had died. Now I revealed to Sylvan not only the facts of my mother's illness but also how I felt when she became ill, and how I had tried, in an attempt at survival, to banish her from my life. Sylvan's response was greater empathy and understanding than I had ever experienced.

We shared many of our thoughts about the importance of music in our lives, what music we enjoyed, and particularly what piano music most appealed to us. We talked about what we hoped our lives could be like in the future. It was inevitable that my thoughts about taking my life would enter our conversations. We talked about this subject at length as I tried to describe the hopelessness that, until then, had led me to believe that I could never lead a fulfilling life. At some point, Sylvan made it clear that we could only continue to see each other if I could find a way to eliminate these destructive ideas from my thinking. He asked me, "How can we anticipate what life will be like in the future if you continue to doubt the value of life itself? How could you just give up the joy we experience together and the prospect of so much more to come? How can you think of destroying all that?" His reasoning—remarkably wise for someone so young—was convincing enough that I was able to promise him that I would abide by these terms, as difficult as they seemed at the time. I am still bound by that promise.

The more I talked to Sylvan about trying to be free of my self-destructive thoughts, the more I thought that I should get professional help. Sylvan agreed that it was a good idea. After contacting one mental health clinic after another, and finding none that could give me an appointment, I finally found a reputable clinic that could schedule a meeting for me with a therapist. With much trepidation, having never been to one before, I sat down across from a bland-looking man—bland-looking clothes, bland-looking facial expression—and attempted to describe my feelings of depression. After about half an hour of talking to him, in which he asked questions like "Are things really as bleak as you describe them?" I came to the conclusion that he was completely incapable of understanding what I was saying. As I left, totally frustrated by his incomprehension, I fully expected to hear him break into a chorus of "Pack Up Your Troubles in Your Old Kit Bag." I wanted nothing more to do with mental health clinics.

Fortunately, Sylvan was able to get the name of a private psychiatrist whom one of his relatives recommended. Dr. T. agreed to overlook his usual rule about seeing patients at least three times a week and accepted me for once-a-week sessions, since that was all I could afford. For the first several weeks of my visits, I was unable to say a word to him, as I sweated through each anxiety-filled hour. He, in turn, said nothing more than an occasional "What are you thinking?" as he sat there, chain-smoking incessantly and coughing occasionally. He followed the Freudian custom at the time of having patients lie on a couch while he sat behind them, so I was unable to see his face, while he was able to see mine. I thought that was unfair. When I did see him, he looked to me like a Mafia don. Of course, being frozen with anxiety I was unable to say anything about my discomfort.

After each session, without even uttering goodbye, I left his office wondering what benefit I could possibly be getting from spending an hour with a therapist without saying a word. Somehow, after weeks of frustrating silence, something clicked and I started talking. I think my inability to speak to him was so obviously related to my early childhood experiences that it required no examination. Eventually, my sessions began to produce results that enabled me to feel more confident that I could keep the promise I had made to Sylvan.

I saw Dr. T. on and off for the next year, and began to see him not as a Mafia don but as a warm and supportive person. My work with him freed me from the worst constraints of my depression. It's hard to separate the results I achieved through therapy from the emotional growth that I experienced in my relationship with Sylvan. I think, ultimately, the two had a synergistic effect that allowed me to envision the possibility of leading a fulfilling life.

While my overall outlook was improving, I was discouraged by what I perceived as my less-than-stellar performance at the piano. Practice hours were painful and I often ended in tears as I felt unable to reproduce on the piano what I could hear in my head. Nonetheless, my piano teacher, a man with infinite patience, seemed satisfied with my progress and continued to offer me encouragement in spite of my dismal self-evaluation.

Weekdays were taken up with studies, but on weekends Sylvan became my guide as we roamed the city, about which I still knew very little. New York opened up to me as I became familiar with neighborhoods that until then had been only names: Greenwich Village, the Lower East Side, Chinatown, and Little Italy. Sylvan delighted in taking me down streets that he knew well as a native New Yorker and introducing me to the maze of the city's bus and subway systems. Riding on the upper level of a Fifth Avenue bus was as exciting as a trip down the Nile. We went to little bookshops where we could browse endlessly amid new and used books that we could actually afford. He showed me where music and theater productions were available at minimal cost. We visited museums and art galleries, where I became familiar with the amazing art that was proliferating at that time. He took me to delicatessens known for making the best corned-beef sandwiches in New York, and told me which store on Houston Street was the best place to buy smoked salmon and sturgeon. "And for God's sake, it's How-ston not Hewston!" (My Canadian pronunciations and expressions were a constant source of amusement for Sylvan for the few years they lasted.)

The city that had once seemed like a formidable opponent became an unlimited source of pleasure and excitement. But, most important, I now had the sustenance of a relationship that gave me the kind of security I had never before experienced, that made these explorations possible. The paralyzing fear that had been with me for so long was gone.

During this time, I also increased my knowledge of the musical literature, of which I knew so little. My exposure before coming to New York had been limited to hearing music broadcast on the CBC, an occasional performance of the Toronto Symphony Orchestra, and piano music at Gordon Stanley's student recitals. Now Sylvan and I were going to every recital and concert that Juilliard offered, as well as everything else we could afford at Carnegie Hall, Town Hall, and smaller settings around the city. These performances, combined with recordings that were available in the public library, allowed us to hear the outstanding soloists and orchestras of the time. In a matter of months, I had the electrifying sensation of hearing the Brahms symphonies in live performance for the first time; was swept off my feet by the ravishing Rachmaninoff piano concertos; discovered the world of Debussy and Ravel and other twentieth-century French composers; fell in love with chamber music; and was astonished by the sounds of Stravinsky, Bartok, Hindemith, and Copland—there was no end to what I had yet to hear.

Beyond the great enjoyment of listening to music were our discussions that either accompanied or followed the performance. These probably contributed as much to our musical growth as many of the classes we were taking at Juilliard. Sylvan's knowledge of music was much greater than mine, since he had had the advantage of being able to listen to all the radio stations that played classical music in New York in his childhood, having heard live performances from an early age, and, of course, being in his third year at Juilliard. On the one hand, this enabled him to lead me in understanding the structure and nuances in music that were already familiar to him. On the other hand, I could provide him with the reactions of someone who had not heard these great works before. I could tell him about the chill going up my spine as I first heard the astonishing beauty of an unexpected modulation in a Brahms symphony, an experience that for him had now been replaced by the pleasure of hearing a familiar passage. Most contemporary music was new to both of us, and we ventured into this unexplored territory together, trying to make our way through the thickets of the twelve-tone system and the complex harmonies of Bartok quartets. Every piece of music that we heard was marked indelibly with the imprint of having experienced it together. There is no piece of music I can hear today that doesn't bear that immutable association.

For the first time in my life, I was experiencing joy—the limitless exhilaration of being with someone who offered me the security of his presence. I felt safe, a feeling that is common in the early years of most people but was a newfound experience for me.

Looking back at who I was at that time, I have tried to identify what it was that Sylvan found attractive in me. Perhaps it was that I had survived a particularly difficult childhood but still had an insatiable desire to explore the world; perhaps it was my Canadian reserve and decorum, combined incongruously with eruptions of outrage over injustices of society; perhaps it was the signs of an innate intelligence waiting to be developed; the sense of humor we recognized in each other from the time we met; and of course my passion for music, equally strong as Sylvan's. Perhaps most important, there was the fact that I accepted Sylvan as he was, without any reservations, convinced that his talents and abilities would come to fruition. I think that we both saw beyond the outer surfaces of ourselves to the inner cores that were still to be developed.

By the end of the year, Sylvan was spending many nights at my apartment. It was certainly easier to spend time together if he didn't have to face the prospect of a long subway ride back to Brooklyn. And during the Christmas break, we had the luxury of having the apartment to ourselves while Juliene spent the holidays at home in Jacksonville, Florida. We were able to spend whole days and nights together without the demands of classes, and without worrying about disturbing Juliene.

Those weeks we had together were filled with the excitement of youthful sexual exploration, intimacy, and freedom that allowed us to reveal ourselves more completely to each other. As we grew closer, we began to see the world through the eyes of "us," no longer as the separate Sylvan and Gloria who had existed before. We had started on a route that we would follow for the rest of our lives, marked by the wonder of continuous exploration of each other and the world.

In contrast to the pleasures we were experiencing during that period, Sylvan's parents, in response to his increasing absence from home, began expressing concern that spending so much time with "this Canadian girl" would adversely affect his studies and his future. His father decided that he had to have a talk with Sylvan to investigate the situation and possibly bring an end to our increasingly close relationship. He asked Sylvan to come down to where he worked on Canal Street, in lower Manhattan, to have a talk with him. I, of course, was not invited. The meeting occurred in the early evening at the beginning of the worst snowstorm of the decade. I accompanied Sylvan downtown, watched the snow accumulate at a furious pace that made the streets impassable, and, feeling like the Little Match Girl, waited in a coffee shop nearby while Sylvan met with his father.

Sylvan sat down across from his father and opened the conversation. "You said you wanted to talk to me. So what's it about?"

"I want to know who this girl is that you're spending so much time with."

Sylvan tried to maintain his composure. "This girl, as you put it, is named Gloria. She's a piano student at Juilliard. We met a couple of months ago. We have a lot in common and enjoy being with each other."

Louis continued his interrogation. "It seems like you enjoy spending time with her so much that we hardly see you anymore. When was the last time you were home?"

Sylvan struggled to remain calm. "Is that really important?"

"Yeah, it's important because you're our son and we wonder where you are and what the hell you're doing. We worry about you. We worry that you're so busy with this Gloria that you're not spending enough time at the piano and not concentrating on your work."

"If it makes you feel any better, I'm doing just fine with my work and doing more than enough practicing at Gloria's apartment."

Louis looked taken aback. "She has her own apartment? And a piano? What about her family? Do you know anything about them?"

Sylvan tried to control his growing irritation. "Yes. I know enough about her family and, more important, I know she's become very important in my life."

"I hope she hasn't become so important that you're getting distracted from your studies—"

Sylvan sighed as his frustration grew. Then, drawing a deep breath, he responded: "Look, I'm not getting distracted. You know, I think it would be a good idea for you to meet her and see what kind of person she is, and that we're serious about pursuing our work at Juilliard and going on to do more. How about we both come over for dinner some evening?"

Louis hesitated briefly and then said, "I guess that would be okay. I'll talk to your mother and see what she wants to arrange. So, are you coming home tonight at least?"

Unhesitatingly, Sylvan answered, "No, Gloria is waiting for me across the street and we're going back uptown to her place. I better get going. The snow is getting heavier every minute. I'll call you in a couple of days and you can tell me when you want us to come for dinner." On that not completely conciliatory note, their conversation ended.

When Sylvan rejoined me and told me what he and his father had talked about, and the likelihood of an upcoming dinner invitation, I told him I was afraid I would be received as a disreputable hussy. "Do you really think it's a good idea?" I asked. Sylvan assured me, "Don't worry. They'll get to know you. They'll see what you're like. It will be okay."

Making our way back to my apartment was a struggle as we plodded through the snow, which by this time had knocked out most public transportation. After unsuccessfully trying to find a subway or bus, we resorted to trudging in deep snowdrifts in the middle of unplowed streets. We finally reached my apartment, hours later, having walked from Canal to 113th Street. When we got to bed that night, we basked in the satisfaction of knowing that not only had we weathered an incredible snowstorm but that we had also made some progress in dealing with the problem of parental objections.

The dinner that Sylvan had proposed during his conversation with his father was arranged shortly afterward. I was invited to his parents' home, on East 56th Street in the East Flatbush section of Brooklyn. A compact, semidetached brick house in a predominantly Jewish neighborhood, it was occupied at that time by Sylvan's parents, his grandmother, and Sylvan, when he was home. Sylvan escorted me into the house and introduced me to his parents and grandmother, as we sat down in the living room. It was a modest, bright, comfortably furnished room, obviously well cared for, that had been readied for guests by the placement of several dishes of Jordan almonds and candies, as well as several immaculate ashtrays. Sylvan's baby-grand piano, covered with stacks of music, occupied the place of honor in one corner.

Soon after my arrival, his grandmother made a quick retreat into the kitchen, where she remained for the rest of the evening. Never before had I felt responsible for driving somebody away in such short order. The rest of us sat around rather uncomfortably, trying to make small talk while verbally circling each other with caution, like animals not sure if the others could be trusted. I tried to tell them something about Levack, the isolated mining community that was my home. It was hard for them to grasp that a Jewish girl could come from someplace in Canada other than Montreal or Toronto, cities that they had at least heard of. What was my father doing in some godforsaken place like that? I detected some doubt that I was even Jewish and that my father really existed. Trying to explain the whereabouts of my mother was even more difficult. I could only say that she had been hospitalized for several years. My failure to provide any further explanation aroused even more suspicion. Talking about my mother caused me great anxiety, as it always did.

My Canadian accent probably struck them as strange, as did the slow pace and muted volume of my speech. At least I had impeccable manners, perhaps too impeccable and formal for their tastes, but we did manage to get through dinner. Sylvan and I talked about our goals of performing, perhaps in a chamber group, and perhaps of doing some teaching. We made it clear that we wanted to continue our education. That seemed to provide them with some reassurance, but I felt once more like an alien in unfamiliar territory.

Notwithstanding the limited success of my first visit, we continued to make efforts to expand our mutual understanding. I became a fairly regular guest at the Fox household, and met other members of the extended family. Before long I was introduced to Sidney, Sylvan's older cousin, who for many years as a youth had lived in the house with him. He was, in effect, an older sibling, with all the usual attachments and rivalries such a relationship entails. Sidney could already see that Sylvan's talents and adventurousness far exceeded his own, and this awareness created a certain competetiveness that continued throughout most of their lives.

Sidney had sought security in a civil service job as a social worker for the department of corrections in what was euphemistically called a boys' training school, more realistically a reform school. He and his family were living at the time in Brooklyn. Sidney's wife, Ruthie, an affable young woman with whom I soon became friendly, and their infant daughter, Debbie, were part of the family circle I was beginning to know.

Most prominent in the group was Annie, Sylvan's aunt and Sidney's mother, who was frequently described with affection as a "tough broad." She looked the part; she was a short, stocky woman with the bearing of a Mack truck and a firmly set mouth that rarely broke into a smile. But I found her to be a most understanding and accepting person with whom I quickly felt at ease. Annie had spent many years living intermittently in Sophie and Louis's home while weathering a marriage to a small-time conman who spent his life alternately in and out of prison. I also learned that, according to family lore, Annie was the one who, when Sylvan was born, selected the name Sylvan because she thought it would look good in print.

Sidney's older brother, Lester, and his wife, Isabel, were also occasionally on the scene. Sylvan's relationship with Lester was never as close as the one with Sidney. It was some time before I got to know him at all, and Isabel was soon out of the picture when she divorced Lester.

Sylvan's grandmother, who had remained in the kitchen throughout my initial visit, never could believe that I was really Jewish, since I didn't know a word of Yiddish and was totally ignorant of the religious rituals and traditional dietary customs that were such an important part of her life. She was appalled at the number of times I inadvertently broke the rules of her kosher kitchen. As long as I knew her, she was suspicious of who I was and I think was always convinced that I was a "shiksa." With her knowledge of English so limited and mine of Yiddish nonexistent, communicating with her was always difficult.

Another eight or ten supporting characters were in and out of the household, many of them Russians who could easily have stepped off the stage of a Yiddish theater.

One of them, Tevel, who if I remember correctly was Sophie's cousin, had a particular fondness for Sylvan. Small and compact, he had a leathered face and the body of a boxer. I never saw him without a cigarette, with a long ash, drooping from one side of his mouth. His demeanor suggested that he had experienced more than his share of rough times. Whenever he and Sylvan were together, their conversation inevitably focused on how Tevel might get back to his family, who had remained in Russia, not an easy feat in the years immediately after World War II. He placed great value on Sylvan's reasoned suggestions in spite of their age difference. Some years later, we were happy to learn that Tevel was eventually reunited with his wife and children in the Soviet Union. We were never able to see him again.

As I got to know the Fox family, I became increasingly impressed with Louis's warmth and hospitality. Without hesitation he was always able to find room for another plate at the table or a place to accommodate a family member who needed somewhere to sleep. He managed to expand the walls of his small house whenever the need arose. In a short time, I too became a recipient of the generosity he extended to those he was close to.

Louis had not had an easy childhood himself, having grown up in near poverty on the Lower East Side of New York, with a tyrannical father who refused to allow him to further his education after high school. Louis had been accepted into Cooper Union, a prestigious school that charged no tuition, where he hoped to study engineering. But his father, proclaiming that continuing to go to school was a waste of time, refused to allow him to attend and insisted that he go to work for him in his repair shop. Speaking of these painful events more than fifty years later, he was still moved to tears.

When he was finally able to get away from his father, Louis, relying on his keen mind and strong determination, worked his way up in a small company that made and repaired electrical equipment, eventually reaching a level where he was functioning as an electrical engineer, although without the formal qualifications. His success culminated in later years when he bought out the owner of the company and established a business profitable enough to allow him a comfortable retirement.

Sylvan's mother, Sophie, was more difficult to read. She usually complied with Louis's wishes, but always with an implicit sigh. She didn't seem to find much enjoyment in her daily life, for reasons I couldn't understand. And I had the impression that she wanted to keep her distance from me. At one point I confided to Sylvan, "I don't think Sophie likes me," to which he replied, "Don't worry about it, she doesn't like me either." It took some time for me to gain some understanding of her and not be bothered by her sometimes off-putting behavior. She often spoke of her unfulfilled dreams, but neither Sylvan nor I could ever determine what prevented her from making them a reality.

I gradually came to realize that each member of the Fox family occupied a unique place on the political spectrum, ranging from moderate liberalism to outright Marxism, with all of them vehemently expressing their opinions, which were frequently revised and re-revised over time. Given this background, Sylvan was exposed as a child to heated political discussions and a house full of an assortment of newspapers that ranged from the *Daily Worker* to the *New*

York Times and *Herald Tribune*. It was not surprising that, after becoming a regular newspaper reader and honing his debating skills at an early age, Sylvan was a master of political argument by the time I met him. Whenever I found myself in the midst of a heated family discussion, I knew that as a neophyte I could be only a silent observer, impressed by the formidable oratorical talents of the whole family.

Throughout this time, although my father was giving me money, covering even my basic expenses was getting harder, particularly when I was seeing a therapist.

I decided to find a part-time job that would provide me with some additional income. From the notices on the student bulletin board, I found a position as a companion on Saturdays to an eleven-year-old girl whose parents, for whatever reason, were rarely available to her on the weekend. Patty lived a privileged life in a luxurious Fifth Avenue apartment and attended an elite private school, but she was a lonely, rather sad little girl who seemed to get minimal attention from her parents. I found it easy to empathize with her and offer her my friendship, to which she seemed eager to respond.

My responsibilities included supervising her homework preparation and her piano practice, taking her to lunch at one of the fashionable restaurants in the neighborhood, and accompanying her to Saturday matinees at the theater. With her, I saw the best musicals and light comedies of the season, featuring stars such as Mary Martin and Ethel Merman. While the job was enjoyable and allowed me to establish a warm though brief relationship with my charge, my services were required only until the end of the school year, thus ending my regular theater attendance. After cursory goodbyes, Patty and I never saw each other again.

As the weather got warmer, Sylvan and I spent many free days at his family's home. Sylvan's piano was a fine instrument that we enjoyed playing, both solo and together in music for four hands, for hours.

At other times, as a change from our musical activities, Sylvan invited his friend Bert over for a strenuous game of stoopball. Their skills had been perfected over years on Brooklyn streets, where they had played not only stoopball but also stickball and many other sports known only to city kids. I was a fascinated spectator, eager to learn the rules and fine points of this and other urban games that I had never before encountered. I loved to watch Sylvan as he played with boundless enthusiasm and the grace of someone with natural athleticism. Sylvan and Bert were back in their childhoods as they smacked the red Spalding ball ("It's pronounced 'spaldeen,'" Sylvan informed me) against the stoop (another term I was not familiar with). We usually ended the afternoon by cooling off on the back porch, often with an egg cream—the quintessential New York drink that was another newfound discovery for me—planning where we would have dinner and which friends we'd invite over for an evening of conversation. Sylvan had known many of these friends, like Bert, from elementary or high school. They were all extremely bright young men from middle-class Jewish neighborhoods who were striving to pursue careers in a variety of fields that included psychology, political science, education, and music. I couldn't fail to notice that even in a gathering of his intellectual peers, Sylvan usually expressed the most articulate, convincing arguments.

Warm weather meant the beginning of the baseball season. Growing up in Brooklyn, Sylvan was an avid Dodgers fan and passionate about baseball. Sylvan took me to my first game at Ebbets Field, where he patiently tried to outline the intricacies of the game and to explain the importance of seeing Jackie Robinson, the first black player in the major leagues, as a member of the team. It was an act of love on Sylvan's part to endure my innumerable stupid questions during a game on which he would surely have preferred to concentrate without my constant interruptions. ("How can someone not know the difference between a strike and a ball and a walk?" he had to wonder.) And it was a testament to the strength of our relationship that it was able to survive the ordeal of introducing me to the sport. The happy outcome was that with time my love of baseball became almost as great as Sylvan's.

As I watched the game with regularity, it occurred to me that Sylvan had the physical characteristics of a first baseman: medium height, lithe, muscular, fast moving, and always poised to leap up to catch a ball in midair. But, beyond that, Sylvan had his own unique characteristic: he walked with a bounce, so that he sometimes looked as if his feet weren't touching the ground. I could always recognize him from a distance simply because of his walk.

It was during the spring semester of 1948 that Sylvan began to consider changing his major from piano to composition. Composing, he thought, would provide greater opportunities to be creative than piano performance. Consultations with several faculty members at Juilliard supported the rationale of his decision. Before the end of the semester, he officially switched to composition, although completing the requirements for a degree would extend his studies by an additional year. Convinced that composition was the route he wanted, he accepted this.

At about the same time, Sylvan and I realized that our feelings for each other had grown into what could only be described as profound love. Although we were still teenagers, yet intelligent enough to know that youthful passions can be intense but short-lived, we firmly believed that we had found with each other something precious that we wanted to continue for the rest of our lives. I knew that for the first time in my life I felt safe and loved, able to trust someone completely—indescribable feelings that I had thought I would never experience. And Sylvan's love was as great as mine. We knew with absolute certainty that we wanted to make a lifelong commitment to each other. There was no need for a formal proposal of marriage. Sylvan didn't have to ask me to marry him. We knew what our decision was: we would get married in the fall.

When we told our families about our plans, we were met with objections from almost everyone. The opposition, expressed in many ways, was based, not surprisingly, on our being so young. From Sophie and Louis, we heard, "The two of you are way too young to get married. My God, Sylvan, you're only twenty, and Gloria's not even eighteen. Have you thought how getting married will affect your education?" To this, we responded, "It's not going to interfere. Why do you think it would?" To which we got no coherent reply.

Sylvan's cousin Sidney solemnly predicted that because of our immaturity the marriage would last no more than a year. He also told Sylvan privately that he was concerned that my mother's mental illness did not bode well for our future. He seemed to think that I came from "tainted" stock that would affect any children we decided to have.

(Years later, when Sylvan and I had been married for more than fifty years, we teased Sidney that we had stayed married this long just so we could prove him wrong. And he needed only to look at our daughter, Ricki, to see how false his warning had been about the effects of my "tainted" stock.)

My brother Bob, in his last attempt to influence my future, warned us that our marriage plans could result only in dire consequences. He foresaw marriage at our age as leading to both of us being hurt emotionally. My father, who had never met Sylvan, and in effect knew me very little, was the only one who expressed no real opposition, probably because he assumed that I would do what I chose anyway; and from his perspective, marriage was not the worst fate that could befall me. In spite of all the objections, we remained firm in our decision.

Next, we had to face the fact that I would have to go back to Levack to stay with my father for the summer, since I had the apartment only until the end of the term. The plan was that I'd stay at the camp during this time and that Sylvan would drive up for a visit in late August with our friends Bert and Mary, after which I would return with them to New York.

Both Bert and Mary welcomed the invitation enthusiastically. Bert had never ventured far from New York City and looked forward to exploring the wilds of Ontario. Mary, an emigrée from Palestine whom I had met at Juilliard, was also eager to get away from the confines of the city for some fresh air in the north woods but dreaded the idea of facing immigration officers at the border. Her family had fled from Berlin to a series of other European cities until finally arriving in Palestine before the beginning of World War II. Her experiences with border crossings had left her with extremely disturbing memories and much anxiety when confronted with uniformed men demanding to see your papers. We had to convince her that the immigration officers she would face when crossing into and out of Canada would not be the menacing fascists she remembered.

Sylvan borrowed his father's car for the visit, and then, since neither Bert nor Mary knew how to drive, did all the driving on the two-day trip. An overnight stop in Toronto was followed by a more arduous drive on smaller roads, which in 1948, before the construction of an expressway, were the only way to get to Sudbury. When the three of them finally arrived in Levack, Sylvan, exhausted from driving, began to understand the discomfort imposed by inaccessibility.

Sylvan's fatigue quickly disappeared when we rushed to greet each other. We hadn't seen each other for several weeks and we were giddy with being reunited. The feelings we had before our separation were strengthened even more now that we were together again, and confirmed for us that we were right in planning to get married.

The trip enabled Sylvan to meet my father and to see what had been my home. I think that until Sylvan saw Levack for himself, which until then he was able to imagine only from my description, he couldn't fully appreciate its isolation. My father and Sylvan hit it off well—to my surprise—and, after being assured that Sylvan would be able to support me after completing his education, my father appeared to accept Sylvan as a future son-in-law with no reservations.

Now it was my turn to act as a guide. I introduced Sylvan, Bert, and Mary to experiences they had never had before: long swims in the lake with no other humans around; the eerie calls of the loons interrupting the still of the night; the magnificent display of the aurora borealis; and bears foraging for food near the house. We filled buckets with wild blueberries growing everywhere in profusion; we read by kerosene lamplight and cooked on a woodstove. What I had experienced before in lonely isolation was now shared with newfound enjoyment with Sylvan and our friends.

Sylvan and I found secluded places to be alone, to reconnect with each other and to satisfy the longings we had felt during the summer. I had never seen beauty in the camp, the lake, and everything surrounding it as I did now with Sylvan.

My father, who seemed pleased to have the company of guests, demonstrated a charm I had never seen before. He obviously enjoyed showing the "Yanks" how you could live comfortably without electricity and running water, although his guests had some difficulty appreciating the joys of outhouses. For the first time, I saw my father chuckling and making jokes. Perhaps he was happier because he had the company of young people in an environment where he felt comfortable; perhaps it also gave him pleasure to see Sylvan as an acceptable son-in-law, and to realize how happy Sylvan and I were together.

When we left Levack, I realized that I was saying goodbye to what had previously been my life, not only to the scars from the losses I had known, but also the sweeter memories of my brothers, my mother, and yes, my father. I was surprised that along with the happy anticipation of what awaited me in the future, I also felt considerable sadness in shutting the door to the past, knowing that I would no longer think of Canada as home.

Chapter 5

Back in New York, we lost no time in making arrangements with Bert's brother, Morrison, who was a rabbi, to marry us in his study. On September 8, 1948, with Sylvan's parents and with Sidney and Ruthie and Bert in attendance, we became man and wife in a simple Jewish ceremony followed by a celebratory lunch in one of the nicer restaurants in Brooklyn. We were both happy with the simplicity of formalizing our commitment to each other, but we went along with Sylvan's parents' wish to make a wedding dinner a few weeks later to present us as a couple to their friends.

It was time to start another academic year. We were living with Sylvan's parents in the room that until then had been Sylvan's and trying to bring in some income with part-time jobs and by giving private piano lessons. I didn't particularly like teaching kids who had little interest in the piano, but it was better than anything else that was available. Sylvan, as I recall, found some part-time clerical work. It wasn't easy managing work and the demands of Juilliard, but, thanks to Louis's generosity, at least we were living rent-free.

Sylvan was pleased he'd made the switch to composition, which now allowed him greater opportunity to express his musical creativity. He was happy to have replaced his weekly piano instruction with individual composition lessons; his initial forays into composing met with encouraging praise from his teachers. Meanwhile, I was making good progress in my studies, although I still wondered whether I had any future as a performer. I began to have serious doubts that I had the temperament for a concert career. In particular, playing in front of large numbers of people, certainly a necessity for a performer, made me very uncomfortable.

I don't remember exactly when we began experiencing dissatisfaction with the liberal arts classes at Juilliard. Because it offered a B.S. degree, the school required students to complete a certain number of nonmusic courses. These included some rather unchallenging classes in literature, sociology, and American history. Both Sylvan and I believed that the value of our independent reading, combined with the discussions we had between us and with our friends, far exceeded the stimulation of the formal offerings. Their mediocre quality was due in large part, I think, to the limited academic background of the teachers and the lack of importance placed on these courses.

In spite of its efforts to appear to provide a well-rounded education, Juilliard was ultimately a conservatory.

As the year progressed, we agreed that we had both underestimated the value of a liberal arts education when we had opted for Juilliard. We scoffed more and more at the reading assignments and the discussions in the English and sociology classes, where raising a point for consideration was usually met with yawns and looks of boredom from other students and the faculty member. "This is an insult to our intelligence," Sylvan proclaimed at one point. "Hell, we have more meaningful conversations on the subway than we do in those classrooms."

The question became, How do we improve our educational opportunities yet still continue our musical studies? Although we wanted to get away from the restrictive atmosphere of Juilliard, we were not yet sure where we wanted to pursue our academic careers. We needed some breathing space, and more than anything we felt a strong desire to explore the world. Spending time in Paris, whose magic had lured so many Americans since the early nineteenth century, was attracting us as well. A center of intellectual activity in those postwar years, Paris was alive with creativity in literature, music, and the visual arts and had become a magnet for expats from throughout the Western world. We grew convinced that we wanted to be there, to immerse ourselves in French culture and take classes at the Sorbonne, and possibly at the Paris Conservatory, for whatever length of time our funds would allow. We knew that doing this would be a temporary interruption in our musical studies, which we did not want to abandon, and would mean detouring off the prescribed course we had been following. The move would be a risk for both of us; but ultimately, it was the leap we chose to take.

At the end of the spring semester, as we were making plans to leave for Paris, Sylvan received an introduction to the eminent composer Roger Sessions, who agreed to accept him as a private student in composition for the summer. While this was an exceptional opportunity, which Sylvan was eager to take, it did not change our decision to go to Paris in the fall. Sylvan always looked back at his time studying with Sessions as among the most exciting experiences of his musical education, a rare opportunity to study with a great twentieth-century composer.

The summer found us trying to earn enough money for our Paris trip. Again, I managed to find as many private piano students as I could handle, and Sylvan found some temporary work. We managed to accumulate a sum that would support us for several months if we were frugal; a longer stay would mean finding an additional source of income.

All I remember about the preparations for our trip is the intense excitement we felt before our departure. Unexpectedly, my father, having come to New York on business, was able to see us off, along with Sylvan's parents, as we were about to set sail on the *Queen Elizabeth*. It was the only time that the three of them met each other, a brief but amicable get-together. I like to think that my father found an excuse to be in New York to bid us a bon voyage, rather than just accidentally being in the city. Looking back, I am saddened to think that in the difficult circumstances of my childhood I had underestimated his affection for me, and it was only in adulthood that I was able to acknowledge it. I was touched by his presence as we prepared to leave.

In the late 1940s, a trip to Europe was still looked upon as a major event, in part because it required a lengthy sea voyage. Goodbyes such as ours at dockside marked the beginning of a significant transition to something new and untested. For us, the departure was a momentous event.

In spite of a stormy transatlantic crossing, we were thoroughly enthralled by our introduction to an ocean voyage. Although we were traveling tourist class, which meant that we had a small cabin, we discovered the endless pleasures of a major ocean liner: the brisk walks on deck, watching the sea swelling around us; the opulent public rooms resplendent with gleaming mirrors and luxurious leather sofas; the vast dining rooms, fitted with the most beautiful furniture and tableware, in which we were served copious amounts of excellent food; and the impeccable staff, ready to take care of our every wish. We had never experienced luxury like this before.

We had as shipmates Sylvan's friend Michel, a pianist from New Orleans, and his wife, Gwendolyn. Michel and Sylvan had known each other in their first year at Juilliard, after which Michel returned to New Orleans to continue his education. He and Gwendolyn had been married for a few months and were also headed for Paris, where Michel planned on pursuing his piano studies. Sylvan and I found

Gwendolyn, who came from a wealthy New Orleans family, particularly unattractive both in personality and appearance. In addition to being terribly overweight, she seemed determined to present herself in the most slovenly, unkempt fashion possible, an image that I think she wished to convey as somehow expressive of her politics. A dogmatic belief in communism (yet able to accept her parents' funding of her and Michel's trip to Paris) completely enveloped every aspect of her thinking. It was inevitable that she and Sylvan would get into heated political discussions in which she was unable to present any rational defense of her beliefs, sometimes showing a shocking lack of historical information. Sylvan managed to destroy her pro-communist arguments with little difficulty. It was apparently the first time that she had found herself in a political argument in which she was totally unable to defend herself. She responded with outbursts of anger followed by tears as she retreated to lick her wounds. In spite of these episodes, Michel, Sylvan, and I had enjoyable conversations that helped pass the hours, with Gwendolyn joining in when she could manage to control her political diatribes.

We could never figure out what attracted Michel to Gwendolyn; there were such differences in their personalities and approach to life. We didn't see much of them in Paris, since their budget allowed them a more luxurious lifestyle than ours. We learned that they divorced a few years later, unfortunately after having had a child.

When we docked at Le Havre, it was astonishing how different everything felt compared to our familiar surroundings: the light, the colors, the air, and even the sounds had a different quality. We were keenly aware that we had been transported to another continent. A seven-day ocean trip provides a much more profound sense of the distance and contrast between two places than a trip by plane. We never had the same experience in later years when we traveled to Europe.

We took the train from Le Havre to Paris, arriving, as I recall, at the Gare St. Lazare. From there, we made our way to the little hotel on rue Monsieur le Prince where we planned to stay. We had found the name of the hotel before we left New York, the very low rates being its major attraction. Our room, not surprisingly, was small and spartan, furnished with a bed barely big enough to accommodate the two of us; a small armoire; a sink; and a bare low-wattage bulb that served as the only lighting fixture. At least the room was reasonably clean and, in spite of the street's reputation for having the most rats in Paris, free of wildlife. (We learned many years later that rue Monsieur le Prince had a better reputation in the nineteenth century, when it was the address of a number of well-known American émigrés.)

The W.C. was down the hall, literally a closet, unlit, with imprints of two wooden feet on either side of a gaping hole, and a chain that when pulled brought down a cascade of water over the hole in the floor. Operating the contraption required a quick agility if you didn't want to be showered by the water as it poured down from the ceiling. Before long, we began planning our schedules to make at least one daily visit to the central American Express offices, which had fully equipped public restrooms.

Our uncomfortable living quarters were of little importance as we began to explore the city. I had a fair knowledge of French, having studied it as a child. However, Sylvan, who had studied German but never French in high school, had to start learning it from the beginning. Children's primers served as good basic introductory texts for him, and the waiters at the local cafés, eager instructors in colloquial spoken French, patiently introduced new words into our vocabulary and corrected Sylvan's pronunciation, which was always inflected with German. (He never lost that accent even when he was almost fluent in French.) We spent many hours retreating from the damp chill of November warming ourselves with a cup of café au lait while receiving private instruction from one of the waiters who had befriended us. We gradually came to understand more of what was being said as we got used to the fast pace and often slangy French spoken by many Parisians. Before long, we progressed to reading newspapers and magazines and watching the occasional movie. Total immersion had quickly been effective.

As we explored the city, we saw innumerable scars of World War II, which had ended only four years before. On the exterior walls of many buildings were holes that clearly had been caused by rifle fire; and above many of them were small brass plaques reading "Ici est tombé" followed by a name. We could only imagine the battles of resistance fighters that had ended in the deaths commemorated so starkly there. Most buildings had still not received the much-needed cleaning and renovation that had been impossible to carry out during the war years, and there was still a shortage of electricity, which marred the image of Paris as the "city of light." Nonetheless, the city was incredibly beautiful and bedazzled us at every turn. Like so many others before us, we had fallen in love with Paris.

Walking became one of our greatest pleasures, even as the cold of winter progressed, and we became familiar with important boulevards of the Left Bank, Boulevard St. Germain, Boulevard du Montparnasse, and Boulevard St. Michel, as well as the maze of smaller streets that revealed their secrets only after strolling them repeatedly. Our walks led us by the landmark cafés—La Coupole, Le Dôme, Le Select—that had been frequented by the literary giants of the past. We allowed ourselves the occasional luxury of basking in these storied places, lingering over a cup of coffee and imagining who had sat there generations ago.

There was so much to learn, so much to see in every part of the city. Turning a corner opened up new vistas to be explored: the history of this boulevard, the architecture of this building, the people who lived on this street. We returned again and again to the endless wonders of the Louvre and visited cathedrals, palaces, and splendid performance halls. The curiosity that was awakened at this moment would extend throughout our lifetimes.

Whenever we could, we struck up conversations, in our less-than-perfect French, with shopkeepers, museum guards, garrulous waiters, and anyone else we could collar. At that time, the attitude of Parisians toward young foreigners was much more welcoming than it was later. We almost always met with encouragement as we struggled to express our curiosity and interest, and the wealth of information we gained from these exchanges matched what we were absorbing from our reading and walks.

Since we had limited money for meals, we were delighted to come upon a soup kitchen, operated by one of the international relief organizations, that served tasty, nutritious soups every day for a small fee. In the huge room, filled with communal tables and a serving counter against one wall, the air was redolent with the aroma of simmering soup and the smoke of Gitane cigarettes. Armed with a fresh baguette from the local boulangerie, we could make a satisfying meal of a bowl of hearty soup and bread.

The mealtime crowd of diners, representing the spectrum of displaced persons of Europe, included academics whose careers had been cut short by the war; former professionals of every kind, some from places that no longer existed; concentration camp survivors whose countries no longer existed; and former students whose education had ended either with conscription into military service or flight from it. Because the citizenship of so many of these people could not be determined, the French government issued them identification cards instead of passports, requiring frequent checks and periodic renewal. Rarely could they give a permanent address, country of origin, or occupation, but in answer to "Purpose of your stay in Paris?" most would have replied, "To search for a new beginning."

The patrons of the soup kitchen also included a more fortunate minority of bright young graduates of Oxford and Cambridge and a few Americans like us, looking to be educated by the city of Paris. We became friendly with many of the regulars and tried to gain some understanding of the challenges they faced as they attempted to re-establish an identity destroyed by the war. At the same time, we carefully avoided the figures seeking privacy behind a wall of silence.

One of the most memorable people we met at the soup kitchen was Batya. A young woman of Jewish parentage, she told us that she had been born in Germany (maybe), had spent her early years in a number of European countries (possibly), and then lived in Palestine (probably) before arriving in Paris. She spoke several languages and was erudite, charming, a witty conversationalist, and a will-o'-the wisp when it came to revealing information about her past and current life. She was known to have frequently altered the facts that she told immigration authorities, with the result, she confessed to us, that on one occasion the Paris police had told her: "Mademoiselle, you cannot change your identity the way you change your chemise." Yet she continued to do so in spite of the warning. We lost contact with her, as we did with other people we knew in Paris, in her case when she no longer appeared at the soup kitchen and disappeared from the quartier. We assumed that she went in search of another setting where she could alight temporarily to make a new home.

Also during this period, we made an effort to attend some classes at the Sorbonne. There were few obstacles to sitting in on lectures, though I recall little of their content or what significance we attached to them. In any event, pursuing a degree at the Sorbonne, an idea that became less and less attractive, would have required staying in Paris for several years. This was certainly not possible, considering our limited financial resources and the goals we had set for our musical development. And we were acutely aware of not having touched a piano since our arrival.

We would not be awarded an academic degree for what we had learned in Paris, for the experiences that would forever change the way we saw the world. However, our time there was one of the most enlightening periods of our lives. In part, we realized that if Sylvan wanted to get back on a serious educational track, the best course of action was to return to New York as soon as possible, so that he could pursue a bachelor's degree at a liberal arts college. He was able to contact Brooklyn College, which agreed to accept him at the beginning of the spring semester. It meant that we had to move quickly to arrive in time.

And what about me? Amid our preparations to leave, we discovered that I was pregnant. Our reaction was a combination of great joy and anxiety as we considered our new responsibilities. We talked about the difficulties we would face in caring for a child financially and the demands of being the emotionally supportive parents we envisioned. There was never any doubt, however, that we would succeed in meeting the challenge, convinced, as we were, of our resourcefulness and determination. And there was never any doubt that I would continue my education after becoming a mother.

We cabled Sophie and Louis to ask them if they could expand the walls of the house a little more to accommodate Sylvan, me, and a baby. Once more we had no doubt how Louis would reply. He and Sophie seemed delighted with the prospect of becoming grandparents, although I'm sure they also had some serious worries about how having a child would affect our lives as well as theirs.

As the time drew near for us to leave Paris, we realized that we had never ventured outside the city limits. We quickly planned an overnight trip to London by rail and channel boat. We spent the first night on the boat and then, after a short train ride, arrived in London. In the span of a day, we managed to race around the city, marveling at its spectacular sights. As evening approached, we found a pleasant little restaurant where we had dinner before returning to Paris. We left London with no souvenirs other than the violent eruption of food poisoning, acquired from what seemed like our good dinner at that pleasant little restaurant. Between our gastrointestinal symptoms, which manifested by the time we reached the boat, and the rough waters of the English Channel, we had a thoroughly ghastly trip back to France. We vowed that it would be a long time before we sampled English cooking again, and it was.

We booked passage on the *Ile de France* back to the United States and regretfully bid Paris farewell. Even though we had not completed a formal course of study, we felt that we had achieved something more important: the experience had opened our eyes to a world wider than the one we had previously known. Without realizing it, that was probably what we had been looking for anyway, in our own incompletely formulated way. We came away from Paris with a different view of the world and the addition of a significant chapter in our lives.

Shortly after we started our voyage, we encountered gale-storm winds, which, to our horror, repeatedly plucked our huge ocean liner out of the water and slapped it back down, like some crazed giant playing with a toy boat. The ship stewards, seeing the fear on our faces, assured us that storms such as this were not unusual and that we were in absolutely no danger. We believed them, since they, after all, were seasoned veterans of the sea. However, not long afterward, one early morning, we felt the ship give an even more violent shudder, heard a loud crash, and found ourselves in total darkness. Somehow, we got to the nearest corridor and, in a blur of activity, heard the crew being told to report to their stations and the passengers to sit calmly until further announcements. Emergency lights went on very quickly. We were informed that the ship had sustained some damage from the force of the wind but that it could operate safely and we would not be unduly inconvenienced. (I wondered if that was what the passengers on the *Titanic* had been told.) Since we were in mid-route, the captain had to consult the administrative headquarters in France to receive directions as to whether to return to the French port for repairs or to proceed to New York. Returning to France would have meant a disruptive delay in our schedule, so it was with great relief that we learned that we were heading for New York.

The gale-force winds subsided only slightly as we proceeded westward, causing the ship to pitch and roll continuously. By this time, the number of people appearing at the dining tables had diminished considerably. Seasickness had taken its toll on all but the sturdiest passengers, a group that included Sylvan, me, and two others at our table. We were treated to meals prepared with meticulous attention, accompanied by complimentary delicacies, in tribute, I suspect, to our perfect attendance in the dining room and unfailing appetites. When I look back and remind myself that I was three months pregnant, I am impressed with what must have been my very strong constitution. We completed the voyage, well fed with superb French cuisine, and in good health.

The ship finally lumbered into the port of New York. As part of the usual questioning at the immigration counter, we were asked the purpose of our trip abroad. We answered, "Education," to which the immigration agent snidely responded: "So, what did you learn?" Sylvan and I looked at each other in disbelief, wondering how we could possibly describe in a few sentences the growth and changes we had undergone. Not wanting to prolong our interrogation, we offered a brief answer: "Some interesting things about France."

Chapter 6

As soon as we got back to New York, Sylvan enrolled at Brooklyn College, with a major in philosophy. He was granted credit for a large part of his work at Juilliard. With that concession, by taking a heavy course load in the spring, and enrolling in both summer sessions and the following winter semester, he would be able to graduate in one calendar year. He eagerly began his studies, like a man finding the cold water of a spring after a long trek in the desert. Heavy reading assignments, which may have been burdensome for a less agile mind, were a challenge that he welcomed and thrived on. The intellectual stimulation that he had missed so much at Juilliard was now available to him.

I decided to defer college classes until after the baby was born and instead find a teacher with whom I could continue my piano studies.

My friend Mary recommended that I contact Irma Wolpe, the wife of the twelve-tone composer Stefan Wolpe. Mary had studied with Irma for some time and described her as a vibrant, caring woman who had a reputation as an outstanding musician and pianist. After a brief audition and conversation with her, she accepted me as a pupil.

Studying with Irma was a completely different experience from my piano instruction at Juilliard. She had a passionate love of music that was expressed in everything she did. She insisted, "You must have a thorough understanding of the structure of the work in order to perform it. You must spend time studying the score before you approach the piano to play it." With her assistance, I came to see much more of the inner workings of what I intended to play, and started to realize that it was not enough to simply acquire technical mastery of a piece. Beyond that, she also coached me in the physical mechanics of playing, instructing me how to use my hands and fingers for greater ease in performance. As a result, I began to enjoy the experience of playing much more than I ever had before, and consequently played better. I'm sure that my enjoyment was also enhanced because I was no longer consumed with anxiety about receiving an end-of-term grade that would pronounce my failure. This meant I was no longer shedding tears during my practice sessions.

My pregnancy, which fortunately did not include the common discomforts experienced by many women, progressed remarkably smoothly, enhanced by the pleasures playing the piano gave me. I must say, though, that the constant exposure to music in utero did not have a lasting effect on the baby who was exposed to it, as far as resulting in as intense an interest as I had.

Early in the morning of July 9, 1950, I went into labor, and within a few hours, with Sylvan pacing anxiously in the waiting room, had an easy delivery of our daughter. There is no way I can describe the wonder of bringing into the world a tiny, flailing creature who, with its first breath, miraculously becomes a human being. I was overwhelmed by the miracle of the event, and with the happiness that was greater than any I had ever experienced. It remains the most memorable experience of my life.

We named our daughter Erica. She was small—only five pounds, eight ounces—but thankfully in perfect health. With the usual discussion of whom she resembled, we could only conclude that she had my blue eyes. Sylvan was as overwhelmed with her birth as I was. Seeing him holding her with gentle caution was a beautiful sight that I remember to this day.

I was ready to go home the next day, but at that time new mothers had to stay in the hospital for six days, something that is, of course, unheard of in this cost-conscious era. So I waited impatiently until we could take our new daughter home to the house that was now shared by four generations: Sylvan's grandmother, his parents, Sylvan and I, and Erica, whom we soon started calling Ricki.

Among the memories of that summer when Ricki was born: the intense New York heat, unrelieved by air conditioning; sitting on the back porch with her cradled in my arms, a wee thing, feeling the cool of the shade and a light breeze, but still with sweat trickling down my face onto Ricki. I was overwhelmed by my feelings of motherhood: the joy of seeing the child that was of us, the abundance of love that poured out to her, and the wonder of how our lives were now so enriched by this new person. And then the images of Sylvan: sitting on the floor, gazing at Ricki lying on a blanket next to him; of him singing to her as he fed her a bottle; of settling her into her crib at night. Clearly, he was savoring the experiences of parenthood as much as I was.

Whatever doubts I had about being able to respond adequately as a mother were dispelled during those first few weeks. There must have been ample love from my own mother in my early years that I was now able to draw upon, even though that mothering was taken from me too soon. I vowed that I would do everything I could to prevent that from happening to Ricki.

I was able to continue my piano studies with Irma. Now, when I practiced, Ricki lay next to me in her pram, usually sleeping peacefully while I delved into the intricacies of a Bach fugue. It was a wonderful combination of music and motherhood.

When the fall came, Sylvan continued the heavy load of courses at Brooklyn College that would culminate in his graduation in January 1951; and, finally, I was able to take some liberal arts courses there, too. As I recall, they were in political science and philosophy, the content of which, over the years, got blended into the eclectic stew of my general education. We arranged our schedules so that one of us was always at home to take care of Ricki, and of course we had the additional support of Sophie, who had found true happiness as a grandmother. Although she was extremely diplomatic in her suggestions to me about my parenting practices, we did differ in how much attention to give Ricki. My position was that there should be no arbitrary restrictions when it came to meeting her needs, while Sophie worried that there was a danger of "spoiling" her. I held my own in this disagreement, I think without any untoward effects for Ricki or Sophie.

In addition to the attention we were giving Ricki, we were focused intently at that time on Sylvan's getting his B.A. He had been accepted as a candidate for an M.A. in musicology at the University of California, Berkeley, contingent on his completing his degree.

Because Berkeley had an impressive composition faculty, doing graduate work there seemed like an ideal way for Sylvan to continue composing while also pursuing a theoretical/academic course of study. He was eager to get back to the world of music, which had been set aside during his time at Brooklyn College.

Looking back on those years, I am struck by the conflicts we both experienced between our devotion to music and our desire to broaden our lives.

It was only many years later that we each found a way to reconcile these two forces. In Berkeley, Sylvan would be totally caught up in music, while I turned my attention to acquiring something of a liberal arts education.

Chapter 7

Venturing off to Berkeley marked the first time that the three of us had to face the challenges of setting up a household in a new place. It was February 1951 and Ricki was just seven months old when we bundled her up in her snowsuit and boarded the plane to take us from New York to San Francisco, making the necessary stop to refuel in Chicago, which, as I recall, was in the middle of a snowstorm. Arriving in the San Francisco airport, we delightedly shed our heavy winter clothing before heading to Berkeley, where we spent a couple of nights in a downtown hotel looking for an apartment, while adjusting easily to the mild temperatures of California.

We quickly found a small, furnished apartment where we were able to set up a comfortable household on the upper floor of a house not far from the campus. We had the luxury not only of a tiny back porch that looked out over the Berkeley hills but also the use of a backyard with lovely trees, where I was able to sit with Ricki on the lawn. The one important item that was missing was a piano, which meant that Sylvan had to use one on campus and I was unable to practice at all.

Our time in Berkeley was marked by so many vivid images: the beauty of the physical environment, which was a constant source of pleasure; and the university itself, which was a place of wonder. I still remember walking up Telegraph Avenue for the first time, approaching the Sather Gate, seeing the campus like a splendid citadel in front of me, and imagining the treasures that lay inside. I was excited that I was going to be attending such a prestigious institution. With credit for my work at Juilliard and Brooklyn College, I was enrolled as an upper-level junior; under the circumstances, the absence of a piano became less important.

Sylvan was delighted with his composition classes, but the musicology courses, which were probably more demanding than anything he had previously encountered, caused him a great deal of concern. I think it was the first time that he worried about being able to meet the intellectual expectations of someone other than himself. It didn't help to hear that many competent students had been forced to leave the program because they were unable to pass the dreaded orals, a requirement to begin your thesis. Talking with me about his concerns didn't seem to offer any relief, and one day his anxiety increased to the point that his symptoms were so severe that we rushed to the emergency room of the local hospital. He was kept overnight to rule out physical illness as the source of his rapid heartbeat, pallor, profuse sweating, and dizziness. The next day he was sent home with a diagnosis of "severe anxiety attack" and a prescription for a tranquilizer. I'm sure that anxiety attacks were the most common reason for visits to the emergency room of that hospital, which served the entire anxiety-ridden student population. The antianxiety medication took the edge off his discomfort, but it certainly did not eliminate it completely.

While the demands of the academic program as well as the implications of its outcome (what would happen if he was not allowed to continue in the program?) created almost overwhelming pressure on Sylvan, I was not weighted with that burden and could derive enormous pleasure in watching the wonders of Ricki's development, while, at the same time, indulging in the wealth of educational possibilities available at Berkeley. It would be hard to say which was more enjoyable, watching Ricki taking her first steps or attending an exceptionally stimulating seminar in American literature. Both were rewarding. We were able to arrange our schedules so that one of us was always home with Ricki, thus eliminating the need for a babysitter, services we preferred not to rely on even if we could have afforded them.

When it came time for Sylvan to take his orals, he sailed through without a problem. He still had a long way to go to complete his master's, but at least he was over a major hurdle.

Fortunately for Sylvan, he could escape from the daily grind of study in moments of complete delight: watching Ricki explore the feel and smell of a wild flower, chortle with glee as our landlord's Irish setter covered her with wet dog kisses, or cuddle on my lap in rapt attention, as I read her a bedtime story. Ricki was such a delightful, even-tempered child; I often wondered how well I would have managed with a child who didn't have her sunny disposition.

To pay for our stay in Berkeley, we had asked Louis for a loan, which he gave us unhesitatingly. However, he told us that he preferred to consider it not a loan but an investment that would bring him, most importantly, the return of seeing the benefits we would derive from our education. Louis could afford to lend us only enough money to cover the bare necessities, and so, like most other graduate students, we were always short of funds. I became very creative at stretching a can of tuna—I could have written a thesis about one hundred and one variations on a tuna casserole—while resisting the common practice of eating inexpensive horsemeat, which was readily available in local supermarkets. Somehow we managed to emerge without significant nutritional deficiencies, and with our respect for horses still intact.

We didn't have a car while we were in Berkeley, and had so little money that we couldn't even afford to take public transportation into San Francisco. We managed to get there once when a friend of the family invited us to dinner when he was in town for a few days. Not only did he treat us to a sumptuous dinner—anything other than tuna casserole would have been—but he sent us home in a cab. That was our one big night on the town during the eighteen months we were in California.

When Sylvan was in the home stretch of his studies, his thesis adviser and some other members of the music department told him that if he went on to get his Ph.D., he would have a good chance of landing a teaching position in the department. The possibility of his being on the faculty at Cal and the life that would be available to us—having a house in the Berkeley hills, my being able to get a degree there, moving in a circle of some of the best minds in music—was a dazzling lure. At the same time, there were conflicting factors that made the idea less attractive, most significant, the major decision Sylvan had to make as to whether he wanted to continue a career in music. To make an adequate income, he knew he would have to take a teaching position if he wanted to continue composing. Yet he also had a desire for a life beyond the walls of the classroom and the library, a life that encompassed the wider world that we had begun to know in Paris. There had to be some way of achieving this other than getting a Ph.D. in musicology. At the same time, could he disregard the time and incredible effort he had invested in his studies over the past year and a half? I think he was also beginning to question whether musical composition was the most appropriate means for him to express his creative impulses.

During the weeks leading up to graduation, we spent endless hours discussing the pros and cons of the possibilities that lay before us. Each day we were pulled from one choice to another, continually finding new reasons to support our decisions. Our strong desire to get back to New York was another significant factor. As attractive as California was, we were not sure we wanted to live there permanently. Finally, we made the decision: we would leave Berkeley, fully aware of what we were giving up but confident that we should "go home." Looking back on that period, I can see the development of an important dimension in our marriage: I was able to provide Sylvan with strength and support in a way that I hadn't been able to do before then. I could offer him reassurance as he wrestled with the difficult decisions he had to make about his career, and affirmation of decisions when he made them. I was willing to take the risks we would have to face in leaving Berkeley, if we took that path. Most important to him, I believe, I had an absolute belief that, regardless of his decision, he would discover the best way to develop his talents intellectually and creatively.

We knew that returning to New York, without any plans for how we would support ourselves, would cause serious problems, the first of which would be telling Sylvan's parents of our decision. They had provided us with financial support during our time in Berkeley with the understanding that Sylvan would pursue a career in music. They were dumbfounded when he told them that he was not only giving up the idea of continuing graduate studies but of teaching music. They had driven out to Berkeley, planning on our driving back to New York with them for a few weeks' vacation. Instead, we told them that we were going back to New York to stay and that Sylvan was adamant about not taking a teaching position. It was only the joy of seeing Ricki again after a year and a half that kept Sophie and Louis from exploding in frustration and disappointment. They were, quite understandably, very concerned about how we would survive. We were concerned too, but we were also convinced that Sylvan would eventually find work that would provide him with some satisfaction and that between us we would be able to manage financially.

Over the next two years, Sylvan had repeated conversations with Sophie and Louis about our future. They all went something like this:

"I don't understand why you won't even consider a teaching job in the city school system," Louis would say. "It would provide you with decent pay and security."

"I told you why I'm not about to consider a job teaching in a city high school when I decided against the possibility of teaching in Berkeley," Sylvan would answer.

"Have you considered what you're putting Gloria and Ricki through?" asked Sophie.

"They're not being put through anything. Gloria and I made this decision together and we're doing fine."

"You were always such a brilliant kid," Louis would say, "and we looked forward to what you would become. And you've worked so hard to get a terrific education—just to throw it away? I wish you would change your mind."

"I'm sorry I haven't lived up to your expectations. But I'm not changing my mind."

A recurring theme from Sophie: "You are so stubborn."

When we got back to New York, we found a cheap basement apartment in Cobble Hill, a working-class neighborhood of Brooklyn that has since become gentrified. With some secondhand furniture, cinderblock bookcases, a borrowed sewing machine to make some colorful furnishings, and a fair amount of creativity, we constructed a reasonably comfortable place to live. While Ricki had a proper bed, Sylvan and I got used to sleeping on a mattress on the floor, and seeing from our window the feet of pedestrians passing by. The saving feature of the place was that the rear of the apartment faced a patch of backyard that had some trees in it, as well as a lot of overgrown weeds.

Our biggest problem was finding work. I gradually acquired enough piano students to provide us with some income, and Sylvan began a series of temporary jobs that included dealing on the phone with people who were not making their payments to a collection agency; managing the office of a second-rate furniture store; working in a juvenile detention facility, in hopeless conditions; and fielding the complaints of dissatisfied insurance customers. There seemed to be no limit to the availability of dead-end jobs involving the poor and unfortunate. With our combined incomes, we were able to maintain ourselves just above the poverty level, but we were constantly worried that we would be permanently mired in this position. Although many years later we looked back and said that a life of poverty could never have been our fate, at the time we were not so sure. I can't say we were optimistic that Sylvan would find work that was satisfying;

the more precise word would be "hopeful." We told ourselves repeatedly that something would present itself and we had to be patient.

Sylvan began making his first attempts at writing prose, mostly short fiction, during that period, but he was unsure whether he could express himself in this medium and whether the creativity that he had demonstrated in music composition could survive the translation. None of those early efforts remain, unfortunately, because he was never satisfied with what he was producing and consequently destroyed everything he wrote.

In addition to writing, he came up with the idea of making a radio documentary about Coney Island. The project consisted mainly of a series of interviews with the owners of various businesses along the boardwalk, from hot-dog stands to freak-show houses and Ferris wheels, with the varied assortment of people who worked there, and with the fascinating mix of customers who frequented these establishments. He rented a huge tape recorder, which was considered portable by the standards of the day, and enlisted his friend Bert to assist in operating it while Sylvan conducted the interviews. He managed to create a colorful picture of the characters who populated the neighborhood. Even then the locals were bemoaning the loss of the "old Coney Island" and of how the current scene didn't have the flavor of the old days. The sound of calliopes and barkers that was picked up during the interviews created a particularly effective background for the rasping voices of the locals, who were more than willing to answer Sylvan's questions and make themselves heard. Sylvan spent hours talking with them, and when all the raw material had been collected, he edited it, wrote additional narrative, and produced a finished product that was remarkably well done and extremely entertaining. But without an agent or connections to someone who would be interested in listening to the recording, he was unable to market it; the tape never received a public airing and ended up languishing on a shelf. It survives to this day, in a long-outdated format.

As the months went by, Sylvan continued to search the help-wanted ads of the *New York Times*, hoping to come across something that might provide more than grinding boredom and a dead end. With each day bringing discouraging results, we kept telling ourselves that something would show up.

Although it was a difficult period, it was made more tolerable by spending time with friends and with those relatives who could withhold their criticism long enough for us to enjoy their company. In spite of Sophie's and Louis's frustrations with the course our lives had taken, we often drove with them to visit Sidney, Ruthie, and their two daughters, who were living in Warwick, New York, where Sidney was the superintendent of a state training school, or reform school, as it was more commonly referred to. Sylvan and I spent many hours engaged in lively political and ideological debates with Sidney and Ruthie, with whom we developed a lifelong relationship, and with whom we shared active, sometimes heated, conversations throughout our lives. Meanwhile, the three girls—Debbie, Lisa, and Ricki—who had also developed a close attachment, enjoyed playing happily together, sublimely oblivious to the adult problems surrounding them.

Sophie and Louis continued to have a hard time understanding why Sylvan refused to consider teaching in the city school system, which they reasoned would at least provide some security and respectability. They were both worried that instead of taking advantage of the opportunity to make comfortable lives for ourselves, we would end up trapped in a life of deprivation. I sensed that Louis, who had a firm belief in Sylvan's potential, was particularly saddened to see him working in jobs that held no future. Sophie, for her part, seemed most bothered by how she could answer the queries of her friends at the bridge table, whose sons had now become lawyers or up-and-coming businessmen. In addition, both Louis and Sophie were terribly concerned about how our situation was affecting Ricki. We, on the other hand, didn't feel that she was showing any adverse effects from our financial limitations. With an abundance of love and attention from parents and grandparents, she seemed as ebullient and outgoing as ever.

Chapter 8

After almost two years of discouraging, fruitless job hunting, Sylvan saw an ad in the *New York Times* for a job as a reporter on a small newspaper in Little Falls, New York, no experience required. His face lit up as he showed me the ad and excitedly told me that this was something he really wanted to try; I could hardly contain my hopes that maybe our luck was finally changing. He quickly dashed off a letter in response to the ad and within a few days got a reply from the editor of the paper, John McGuire, inviting him to come upstate for an interview. We got out a map to locate Little Falls, which sits on the north side of the Mohawk River, about halfway between Albany and Syracuse and a few miles east of Utica. We discovered that the town's chief feature was being the site of one of the locks on the Erie Canal, still used at that time by slow-moving barges carrying cargo up and down the river.

This was before the construction of the New York State Thruway, and the drive from Brooklyn to Little Falls was an arduous one that took four to five hours along winding roads. The meeting with McGuire obviously went well because Sylvan came away with an offer to start as soon as possible as one of the five members of the staff of the *Little Falls Evening Times.* Sylvan was enthusiastic about testing his skills in reporting on the variety of subjects that the paper covered—everything from school board meetings and church socials to breakdowns in the local lock, which caused a crisis in the operation of what county residents considered a major transportation system.

We agreed that it would be foolish for the three of us to move to Little Falls if there was a chance that the job wouldn't pan out, or if it was just another dead end. It seemed that the only reasonable course of action was for Sylvan to live alone for a while, to see if he liked the job and passed muster as a reporter. This meant the unattractive prospect of our not living together and of Sylvan taking a furnished room in town. And then there was the question of what we'd do if the job did work out. Could we manage to live in Little Falls for any length of time on Sylvan's extremely meager salary and without my income from teaching?

After many hours of talking it over, we decided that, although it meant some sacrifices, it was worth taking the chance that the outcome would make it worthwhile. So Sylvan told McGuire he was ready to start. Sylvan would drive down to Brooklyn each week so at least he could be home with Ricki and me on weekends, even though this meant making the tiring trip alone after working all week. He found a habitable furnished room in Little Falls with no difficulty and survived on the food in the local diner with the anticipation of better food over the weekend.

Within a couple of weeks, Sylvan was turning out stories that far exceeded the editor's expectations. A savvy guy, in spite of living most of his life in Little Falls, McGuire had a sophisticated appreciation of good writing in any form and soon was giving Sylvan the choicest assignments and commending him for his rapid adaptation to the work. Meanwhile, each time he came home, Sylvan reported more enthusiastically on what he was doing. He couldn't wait to show me his first byline on the front page, on a story about a breakdown on the lock that caused a day-long disruption of traffic on the canal. This had involved his going to the scene to cover the story and then racing back to the office to write a polished, professional article. There was no doubt that he had found an occupation in which he excelled and that he thoroughly enjoyed; he had succumbed to the siren call of the newspaper business. We were overcome with elation as we allowed ourselves to think that our fortunes had finally changed.

These developments meant that we had to make plans for Ricki and me to move to Little Falls so that we could all be together. With the limited money we had available, our choices of an apartment were extremely restricted. We packed up our basement apartment in Brooklyn and found another basement apartment in Little Falls. Even less attractive, it was at least on a pleasant, tree-lined street. Since it was summer, Ricki and I were able to take long walks, which provided some exercise and a chance to explore the few streets of the town. On most nights, when Sylvan had finished work, the three of us had a bite to eat, then got into the car and ventured into the Mohawk Valley. The area was totally unfamiliar to us and presented a lush panorama in the full bloom of summer. We discovered the network of roads that meandered through the adjoining towns and hamlets, and came upon charming old stone houses and small farms that appeared untouched by the twentieth century. These evening drives made living in a cramped apartment much more tolerable.

On several occasions John McGuire and his wife invited us to have an outdoor dinner at their house. They were a well-educated, gracious couple in their fifties who seemed happy with the quiet life they had led for many years in Little Falls, where John had been the editor of the paper for most of his adult life. While they were both involved in local politics, they were equally interested in the affairs of the broader world, although neither seemed eager to spend any time in big cities like New York. We spent many delightful hours with them learning not only about upstate New York but also about what might be available to Sylvan as a journalist. John was unhesitatingly supportive, encouraging him to set his sights on a larger paper, although he knew that would mean losing a reporter whose talents far outshone those of the other three members of the staff.

Sylvan soon discovered that he not only had a natural facility for writing but that he could write almost as fast as he could think. What he had been searching for during his years at Juilliard and Berkeley had finally been revealed. The success of his initial efforts and the encouragement of John McGuire became the impetus to find a way to move up to the next level in his career—a larger paper.

After about six months in Little Falls, Sylvan set about compiling a list of roughly forty newspapers in upstate New York and southern New England. He and I checked each city's population and the paper's circulation to determine if it presented an adequate upward step without being an unrealistic leap. Sylvan then composed a letter of application, describing his background and experience. Since this was in the days before copying machines, he needed to find a way to duplicate the letter for multiple submissions. The problem was solved when Sophie generously offered to type the letters, one by one. An experienced typist, she accomplished the task efficiently, but, more surprisingly, exhibited a rare moment of pleasure in doing something to further Sylvan's career.

There was a long wait until the responses—a small number out of the total—arrived. Most simply stated that the paper had no openings, while a few referred to what they considered Sylvan's limited experience. However, amid all the rejections were three letters inviting Sylvan to come for an interview.

The one that seemed to hold the greatest possibility was from the *Schenectady Union-Star,* which had a much larger circulation than the *Little Falls Evening Times*. The position was as a general reporter on the local staff.

Sylvan scheduled an interview with the city editor, who was impressed enough that he immediately consulted with the managing editor to get an okay to hire Sylvan on the spot. Schenectady was a thriving community at the time, thanks to the presence of a massive General Electric plant. The demand for news coverage was great enough to support two papers in Schenectady as well as two in Albany, the adjoining city and state capital. We were delighted not only with Sylvan's move upward but with the prospect of an increase in pay, which would allow us to live more comfortably.

For the first time, we could afford a decent place to live—a two-bedroom garden apartment in a newly developed suburban neighborhood of Schenectady. What a relief it was to be out of basement apartments and all they symbolized. At last we could get some comfortable furniture and accommodate Sylvan's piano, which until now had remained in his parents' house in Brooklyn. Most important, we felt we had finally come out of the depths of the painful, unsuccessful searching we had endured from the time we left Berkeley, and we could now anticipate a promising future. The message that kept reverberating in our heads was that we were finally getting affirmation for our decision not to settle for something we knew was not right for us, in spite of all the advice well-meaning people had been giving us. Although we talked at length about our perceptions, there was, beyond our conversation—as there was throughout our lives—an uncanny, unspoken, total understanding of what each of us was thinking.

Sylvan quickly became caught up in covering local government in Schenectady, thereby acquiring a firsthand introduction to upstate politics. Before long, he was familiar with the whole cast of characters who made up the political establishment, ranging from the city councilmen to the governor. He also had his first exposure to the court system, as he was sent to cover several criminal trials throughout the county.

With each of these experiences and his unstoppable curiosity, he was amassing a wealth of information that served him well throughout his career. In later years, his legal knowledge and facility in presenting sound logical arguments was so impressive that people often asked if he had gone to law school.

Meanwhile, during the time we were in Schenectady, my attention was focused primarily on caring for Ricki, who by this time was a delightful four year old. I was convinced that the attention I was giving her at this stage in her life was the most satisfying and important occupation I could have. I enjoyed all the things we did: going to the park, exploring the neighborhood, reading books together, introducing her to the piano. I was acutely aware that there was only a short period of time in which I could have such a significant influence on her, and I wanted very much to take advantage of it. At the same time, while I was so delighted in sharing the successes that Sylvan was achieving, and enjoying the life we were leading, it was easy to postpone considering my own career goals, though thoughts about what I wanted to do in the future were always on my mind.

Sylvan's rapidly developing reporting and writing skills were, of course, noticed by the city editor in Schenectady, who realized that before long Sylvan would probably want to set off in search of greater challenges. He was absolutely right, although he probably didn't expect this to happen so quickly. After about six months at the *Union-Star*—by now it was February 1955—Sylvan was already thinking about his next move. Again, he surveyed papers in upstate New York and New England with even larger circulations and influence. The list of potential employers he compiled was shorter this time and included, as I recall, papers in Boston, a couple in New England, and one in Buffalo, New York. Again, Sophie volunteered for the arduous task of typing copies of the application letter.

The response that offered the most attractive possibilities came from the *Buffalo Evening News*, which had an opening for a general assignment reporter. Sylvan quickly set up an interview with the city editor for the following week. He'd drive to Buffalo on Thursday afternoon, meet with the editor the following morning, and then return to Schenectady later that day. We were looking forward to Sophie and Louis coming to stay with us that weekend.

Sylvan left on the scheduled day, feeling optimistic as he said goodbye to me and set off. Snow had started falling, but even in the snow, the drive on the newly completed New York Thruway would take only a few hours. Sylvan was accustomed to driving in snow, a routine occurrence in upstate New York, so he was not overly concerned about the weather.

On Friday, the hours dragged by as I tried to keep myself busy as I impatiently awaited Sylvan's return. Late in the afternoon, as I was beginning preparations for dinner, the phone rang. My first thought was that it was Sylvan calling to say he was delayed because of the weather; however, when I picked up the phone, I heard the voice of a woman. She identified herself as a nurse in the emergency room of a hospital in Utica and then said that she would let me speak to my husband, whom they were treating.

Sylvan got on the phone and managed to use his most reassuring voice to tell me that he was all right after having been in an automobile accident. While driving home, he had hit an icy patch of snow-covered road that had sent the car into a spin and off the highway. After turning over several times, it had hurtled down a thirty-foot embankment, landing right side up in deep snow at the bottom. Because the thruway had just been completed, there were not yet guardrails to prevent such an accident. Sylvan told me that he had sustained a concussion and injured his left hand but didn't seem to have any other injuries. He was going to be kept overnight in the hospital, and would probably be discharged the next day. "And, by the way," he added almost nonchalantly, "I was offered a job on the *Buffalo Evening News*!" Appreciating the good news was difficult while trying to deal with the flood of anxiety that was enveloping me. I wanted to rush to him, to hold him, and to be sure he was really all right, but that was impossible. Sylvan advised me to sit tight, wait for Sophie and Louis, and drive with them to Utica the next morning to pick him up.

When I got off the phone, I composed myself enough to tell Ricki that Sylvan had been hurt in an accident and we would be going to the hospital to bring him home in the morning. Ricki asked questions but seemed able to absorb the event without undue distress. Within minutes, Sophie and Louis arrived, which meant that I had to remain as calm as possible while telling them what had happened. I gave them the few details about the accident and his injuries that Sylvan had told me, and that he had been offered a job in Buffalo. They were shaken, of course, but agreed that the best plan was to drive to Utica the next day. After a sleepless night, we made an early start to the hospital.

When we finally saw Sylvan, he didn't look as bad as I had anticipated. He had severed tendons in the fourth and fifth fingers of his left hand when a window he was bracing himself against shattered as the car went careering over the embankment; and a suitcase had hurtled through the car from the back seat, hitting him on the head and causing the concussion. But, aside from the left hand, which was heavily bandaged, and a few bruises on his face and arms, he looked pretty intact.

After the doctor examined him that morning, he was discharged with instructions to take it easy for a week, watch for any developing problems from the concussion, and immediately schedule an appointment with a surgeon to care for his hand. While all the final arrangements for his release were being made, Louis and I drove to the lot where the state troopers had hauled the car, so we could make the necessary inspection for insurance purposes. The car had been totally demolished: the body was crushed in, the windows and windshield had been shattered, and pieces of the metal frames of the windows were stabbing through the car interior like bayonets. Louis and I agreed that it was fortunate that we had seen Sylvan before seeing the vehicle, since it looked as though no one could possibly have survived the accident.

We learned that Sylvan had been briefly knocked unconscious as the car hurtled over the embankment. The first thing he recalled as he awoke was two state troopers hoisting him under the arms and "walking" him up the hill to the road (not the most appropriate action to take with someone who has just lost consciousness in a car accident). By a stroke of good luck, the troopers had seen the car go off the road and been able to reach him within a matter of minutes. It was a short distance from there to the hospital. Sylvan always remembered the brief exchange he heard between the troopers and a nurse as they wheeled him into the emergency room. The nurse asked the troopers if they thought this was a "fatal," to which they replied that they didn't think so. For Sylvan, that was all the reassurance he needed for the moment.

When we got home, Sylvan slept on and off for a few days while I watched carefully for any new symptoms, which fortunately didn't appear; and the headache and slight dizziness that he had from the concussion soon disappeared. We were able to get an appointment with a surgeon, who said that the severed tendons were healing well enough that the limitations to the use of the two fingers would probably be no more than an inability to bend the last joints. We were relieved to discover, as the healing progressed, that the injury would in no way affect his piano playing.

Sylvan contacted the editors at the *Schenectady Union-Star*, to tell them that he had been in an accident and to inform them that he would be leaving to start a new job in Buffalo. They were sorry to be losing one of their best reporters, but not surprised that he was moving on. When he left, they graciously wished him well in his new position.

Chapter 9

And so we began another phase in our lives. In less than a year, we had moved from a basement apartment in Brooklyn to Little Falls to Schenectady to Buffalo. During that time, we had become experts at finding a place to live, to packing and unpacking our belongings, and to becoming familiar with new locations. We quickly bought a new car to replace the one destroyed in Sylvan's accident and signed a lease on an apartment in Cheektowaga, a suburb of Buffalo. We had escaped a sentence of eternal stagnation in dead-end jobs and acquired the trappings of a comfortable middle-class life. But Buffalo meant more than joining the ranks of the middle class. When we looked back on that period in our lives, we saw that it also marked important strides in our professional growth: Sylvan had begun a career in which he had already demonstrated considerable success, and I was about to embark on an entirely new one that held great promise.

We moved into one of two units on the second floor of a new garden apartment. Our neighbors downstairs were another young family, Dan and Mickey and their two daughters, who were close in age to Ricki. The three of them were soon running in and out of each other's homes and racing outside together to play in the yard. And Mickey and Dan were compatible neighbors with whom we developed an easy friendship.

For the first time since leaving New York, we were living in a major metropolitan center. At that time, before the death of the Rust Belt, Buffalo, the largest city in western New York, was a thriving community supporting steel production, chemical factories, manufacturers of industrial products, and thriving small businesses. The city had a large population of blue-collar, predominantly Catholic workers, many of them of Polish or German background, as well as a sizable professional workforce. Buffalo was home to a major university, several smaller colleges, innumerable churches, a reputable symphony orchestra, an art museum, and two newspapers. Perhaps most important, as the center of Erie County, Buffalo wielded significant clout in the political operations of the state.

With impressive speed, Sylvan had reached a point in his career where he could legitimately identify himself as a newspaperman (a term he always preferred over what he considered the more pretentious "journalist"). He was working for a highly respected paper with exacting journalistic standards, run by an executive editor with the personality of an obsessive Prussian general. As just one of many incidents he was known for, Alfred Kirkhoffer once almost fired a hapless young reporter for the unforgivable sin of leaving out the second "a" in "Niagara" in a story. When Sylvan had his first interview with Kirkhoffer and attempted to adjust the angle of his chair to prevent the sun from shining directly in his eyes, he discovered that the chair was bolted to the floor so that the interviewee was blinded, in effect putting Kirkhoffer in complete control of the situation. This was a typical Kirkhoffer tactic, which the staff had to accept as a means of surviving on the paper.

After experiencing some anxiety during the paper's required probation period, Sylvan settled comfortably into the routine of local reporting, covering a wider range of subjects than he had in Little Falls or Schenectady. He found himself in a more competitive and demanding environment than he had known before: the paper had several editions, which required frequent updates to stories; a larger, more specialized staff; the unforgiving standards of editors who were under the iron heel of Alfred Kirkhoffer; and competition not only from the other Buffalo newspaper but from local radio and television stations. In spite of, or because of, these hurdles, Sylvan was able to perform even more adroitly. Thriving on challenges became a pattern that would continue throughout his life.

Now that Ricki had started kindergarten and would soon be attending school for a full day, I was at a point where I could think about continuing my own education. As my interests had broadened over the previous several years, I had developed a growing desire to move beyond the sequestered activities that had previously interested me and to become involved in the world in a way in which I could work constructively with people. Because this was such a marked change from what had interested me previously, I had serious concerns about making this transition. I was drawn to pursuing a career in one of the helping professions; I narrowed my choices to either clinical psychology or nursing, which, while different from one another, was each attractive in its own way. To get an advanced degree in psychology, I would have to take further undergraduate courses to complete a major, and then at least three years of graduate work. Getting a baccalaureate in nursing at the

University of Buffalo would take just about as long. Because of the way the program was organized, it would require four years of study even with all the credits I had previously accumulated. The number of years I would have to spend in school to reach either goal was not a determining factor.

There were conflicting pulls in both directions. The psychology professors I spoke with during the summer as I was coming to a decision were adamant in recommending that I pursue psychology. In one way or another, their message was "Don't waste your intelligence in nursing school." They seemed to think that nursing was not a profession for someone with any real brains. I hope that eventually they became better informed about the intellectual challenges nursing could offer. While I was drawn to the idea of providing help to people with psychological problems, I was particularly attracted to the opportunity of addressing someone's physical and emotional needs.

My ultimate decision, to pursue nursing, was influenced in large part by a meeting I had with Ellen McNicholas, a professor in the nursing school at the University of Buffalo. She described to me, with great enthusiasm, the school's baccalaureate program, in existence for only a couple of years, which aimed to incorporate the most progressive, recently developed elements of nursing education. I was impressed with the emphasis that the school placed on rigorous scientific preparation for clinical practice, and the inclusion of psychosocial aspects of patient care throughout all phases of the curriculum. I was equally taken by the fact that she assured me that I would be welcomed as a student who was somewhat older than most of the applicants, and that my eclectic educational background would be seen as an asset. At that time it was not common for a nursing school to admit married students or men. I learned that I would not be the oldest member of the class; one woman and one man were older than I was. However, I was the only one with a young child.

After lengthy discussions with Sylvan, I decided I'd give myself a year to try out the program, to see how well I could manage a schedule of schoolwork with being a wife and mother, and also to see how comfortable I was with my choice of a new career. I had doubts about whether I would be able to handle all my responsibilities, and I vowed that I would not allow my education to cause hardships for

Sylvan or Ricki. I made Sylvan promise he'd tell me if he ever felt that my going to school was causing problems for us or Ricki. He assured me he would, and added, "I want you to achieve what's important to you. We've always helped each other out. We're in this together. Isn't that what it's all about?" Without Sylvan's wholehearted support and determination to help me in every way he could, I would not have had the courage to go through with my plan.

In the fall of 1956, Ricki started first grade and I started nursing school. Because of my previous educational background, I didn't have to take the liberal arts courses that were part of the first-year curriculum, so I was able to be with Ricki when she came home from school. I felt this was an important condition of enrolling in the program.

I found the required science and nursing courses challenging and stimulating, totally different from anything I had studied before, but I also discovered that I had considerable aptitude for them. Within a few months, I was confident that I had made the right decision.

It was an exciting time for the three of us. Each of us was learning and growing: Ricki was doing well in school, Sylvan was proud of what he was accomplishing at the paper, and I was enjoying the expanding world of my studies. I was on the alert for signs that either Sylvan or Ricki was experiencing deprivation of any kind because of my new schedule, but, as far as I could tell, that was not the case, and Sylvan agreed completely.

The months went by in a blur of activity. Aside from being involved in our work and studies, we made interesting new friends, most of them people that Sylvan met at the paper.

A young woman from New Orleans, who had joined the staff about the same time as Sylvan, and her attorney husband became close friends whom we continued to see long after we had all left Buffalo. Another colleague of Sylvan's, a talented young man from a distinguished family in Switzerland, was also a frequent visitor to our home. He often invited Ricki to accompany him on Friday nights to synagogue, providing her with some exposure to Jewish tradition that she wouldn't have had were it not for his generosity, since neither Sylvan nor I practiced any religious rituals. Our circle of friends also included an oboist we had known in Juilliard who had become a member of the Buffalo Philharmonic and had recently arrived in the city with his wife.

Our apartment frequently became the setting for dinners and social gatherings. As a group we had a diversity of professional interests, but what we had in common was intelligence, driving ambition, and a thirst for stimulating conversation. For many of the people we knew at that time, Buffalo served as a steppingstone, as it did for us, leading to more attractive positions. Over the years, as most of us moved to new locations, maintaining contact was difficult and we lost touch with many of the people who had once been close friends. Sadly, this seemed to be an unavoidable penalty of leading a peripatetic life.

Our household was significantly enlivened when we presented Ricki with a beautiful Siamese kitten, Rama, for her fifth birthday. In somber resignation, Rama put up with Ricki dressing him in a doll's baby bonnet and wheeling him around in her toy pram. He maintained his position as a beloved member of the family for more than seventeen years. We considered his intelligence far superior to that of any feline or canine we had ever encountered, and he rewarded us not just with constant affirmations of our belief but with demonstrations of affection remarkable for any animal. Many years after Rama joined the family, we acquired another Siamese cat, Karma, to be his companion. They were a remarkable pair, in their attachment to us and to each other.

On many weekends, though it was a long trip, we drove to Queens, New York, to visit Sophie and Louis in their apartment in Forest Hills. We would bundle up Ricki in her pajamas and put her in the back of the car, where she could sleep while we made the long drive that brought us into New York in the wee hours of the morning. As tired as we were, it was always fun to spend a day and a half with Sophie and Louis before having to make the trip back.

Sophie and Louis were delighted that Sylvan had finally established himself in a profession in which he was becoming increasingly successful; I was continuing my education; and we had acquired the hallmarks of a comfortable middle-class life. Now that we didn't have to contend with their disappointments and concerns about our future, we had a more relaxed relationship with Sylvan's parents. And Ricki had the immeasurably rich experience that a child can only have with grandparents. Since she was their only grandchild, they gave her an overabundance of love and attention, to which she responded enthusiastically. I always believed that the time Ricki spent with her grandparents provided her with some of the most enriching experiences she had.

My mother died while we were living in Buffalo. She had been discharged from the hospital after having had a prefrontal lobotomy, which had erased the symptoms of her depression but also destroyed her capacity for any kind of emotional response and left her able to function only with much assistance. My father had found a foster-home arrangement for her with a family in Montreal, where I visited her once, a year or two before she died. During our brief meeting, she had no reaction to me whatsoever; it obviously meant nothing to her when I explained to her that I was her daughter. For my part, I could not bring myself to recognize her as my mother; my response to her was, in its own way, as devoid of feeling as hers. It was the last time I saw her. I had mourned her loss for so many years that when she died I could not allow myself to mourn anymore. More accurately, I mourned her as I had before.

My father died a couple of years later from a heart attack he had while driving back to Levack from the camp. I was stunned by the depth of grief I felt when my brother Don called to tell me that he had died. I attended his funeral in Montreal, where he was buried next to my mother and my brother Saul. I felt so many conflicting emotions, ranging from regret over the difficulties we had in communicating with each other, to anger about what I felt I had been deprived of, to great sadness over the loss of a man I wished I had known under better circumstances. I could not help thinking about the one time that Sylvan, Ricki, and I had visited him at the camp, when Ricki was about four years old. His obvious delight in being with his grandchild, the ease with which he was able to talk with her and play with her, astounded me. He pulled pennies magically out of his ear, told her about animals that lived near the camp, and had her giggling at silly jokes. I couldn't believe this was the same man who was so frightening to me as a child. That visit was a stark illustration of the ways that grandparents can treat a child so differently than they did their own child, and the impressions that remain from these contacts. Unfortunately, Ricki was so young at the time of the visit that she was left with virtually no recollection of it.

After living in Buffalo for about three years, and getting a little tired of the suburban environment, we moved to a neighborhood in the central part of the city, an area of tree-lined streets with many older, well-maintained, grand houses surrounded by spacious yards. Our apartment, on Summer Street, on the ground floor of a house that had been divided into two apartments, was larger than the one we had had in Cheektowaga, had a working fireplace and many other attractive features, and was more convenient to Sylvan's work and to the university. It was close to the concert hall where the Buffalo Philharmonic played; to the Albright Art Gallery, the major art museum in the city; and to some of the nicer shopping districts. All of this contributed to our sense that we were more in touch with the heart of the city. There was one drawback: Ricki would have to change schools, an experience that, unfortunately, occurred several times during her school years. While she seemed to adapt well, she had to find new playmates and get used to the almost imperceptible but important differences in the school environment.

We had good times when we lived on Summer Street. Sylvan had established himself as one of the most competent reporters on the paper, which meant that he was often given the choicest assignments, more than his share of bylines, praise from a crew of editors who were not known for being quick to give compliments, and, as his success grew, much-welcomed increases in salary.

I was doing well in nursing school, amazed at how much I enjoyed work that at one time was so completely foreign to me. For the first time in my life, I experienced the gratification of being able to ease the physical and emotional pain of someone suffering from a serious illness. As students, carefully supervised by our instructors, we were assigned to give complete care to a small number of patients in the clinical area of our studies. One of my most vivid memories is of caring for a middle-aged man with Parkinson's who was recovering from unsuccessful surgery to treat the disease. His crushing disappointment and hopelessness because of the failure of the operation were as devastating to him as the surgical assault he had experienced, and required at least as much attention. I was proud to think that even with my limited experience I met the challenge of providing him with the best possible nursing care. At the time of his discharge, his wife approached me to thank me tearfully for the care I had given her husband, and to present me with a gift that she insisted I accept: three delicate handkerchiefs that she had carefully embroidered. Although I was aware that accepting gifts from patients was frowned upon, I could not refuse her gracious expression of thanks, given the circumstances. I still have the handkerchiefs tucked away in a drawer.

Each rotation through a clinical area was fascinating and attractive in its own way. I could imagine the possibility of working in any one of a number of specialties: pediatrics, maternal health, or public-health nursing, particularly. But it was my clinical rotation in psychiatric nursing—six weeks at a V.A. hospital and six weeks at the psychiatric facilities of the county hospital—that most interested me. I saw the opportunity to work with people suffering the pain of severe psychological problems as being more challenging and having the potential of providing me with greater satisfaction than any other kind of nursing. There was, of course, the underlying consideration of finally being able to have some understanding of the behaviors I had witnessed in my mother that had so frightened and confused me in my childhood. Most important, in my current position, I was no longer the small child trying to deal with the myth of being responsible for her behavior but an adult finding ways to alleviate severe emotional distress in others.

In retrospect, I am overwhelmed when I think of the boundless energy and optimism Sylvan and I felt during those years. We looked ahead to the endless possibilities the future held, with the youthful exuberance that comes with being thirty. That sense of promise can never be replicated in later life but is wonderful to recall.

***

With his continuing success, Sylvan came to a point where he felt the urge to get back to New York to see if he could make it under the most competitive conditions in the newspaper business. He began making inquiries to the papers in New York, without any positive responses.

I don't remember how he made a connection with someone who was in charge of acquiring the staff for a new weekly newsletter that Cowles Publications, the publisher of *Look* magazine, was starting. Although the job was not on a newspaper, it gave Sylvan a chance to get back to New York and possibly have more successful contacts with the papers that had until then rejected him.

But moving back to New York created a problem: I still had one more year in nursing school. With the help of the faculty, who allowed me to combine all the courses I needed into the second semester, I was able to be free during the first semester. Sylvan and I rented an apartment in Queens, a few blocks away from where Sophie and Louis lived. I made arrangements with a friend of ours in Buffalo, Barbara Ashford—a colleague of Sylvan's at the *Buffalo Evening News*—to rent a room in her apartment while I was completing my final courses.

Sylvan started work at the newsletter, and since I didn't have to worry about classes for the first few months we were in Queens, I had time to get the apartment organized and help Ricki get settled in her new school.

When it was time to return to Buffalo, I spent weekdays completing my course requirements while staying with Barbara, and then flew to New York to be home each weekend with Sylvan and Ricki. It required much skillful coordination and cooperation from everyone to execute Operation Getting Gloria to Graduate: Sylvan had to take over the role of being the available parent to Ricki in addition to holding down a new job; Sophie and Louis were there to provide Ricki with most of her care while Sylvan was at work; Sophie made sure that everyone ate well; and, most important, Ricki had to tolerate this rather unconventional, inconvenient arrangement for the sake of my becoming a nurse. Somehow, we managed to pull it off.

I don't know who the happiest member of the family was on that sunny day in June of 1960 when, dressed in cap and gown, I marched up to receive my diploma. I was filled with immeasurable gratitude to all of them for what they had done and for what they had given me. It was a moment in which I basked in the warmth of the family surrounding me and contemplated my extreme good fortune in being with them. Later that evening, while lying in bed, I told Sylvan that there was no better way for him to have expressed his love for me than he had by helping me reach this goal.

My brother Bob also attended my graduation. He was as delighted as the rest of us, and his congratulations included his apologies for doubting that I had made the right decision in choosing nursing as a career. As much as he and I had differed over the years about my decisions, he was gracious enough to concede that I had chosen correctly in the most important ones. At about this time, Bob moved to New York, where he began his teaching career at Adelphi University, and we were able to establish a long, close relationship with him that continued until his death.

Chapter 10

Another new phase in our life had begun. Back again in New York, under much better circumstances than before, both Sylvan and I were eagerly looking for ways to pursue our careers. He had become determined to land a job on a newspaper, after concluding that the job on the newsletter was not sufficiently challenging. Through an acquaintance who had some connections with *Newsday*, the Long Island paper, Sylvan got an interview with the managing editor and impressed him enough to be offered a position as a reporter. It was a great achievement to finally be working on a paper that, if not actually in New York City, was at least in the New York area.

Meanwhile, heeding the advice that had been given to nursing students who were about to graduate—get some experience in medical-surgical nursing before going into a specialty—I found a job on a medical unit of a small hospital in downtown Manhattan. As a new graduate, I was assigned to the least attractive shifts, rotating between nights and evenings on an irregular schedule, with little time for an adequate orientation period. To add to my misery, the hospital was without air conditioning. In the mid-summer heat, usually exhausted from not sleeping well, often with few nursing assistants, and with little supervisory support, I found myself wondering: "Is this the best way to begin my nursing career?" After a few weeks, I decided that I would forgo any further attempts at increasing my skills in medical nursing and go the route I had wanted to take initially: looking for a job in psychiatric nursing.

Without much difficulty, I found a job as a staff nurse at Payne Whitney Clinic, the psychiatric division of New York Hospital. At that time, Payne Whitney was primarily providing long-term treatment lasting up to two years to a select group of patients who, in addition to being able to afford to pay for private care—health insurance was nonexistent then—were considered capable of benefiting from psychotherapy and adjunctive treatments; psychotropic drugs were not yet widely available. Each patient saw an individual therapist several times a week, participated in group meetings, and had regularly scheduled occupational and physical therapy. All of this was conducted in an elegant building, tastefully furnished in a style befitting an upper-middle-class residence, with sweeping views of the East River. Meals were served to all but the most disturbed patients in a comfortable dining room with snowy white tablecloths and attractive silverware. (I was saddened to see, many years later, that the building was demolished and replaced with a generic-looking modern addition to the main hospital.)

I was attracted to working at Payne Whitney because it was a teaching hospital, used by both the medical and nursing schools of Cornell University, and in addition participated in a number of research projects in psychiatry. It also had an excellent reputation for offering opportunities for development to the nurses on its staff. It seemed like an ideal environment to further my professional growth. In 1960, the clinic was still headed by Oskar Diethelm, a protégé of the noted psychiatrist Adolf Meyer. Diethelm had been there since 1936 and continued to be a formidable, sometimes frightening presence who met with every resident physician and every patient at least once a week; and when, during his rounds, he entered the nursing station, everyone quickly snapped to attention to await his interrogation.

Payne Whitney provided me with ample opportunities for professional growth: I had the satisfaction of working with patients with a variety of diagnoses, under the guidance of experienced supervisors, and I participated in staff meetings and attended clinical conferences with members of other disciplines. I was acquiring increasing understanding of the manifestations and treatment of psychiatric illness. Energized by the stimulation of work, I hardly minded the long commute from our apartment in Queens to the East Side of Manhattan.

Meanwhile, more and more, Sylvan was feeling the urge to move from working in the suburbs to being on the staff of a newspaper in New York. While searching for a way to accomplish that, he heard that the *New York World-Telegram and Sun*, a daily evening paper, was accepting applications to try out on the local staff. When he spoke with the city editor, he was told that the paper had one job opening for which it was offering two-week tryouts, at the end of which the applicant would either be sent on his way or offered a job. The chances of the latter occurring seemed rather slim, as Sylvan discovered when he learned that a large number of people had joined the ranks of rejected candidates.

To make the situation more complicated, when Sylvan asked his bosses at *Newsday* if he could take a few weeks' leave for the tryout, they turned him down. As the managing editor told him, he had to decide whether he wanted to make a career at a growing operation like *Newsday*—where he was assured of a promising future—or take a chance on a newspaper in what the editor described as "a dying city." Leaving *Newsday* would mean giving up a secure job for the risky possibility of getting on the staff of the *Telegram*.

During the many long walks that we took on the streets of Forest Hills, agonizing over the choices that were before us, I recognized how driven Sylvan was to take his chances in New York, but I also knew that he wouldn't make the move without my complete agreement.

On one of these walks, I reminded him that if the job didn't come through at the *Telegram,* we could manage on my salary until something else came through.

"This tryout is a chancy thing, you know," he said. "Are you sure you want to take the risk?"

"Yes, I'm sure. And I'm sure that if a job at the *Telegram* doesn't materialize, with your talent and experience, you'll find something else. Do we go by the old saying 'A bird in the hand is worth two in the bush' or by the other one, 'Nothing ventured, nothing gained'? I like the second one better."

"Me, too," Sylvan answered.

In many ways, this quandary was similar to the one we had faced when Sylvan had completed his degree at Berkeley: should we give up the security of what we have and the promise of something even better for a risky leap into the unknown? We opted for Sylvan quitting *Newsday* and trying out at the *Telegram*.

***

With great trepidation, Sylvan started his tryout as a reporter on the *World-Telegram*. He thought he was handling the assignments well but had few clues from the city editor, who gave little indication of his opinions. After he had been there a week, Sylvan saw the fellow who had preceded him being beckoned to the city editor's desk and summarily told that he was finished. At the end of the second week, with the memory of the previous week's scene fresh in his mind, Sylvan was called up to the city editor's desk. "Are you available for another two weeks?" the editor asked. Sylvan responded that he had no other commitments so he was free to continue.

We still didn't know how the situation would play out, but at least Sylvan's stay had been extended. Having gained some familiarity with what was expected of him, his increasing confidence was reflected in his writing. His performance impressed the city editor enough that at the end of the second tryout period he again summoned Sylvan to his desk. "Can you stay on for another two weeks?" he asked. Once again, our hopes rose and fell as we tried to read the significance of these extensions and of every other clue that Sylvan could pick up. This went on for another two weeks until—after eight weeks of uncertainty—Sylvan was finally offered a permanent position as a reporter. At last we had cause for serious celebration, which we did with great gusto and much wine, to hell with the expense, in an excellent restaurant. It was another moment when we were both firmly convinced that this success could not have been possible without each of us having the unqualified support of the other, a leitmotif that ran throughout the course of our lives.

Those were heady times. We both had jobs that, in addition to being challenging and stimulating, validated the wisdom of our decisions. During the next months, Sylvan's reputation at the *Telegram* began to soar, as he quickly became known as a writer of great speed and elegance. He often worked as a rewrite man, which meant writing on a tight deadline while information was pouring in from reporters in the field through a phone cradled between his shoulder and his ear. In the days when the afternoon papers put out seven editions over a few hours, the competition was intense to get fast-breaking stories out ahead of the other papers, which meant that writing speed was of utmost importance. As a rewrite man, Sylvan had to work under much stress, flooded with a lot of adrenaline and too many cigarettes; but he thrived on this pace, which only a young man could maintain.

While Sylvan was experiencing his success at the *Telegram*, I was unexpectedly offered an additional challenge. Having already been promoted to head nurse at Payne Whitney, I was asked whether I'd like to become the clinical instructor of psychiatric nursing for the Cornell students who were having their psychiatric nursing experience at the hospital. This opening had suddenly become available when the previous instructor was forced to leave because of "severe emotional problems." It seems that she had been demonstrating some rather irrational, bizarre behavior that was quickly noticed by the director of nursing, who lost no time in removing her. When I expressed some hesitation, I was told that most of my responsibilities would involve clinical supervision, for which I would get some help from the nursing supervisors, and that course outlines and lecture notes would be available for my classroom responsibilities. Attracted to the idea of teaching, and naively optimistic that I could handle the job, I accepted the offer. Fortunately, the students were bright and motivated; and because they readily rallied to my support in this rather unusual situation, I managed very well, and the students passed their exams without difficulty. Although flying by the seat of my pants was an exhilarating experience, I decided that I didn't want to do it again. I did come away with serious thoughts about the possibility of teaching psychiatric nursing in the future, but with better preparation for the job.

Added to the sweet taste of success that both Sylvan and I were getting from our careers was the joy we had as Ricki's parents. A bright, delightful child, she was moving through fourth and fifth grades in a public school in Forest Hills. Our only cause for concern was that she had already changed schools three times because of our moves. We hoped that the consistent support she was given—not just from Sylvan and me, loving if somewhat unconventional parents, but from Sophie and Louis—compensated for the burden of the upheavals. At least from what we could observe, she seemed to be a healthy, well-adjusted child. Through no choice of her own, of course, Ricki had to put up with parents who were playing their own song.

In many ways Sylvan and I differed from many of the people around us. The security that Sylvan and I felt in our relationship was always more dependent on what we felt for each other than on what our physical environment could provide. As a result, we were willing to make changes and moves in the interest of following our dreams, even if it meant forgoing the stability and financial rewards that could be achieved by sticking to a more predetermined course. We had little interest in marking the passage of time by finding yet a more luxurious house with more luxurious furniture in a more upscale neighborhood. As a result, we probably ended up financially less well off than we might have been, but we considered it well worth the tradeoff.

The next two years were filled with a number of changes. In 1961, we moved from Queens to Manhattan, to an apartment in a new building on 12th Street and Seventh Avenue. It was a great location, in a good section of the Village, close to all the cultural, culinary, and recreational attractions that drew people there, and a short subway ride from the *World-Telegram*. We had finally reached our goal of living in Manhattan. Ricki, unfortunately, had to change schools yet again to attend sixth grade.

We didn't know it at the time, but Sylvan's talents as a rewrite man were demonstrated most dramatically the next year, on March 1, 1962.

As the city was honoring astronaut John Glenn with a tickertape parade, an American Airlines plane headed from New York to Los Angeles crashed shortly after takeoff in Jamaica Bay. All ninety-five people on board were killed, making it the deadliest crash of a Boeing 707.

Within minutes, the *World-Telegram* dispatched a crew of reporters to the crash scene. As they frantically fed fragments of information to Sylvan by phone, as fast as they could retrieve it, Sylvan instantaneously converted the raw material into a coherent narrative. At that time, this had to be done on a manual typewriter, of course, which was a lot more difficult than producing such an article on a computer. Within half an hour, Sylvan had completed a superbly written piece.

As the story unfolded, Sylvan received more information throughout the day, and he continued to make revisions for the six additional editions that were released over the next few hours. It was a reporting tour de force that few writers could have achieved.

Sylvan and I had planned to meet for dinner later that evening when he had finished for the day. I waited for him at the bar of the restaurant that was to be our meeting place, wondering when or if he would be able to get away. Finally, he rushed into the bar, looking exhausted but with a smile of satisfaction lighting up his face. As he settled into a seat beside me, he said, "If I am ever going to win a Pulitzer, I won it today." Laughing at the unlikelihood of this wild prediction, we promptly ordered a drink and sat back as Sylvan filled me in on the incredible events of his day.

In the fall of 1962, I left Payne Whitney to begin a master's program in psychiatric nursing education at Teachers College, Columbia University, with the goal of making a career in teaching. The program demanded far more of my time than my job had, and also required considerable traveling to the various hospitals where I was assigned for my clinical experience. From the beginning, I had misgivings about whether this was the right program for me, but I decided that I should take enough time to explore it.

On December 8, 1962, a newspaper strike began that closed down all the major New York newspapers. Sylvan and his colleagues were out of their jobs for 114 days, until March 31, 1963, when the strike finally ended. It turned out to be the most costly newspaper strike in the city's history, causing not only lost revenue to the papers but immeasurable damage to many related industries. It also forced the closing of the Hearst morning tabloid, the *Daily Mirror*, leaving only two tabloids, the *New York Daily News* and the *New York Post*.

During the strike, Sylvan found work on a paper that had been set up temporarily. Produced by a company that published an Italian-language daily, it was a weak substitute for a major newspaper, but at least it provided the public with a daily source of printed news—and Sylvan and a few others with a decent salary. Not all the employees of the city's newspapers were so fortunate. Being left without a paycheck added to the air of discouragement that hung over what seemed like a never-ending strike. Thus it was an occasion of great jubilation—celebrated in an appropriately well-lubricated style by hardworking newsmen—when the presses started to roll on April 1 and the appetites of news-hungry New Yorkers could be satisfied again.

By the time the newspaper strike was over, my dissatisfaction with Teachers College had led me to the decision that it was not worth continuing in the program. I was disappointed by the instructors, who had less experience in the field than I did, and who had begun teaching as soon as they had finished their graduate degrees. I was even more disappointed by the clinical settings to which we were assigned; a long-term care unit for chronic patients at the county hospital in Brooklyn was one of the main facilities we used. It offered patients little in the way of a treatment program and few learning opportunities for the nurses getting clinical experience there. I deliberated for some time about the pros and cons of leaving the program, and ultimately decided to leave at the end of the semester, with the thought that I'd continue graduate studies elsewhere in the future.

I lost little time in finding a teaching position in the school of nursing of St. Vincent's Hospital. It was known for being one of the best diploma programs in the city. My credentials from Payne Whitney convinced the school's director to hire me, even though I hadn't finished my master's. In my first experience working in a Catholic institution, I joined three other women: two lay instructors and the nun who was the director of the department. I was warmly welcomed and soon felt completely comfortable in this racially and religiously heterogeneous group composed of one African American Protestant, one white Irish Catholic, one secular Jew, and a young, vivacious Sister of Charity whose impish sense of humor couldn't be concealed by her white habit.

The psychiatric division of St. Vincent's, housed in a building called the Reiss Pavilion, offered patients short to moderate periods of hospitalization, depending on their needs. Patients were assigned to units based on the severity of their illness, with locked floors for those who required a more secure environment. By this time, patients' treatment programs included psychotropic drugs, complemented by individual therapy, structured community meetings, and occupational therapy. Electroconvulsive therapy was used only selectively for a small number of patients. The hospital offered a residency training program for physicians, as well as classroom and clinical instruction for the student nurses, who had a twelve-week psychiatric rotation in Reiss. Since it was assumed that most of the students would not pursue psychiatric nursing as a career, much of the teaching program was directed to the psychosocial principles they could apply in any nursing setting.

One of the attractions of working at St. Vincent's was its ideal location, directly across the street from where we were living. I had the rare convenience of being able to go home for lunch, often accompanied by my colleague Opal, with whom I had become close friends.

While I was enjoying my new job at St. Vincent's, Sylvan was continuing his successful rise at the *World-Telegram*, having by this time advanced to being an assistant city editor. One late afternoon in the spring, the announcements of the 1963 Pulitzer Prizes were being made. I was at home when Sylvan called me with the incredible news that he had just been informed that he had won the prize for local reporting under deadline for the story about the American Airlines plane crash the previous year. I couldn't stop jumping up and down in excitement, trying to absorb the enormity of the event. About all Sylvan and I could say over and over, while shrieking with joy, was "I can't believe it! I can't believe it!" Suddenly we both recalled the prediction that Sylvan had made a year ago after he had finished writing the story. Sylvan wondered, "Do you think anybody would believe that I said that then?" "I don't think so," I replied. "It's too fantastic." We agreed that everyone would think that we had simply made up the whole amusing but unbelievable story.

Within moments, we had told Ricki and called Sylvan's parents with the news. It's hard to describe how overwhelmed we all were. For each of us, there was special meaning attached to the achievement, but we all shared a feeling of tremendous joy. Sylvan and I joked that finally Sophie would be able to trump her friends at the bridge table with the news that her son had won a Pulitzer.

That evening the five of us went out to celebrate with a festive dinner, while still letting the news sink in. For me, his winning was the ultimate confirmation of my unfailing belief in Sylvan's immense talent, which I had felt long before he had had the opportunity to demonstrate it. For Sylvan, it was a mark of the highest achievement in journalism, an honor that he would always treasure and that would always enhance his personal and professional life. Someone once wryly remarked that winning a Pulitzer meant that the term "Pulitzer Prize winner" would always precede his name in every conceivable context, including his obituary, and that was absolutely true. The award always remained a source of great pride for Sylvan and me.

***

Our years living on 12th Street were among the happiest of our lives, enriched by the joy of being together, very much in love, with a young daughter who gave us endless pleasure, and careers that provided us with a wealth of challenges and a great deal of fun. We both looked forward to setting off for work in the morning, and to returning at the end of the day, when we could relax and talk about what we had done, what had happened, what was funny, what was exciting; there never seemed to be enough time for everything that we wanted to talk about. But there was always the next day.

For the first time, we were able to take vacations to escape the cold New York winters, usually in the Caribbean, and to afford to take advantage of the cultural life of the city in ways that hadn't been possible before. We eagerly attended concerts and the theater, and we developed a newfound appreciation for jazz that led us to go out many nights to hear the top performers who were appearing in clubs around New York.

Since Ricki had now finished sixth grade, the final grade in the school she had been attending, we had to decide where she'd continue. The nearest junior high school, in a not particularly safe neighborhood and with low academic standards, was out of the question.

As much as both Sylvan and I were strong believers in the public school system, there seemed to be no choice under the circumstances but to find a suitable private school for her to attend. We finally selected the Calhoun School, at the time a small, all-girls school that went from junior high through high school. It promised to be a place where Ricki would receive a solid education in a supportive environment. She was finally able to attend one school for six uninterrupted years, which gave some continuity to her life and allowed her to make lasting attachments, something she had not been able to do until then.

Over the years, people who were raising their children in the suburbs often questioned Sylvan and me about the suitability and safety of raising a child in the Village, to which we answered that the environment that Ricki was growing up in was far richer than and at least as safe as the suburbs. Unlike youngsters who lived outside the city, she had easy access to a wealth of cultural opportunities, including innumerable events especially for children. Among the most enriching of these were the music programs for young people led by Leonard Bernstein, then the conductor of the New York Philharmonic, which she attended. We were firm believers in the value of what New York offered all of us.

Where was our piano during all those peripatetic years? The beautiful brown Hamilton grand, which had been Sylvan's since childhood, had survived the moves with us from one apartment to the next, not much the worse for wear, and continued to occupy an honored place in our home. While neither of us had time for serious practice, we turned to it for moments of enjoyment and relaxation whenever possible. In many ways, it was a greater source of pleasure to us now since we were free of the demands of music teachers and classes. We even managed to find time to do some four-hand playing, which we had always enjoyed and which became even more attractive as the years passed. Our time at Juilliard had given us an education that, although not professionally productive, rewarded us with a dimension to our lives that we would otherwise have never had.

Because of Sylvan's active involvement in the major news stories of the day—whether he was writing a story or planning for its coverage—what was happening in the city and the world had a daily impact on our personal lives. The immediacy and tension of significant events that Sylvan brought home with him imbued our thinking and conversations so much that it became an occurrence we took for granted. The up-side of this was the richness and excitement it brought to our lives; the down-side was the constant pressure that Sylvan had to endure.

The early 1960s were, of course, the time of the Cold War, with the endless threats that accompanied it. International conflicts reached a most dangerous peak with the occurrence of the Cuban missile crisis, in October 1962. As conditions rapidly deteriorated, Sylvan insisted that Sophie, Louis, Ricki, and I go to his parents' weekend house in New Jersey, where he thought we would be safer than in New York should an attack actually be launched against the United States. I initially resisted the suggestion but finally agreed, after much urging by Sylvan, to go. Sylvan remained in Manhattan to cover the story, while the four of us stayed in New Jersey for what seemed like an interminable time until the threat diminished. Being separated from Sylvan under such unsettling circumstances was painful, and it was one of the few times that we were forced to do so. A modicum of sanity seemed to return to the world when the crisis was resolved and we could resume our normal lives.

Not long after that, we rewarded ourselves with a trip to France, starting in Paris and then driving leisurely south to the Mediterranean. It was the first time we had been back in Paris since our stay in 1949. What a contrast this visit was to our earlier one. Now we were able to stay in one of the best hotels in the city, to frequent restaurants that we could never have dreamed of before, and to enjoy the city, which had completely recovered from the devastation of war and had again become the city of light. We revisited many of the haunts that we had frequented years before—the street we lived on, familiar cafés, and the beloved American Express building, whose bathroom facilities had been so mercifully available to us—and marveled at the distance we had traveled in our lives since we had been there the first time. Since these were the promising days of the Kennedy administration, in which the United States and France enjoyed particularly amicable relations, we were greeted more warmly as Americans than we might have been at other times.

After visiting Paris, we spent another ten days or so driving to the Côte D'Azur, stopping as we encountered a village or an inn that looked particularly appealing. It was a glorious trip, unhindered by the necessity of having to make advance plans and reservations, something that was still possible then.

The optimism we and other Americans felt in 1963 came crashing to a halt on November 22, when John Kennedy was assassinated. Sylvan was acting as city editor that day, which put him in the center of the maelstrom of information that had to be processed and reported. While the tragedy was a part of everyone's life during those awful days, Sylvan, like every journalist who was in some way involved in the story, felt the responsibility of trying to present a coherent picture of the events to the public.

Coverage of the events demanded long hours of grueling work under the most intense pressure, and Sylvan performed at his usual level of excellence. The *World-Telegram* met the highest journalistic standards in its reporting on the horrific events of the weekend. The rest of us could only sit riveted to our televisions, transfixed by what was unfolding before our eyes. It was to the print media, however, that we turned for a better understanding of the catastrophe we were witnessing. In the following weeks, the papers and magazines continued to provide interpretations and analyses—some with more sensationalism than erudition—that only partly satisfied the public's need for resolution and closure, a need that for many people was never satisfied completely.

Not long after the assassination, Sylvan took a leave of absence for several months to write a book about the Warren Commission report on the assassination. Entitled *The Unanswered Questions about President Kennedy's Assassination*, the book, one of the first of many about the event, was a critical examination of the deficiencies of the report and posed many significant questions that should have been examined but were not investigated by the commission. Although not a bestseller, the book was well received and went into three subsequent printings. Sylvan was extremely proud to have successfully ventured into a different genre by writing a serious, well-researched book that had greater permanence than a daily newspaper story. It was the only book that he would write.

Shortly after Sylvan returned to his job at the *Telegram*, he was made city editor when the previous editor retired. While the promotion marked another advance in Sylvan's career, directing the coverage of local news came with the burden of additional work and longer hours.

Sylvan's position as city editor placed him in a higher stratum of the news world. He was now attending professional and social affairs to which only editors, distinguished reporters, notables in the community, and visiting dignitaries were invited. I usually accompanied him as his guest and soon became accustomed to meeting the newsmakers and news writers of the world. Shaking hands and making small talk with mayors, governors, and the occasional heads of state became commonplace.

Of all the political figures I encountered, I was most impressed with Golda Meir, whom I met on one of her visits to the city. Her grandmotherly appearance and unpretentious manner belied the influence she had exerted for many years in the government of Israel, part of the time as prime minister.

In contrast, Nelson Rockefeller, who I think was governor of New York at the time, was the consummate politician. He had a smile stretched across his face as he gave his signature greeting of "Glad to see ya" and gave a handshake that left your hand tingling. The excitement of meeting "wheelers and dealers" was an experience that faded quickly.

We were invited to the celebratory inauguration ball for John Lindsay when he became mayor of New York on January 1, 1966. The membership of the Transportation Union had decided to go on strike to coincide with the gala, and, as a result, there were no buses, subways, or cabs operating anywhere in the city, creating what the union hoped for—a colossal problem in trying to get anywhere, including the celebration. A friend, who was accompanying us to the affair with his date, was foresighted enough to contact a car service a few days in advance, but by the time he made the call, all the cars had been reserved and the only vehicle available was a vintage 1920s chauffeur-driven Rolls-Royce limousine, which we, of course, eagerly hired. How could you compare that with some commonplace Cadillac or Chrysler sedan? Needless to say, we made a striking scene: four handsome young people, dressed smartly in evening clothes, looking like an illustration from *The Great Gatsby* as we pulled up to the hotel where the event was being held. I remember less about the ball itself than our sensational mode of transportation and dramatic entrance.

Later in the year, Sylvan faced a serious career decision when the *New York Journal American*, a Hearst newspaper, acquired the *World-Telegram and Sun* to create a much-enlarged joint afternoon newspaper. The owners of the newly merged paper approached Sylvan to offer him the position of city editor on the new paper, which, of course, entailed greater responsibilities with an enlarged staff and a heavier production schedule. When Sylvan inquired about the salary he would receive in this new position, he was told that it would be the same as what he had been getting in his previous job. Since this hardly seemed like fair compensation for what would be a greatly expanded role, he attempted to negotiate with the owners, who adamantly refused to make any compromises in their offer. Sylvan, angered by the attitudes of the Hearst executives, and uncomfortable with the entire atmosphere of the Hearst operation, decided that the time had come to leave, and summarily submitted his resignation.

(The wisdom of his thinking was confirmed when the merged paper survived for only about a year, leaving the city with three papers: the *Times*, the *News*, and the *Post*.)

With a great feeling of relief, Sylvan told me about his decision. I agreed that it was the best move to make in a situation where there was unquestionably an unscrupulous attempt to take advantage of him. Once more, Sylvan was without a job and no immediate prospects, but this time he was armed with extensive experience as a writer and editor and credentials that included a Pulitzer Prize. We had little doubt that attractive offers would present themselves. Sylvan was still hoping that he might be contacted by the *New York Times,* where he had continued to let it be known that he would be interested in working. He had also been in touch with the *Washington Post* for some time, which he considered equal to the *Times'* stature.

The offer he received, however, was from neither the *Times* nor the *Washington Post* but, surprisingly, from the New York City Police Department, asking if he would be interested in becoming deputy police commissioner in charge of press relations. Up until then, Sylvan had been on the other side of the equation as a reporter getting news about police activities. Now his name had been suggested by someone he knew who had formerly held the position as deputy commissioner.

Commissioner Howard Leary, a recent appointee of Mayor Lindsay, thought that Sylvan was a good candidate for the job because of his extensive knowledge of the workings of metropolitan newspapers, which would enable him to act as a successful liaison between the police department and the press. Sylvan was intrigued with the idea of assuming this completely different role, but only for a limited time. He presented this caveat to Leary, saying that he would stay in the position for no more than a year. Leary agreed. After discussing the financial compensation and the perks, which included the use of a police car and a driver during work hours, Sylvan took the job.

We never failed to be amused by the sight of a New York City police car, driven by a uniformed officer, arriving at our apartment building to chauffeur Sylvan to work. Sylvan always declined use of the siren, except once, when he finally gave in to the entreaties of his driver, who thought his passenger should enjoy speeding in and out of morning rush-hour traffic, siren blaring, at least once.

The job with the police department was an interesting one for Sylvan, as it provided him with an intimate look at its inner workings from a totally new perspective. He was impressed by the level of intelligence and sophistication of the high-level officers he worked with, and found that he was able to work comfortably with Howard Leary. This interlude, away from the constant pressure of daily deadlines, gave Sylvan the opportunity to regroup for his next step.

Meanwhile, I was enjoying my work with the students at St. Vincent's. The school had a reputation for graduating skilled, compassionate bedside nurses who were known for the excellent care they provided patients. To its credit, the school's curriculum supported the importance of psychosocial nursing, which was at the core of what we were teaching. I worked most closely with Opal, who had become a close friend as well as a respected colleague. Though she was an African American, she had a greater knowledge of Jewish traditions and the Yiddish language than I did, having spent much of her life in totally Jewish neighborhoods. She jokingly referred to me as her "shiksa" friend.

St. Vincent's was about as close to an ideal work situation as I could have hoped for: I was seeing gratifying results in the development of my students, and at the same time I was aware of my own professional growth, all in a congenial setting. I was grateful that I was not being pressured by St. Vincent's to finish my master's degree. In my scheme of priorities I placed greater value on having time to spend with Sylvan and Ricki; and I was unwilling to take time away from what was most important to me to pursue a master's. I think it was evidence of what was then my somewhat limited professional ambition, of an absence of striving to move ahead to more responsible positions. Although there was a change in later years, at that moment it was how I felt.

After Sylvan had been with the police department for six or seven months, he received a call from the *Washington Post* inviting him to come to Washington to discuss the possibility of a job on the local staff of the paper. Although it would mean leaving New York, Sylvan viewed working for a paper with the prestige and reputation of the *Post* as an attractive way to get back into active journalism, and he accepted the invitation. His meeting with the *Post* editors resulted in an attractive offer that required only attending to some details before final arrangements could be made.

On my part, while I was saddened by the prospect of having to leave St. Vincent's, I was excited by the possibilities that Washington offered, and ultimately had no regrets about leaving my job. Having submitted my resignation in anticipation of the move, I was duly feted with a going-away party where my co-workers and supervisors lauded me for my work and proclaimed that I would be greatly missed.

The biggest problem we had to consider, however, was the impact that the relocation would have on Ricki, who was then in her junior year of high school. Ultimately, we reasoned that the possibilities that a job on the *Post* would offer Sylvan were great enough to outweigh the adjustment that Ricki would have to make to a change in schools. It illustrated once more the difficulties imposed by our being peripatetic parents and the never-perfect attempts we made at resolving conflicting needs.

Having made the decision to move, we began a serious search for an apartment in Washington. Sylvan was ready to make a formal acceptance of the *Post*'s offer, and we were close to signing a lease on the apartment we had selected when Sylvan got word from the *Times* that the editors finally thought he was worthy of consideration as a potential employee. Since that had been Sylvan's goal for so many years, it was impossible for him to abandon it now. A number of interviews with top editors followed. Being hired by the *Times*, regardless of the department or the position involved, required scrutiny by every editor whose judgment carried some weight within the organization. The deliberations, which extended over a couple of weeks, seemed to be more complex than those required for naming a new pope. But finally the decision was made: Sylvan was offered a job as a reporter and rewrite man on the metropolitan desk, which was then under the aegis of Arthur Gelb.

Thus, we stayed in New York. Sylvan left the police department, with the blessings of Howard Leary, I was no longer working, Ricki didn't have to change schools, and Sylvan chose to join the *Times*.

***

On Sylvan's first day at the *Times*, when he was supposed to be getting oriented, word came in that there had been a major bank robbery in Brooklyn. Arthur Gelb unhesitatingly turned to Sylvan and told him to forget about orientation and cover the story. Sylvan got his byline on the front page after being there for less than a day. This was the first of innumerable assignments to write major local news stories that appeared on the front page with his byline. Sylvan was exhilarated by his rapid success, engendered by the enthusiastic approval of Arthur Gelb, who quickly began to rely on Sylvan to write the fast-breaking stories that drew upon his consummate reporting and rewrite skills.

Arthur was known for his constant level of tense excitement, his frenetic activity, and the pressure on his staff caused by his anxious demand for top speed regardless of the circumstance. He was likened to a tornado whirling around the city room, sweeping up everyone in his path.

Working under Arthur on the metropolitan desk was not a job appreciated by many reporters, most of whom were unable to tolerate his often unreasonable expectations. However, Arthur seemed to have met his match in Sylvan, who was unfazed by Arthur's neurotic habits; and Arthur was delighted that he had finally found someone who could keep up with him.

Although Sylvan was working for the metropolitan desk, he was often assigned to cover events occurring outside New York that were of significant interest to the city. It was usually on short notice that he went flying off to another part of the state—to cover a major fire that killed eight students and a professor on the campus of Cornell University, for example—or to more distant parts of the country. These trips were particularly wearing because of the fatigue caused by traveling, often involving driving some distance in addition to plane travel, combined with the effort of writing a story away from the facilities of the office, without the convenience of computers or cell phones. Calling in a story that he himself was writing meant racing to find a public telephone and dictating the copy, word for word with every punctuation mark, to a clerk on the desk. When Sylvan returned from an assignment, there was little time for him to rest before Arthur had another urgent assignment waiting for him.

Sylvan's work and the endless demands made on his time and energy became the focus of our lives—mine as well as his—during this period. Beyond the significance that every major news story carried for the readers of the *Times*, Sylvan's direct involvement with the event produced an indelible imprint on our lives.

During the bitter Columbia University student demonstrations in the spring of 1968, Sylvan was on the scene every day covering the events for front-page stories. The protesters had two primary demands: one was regarding the acquisition of community property, on which the university intended to build a gymnasium that African American students interpreted as having a segregationist design; the other was that Columbia divest itself of investments in companies that were making profits from the Vietnam War and resign its membership in the Institute for Defense Analysis. The Columbia demonstrations—the riots, occupations of buildings, taking of faculty hostage, and shutdown of virtually all campus activities—were among the most far-reaching campus antiwar demonstrations in the country. The protests, which began eight days before the assassination of Martin Luther King, came to an end on April 30, when the police, armed with tear gas, evacuated the buildings that had been occupied by students. Columbia abandoned its plans to build the gym, instead constructing a facility elsewhere on the campus; and it withdrew its affiliation with the Institute for Defense Analysis. In the aftermath of the demonstrations, a number of students walked out of their graduation and held their own celebration elsewhere.

Unfortunately, the date of the Columbia graduation coincided with Ricki's graduation from high school, which was being held at Town Hall and which of course we all looked forward to attending. As luck would have it, Sylvan had been assigned to cover the Columbia graduation earlier in the day. While Sophie, Louis, Ricki's cousin Lisa, and one of Ricki's friends and I were seated in the auditorium, I went through the anguish of wondering if Sylvan would ever get there, and what this would mean to Ricki if he didn't show up. The strains of *Pomp and Circumstance* began, the graduates appeared, and, just as I was about to burst into tears, Sylvan finally arrived, panting so much he could barely breathe. As he slid into a seat beside us, he managed to gasp: "I've never raced so fast to get somewhere as I did to get here. I made it!"

In later years, Sylvan sometimes expressed regret that he was so busy dashing around for the *Times* that he was not available as much as he should have been when Ricki was a teenager. We watched with pride as Ricki marched onto the stage to get her diploma. It was hard to believe how the years had flown by, and that our daughter had now arrived at this point in her life, ready to go off to the University of Wisconsin for college. It was one of the happiest moments in our lives.

After the ceremonies, we all went out to celebrate the occasion with a festive dinner that didn't end until late in the evening. We got home, all of us exhausted, especially Sylvan, who had put in a grueling day of work, and fell into bed.

We had been asleep for a short time when I was jolted awake by the phone ringing next to the bed. I answered it and heard a tense voice on the other end saying it was the *Times* and that I should put Sylvan on immediately because Kennedy had been shot. In the fog of not yet being fully awake, I couldn't make sense of what the person was saying; it was only after hearing Sylvan talking to him that I absorbed that Robert Kennedy had been shot in a hotel in Los Angeles after winning the California primary. Sylvan was called in to the paper to work on rewrite as the *Times* mustered a full battalion of reporters to cover the story from vantages in Los Angeles, New York, and other U.S. locations. I don't know how Sylvan summoned the energy to go back to work at full speed with virtually no sleep, but he did so and kept up the pace for hours. It was his ability to write the most coherent, elegant story in less time than almost anyone else on the paper that earned him the reputation of being the fastest and most respected rewrite man in the business.

During August of that same year, 1968, Sylvan was sent to Chicago to cover the Democratic national convention, during which Mayor Richard Daley unleashed the Chicago police in attacks on antiwar protesters supporting Eugene McCarthy. It was yet another event requiring long hours of intense effort to meet the endless deadlines of the paper. The protests and bloody confrontations with the police in the intense heat of a Chicago summer were far more egregious than what had occurred in the student demonstrations that Sylvan had covered earlier in the year. I worried about him when he was in situations like this: not just about his safety, which was a legitimate concern considering the violent actions of both the police and the protesters, but about the unrelenting stress he was subjected to for days on end.

When he came home from an assignment such as the one in Chicago, he was returning from combat, but without being granted an adequate period of recuperation.

It was during those brief interludes together that I was glad I was available to him, to help him wind down and find some peace, until the next story came up.

Arthur Gelb became accustomed to turning to Sylvan to write nonstop under the most grueling conditions, which sometimes resulted in unfortunate consequences. Once, when Sylvan had been working at a furious rate most of the day on a major story, without stopping to eat or rest, he suddenly collapsed, unconscious, on the floor. A young copy boy, who saw what had happened, reacted in horror and shouted at Arthur: "You've killed Sylvan!" Within minutes an ambulance arrived and rushed Sylvan, who by this time had regained consciousness, to St. Vincent's Hospital's emergency room. Arthur, meanwhile, telephoned me, and, in a voice quivering with guilt, told me what had happened. As soon as I knew that Sylvan was fully alert and apparently having no further symptoms, I found myself, rather than receiving any support from Arthur, in the strange position of reassuring him that the event—not life-threatening—was undoubtedly caused by Sylvan having had nothing to eat and too much caffeine and nicotine while working furiously for hours. Arthur was much relieved that I didn't respond with hysterics or an angry outburst, as he probably feared.

Within a short time, I got to the emergency room to find Sylvan quite comfortable, receiving IV fluids, some solid food, and some much-needed rest. He was kept overnight for observation, then discharged in the morning. That day, in an effort to assuage his guilt, Arthur proposed that Sylvan take a week's vacation with me somewhere where we could relax, at the *Times'* expense. We quickly flew off to the most luxurious hotel we could find on one of the Caribbean islands, where we had a wonderful time as Sylvan enjoyed not only complete relaxation but the pleasure of being away from the frantic atmosphere of the *Times* and Arthur Gelb for a short while.

As Sylvan discovered, being one of the most successful journalists on the most respected paper in the country came with a price. The attitude at the *Times* was that anyone worthy enough to be a member of the esteemed organization should demonstrate nothing less than total, unquestioning devotion. The more valued Sylvan became, the more was demanded of him. He had become a member of the elite circle of writers who were favored not only by Arthur but by Abe Rosenthal, the managing editor. It became common practice not only for both of them to include Sylvan in significant discussions of the approach to be taken in the coverage of major stories, but to invite Sylvan and me to social events at their homes. Those occasions were not particularly enjoyable, since the conversation inevitably centered on *Times* issues. Both Arthur and Abe were so consumed by their work that they seemed unable to turn their attention to other topics even briefly. The cocktail parties and dinners they held were, at least for staff members, extensions of the workday; and for the occasional spouse who was invited, they were wearing periods of trying to be attentive, charming, and fascinated by Arthur and Abe.

After I had resigned from St. Vincent's, when we thought we were moving to Washington, I found that I had little desire either to ask if I could return to my job there or to begin looking for a position elsewhere. Rather, I felt content knowing that not working gave me time to be available to Sylvan and Ricki. Having my days free meant that I could more easily provide Sylvan with a haven of support as he was enduring the stress of work. It was difficult to define exactly how my availability was important to him, but it clearly was, and it was something that both he and I were aware of and valued. In addition, I could give Ricki my unrestricted attention during her final high school days; this too was hard to quantify, but I think it was significant, even though the sometimes stormy parental guidance in adolescence was so different from what was needed in early childhood.

Then there was the luxury of being able to spend hours at the piano again, a totally selfish pleasure that brought me much enjoyment. I was comfortable putting a temporary hold on my professsional goals knowing that I would eventually return to them. In short, I was surprisingly happy to be a full-time wife and mother for a while.

By this time we had moved from 12th Street, when we were confronted by an unreasonable raise in rent, to the Upper East Side, where we found a spacious two-bedroom apartment with a beautiful view in a new building. It was undoubtedly the most comfortable apartment that we had yet had.

Sylvan's career continued to flourish. Since this was the height of the antiwar demonstrations, there were many more major stories about student unrest, which had become something of a specialty for Sylvan. The demonstrations at the City College of the City University of New York, among the most violent and disruptive to the surrounding community, involved demands by African American and

Puerto Rican students for open admission and the establishment of programs in Black and Latino Studies. The events on campus caused considerable damage to the neighborhood, while the intense hostility of the students made it risky for a white journalist to approach the area. Sylvan often had difficulty finding a cab driver willing to take him close to the scene of the action and ended up having to walk for blocks in what was essentially a battle area. He and the photographer accompanying him used to joke that they should be receiving combat pay. Regardless of the danger, though, Sylvan was at the site of the demonstrations every day, covering the events and then rushing back to the office to write the story, which ended when the students' demands were met and the conflict was resolved.

By the spring of 1969, Ricki had finished her freshman year at Wisconsin, where the campus had also been in a state of unrest, and had decided to transfer to Stony Brook, part of the State University of New York. Stony Brook had been in existence for a relatively short time and had not yet reached the size it would in future years. It had already developed an excellent reputation, particularly in some fields, so Ricki's decision seemed sound and we readily supported it, especially since it meant that she would now be closer to home.

At about the same time, Sophie and Louis began looking for a condominium in Fort Lauderdale to use during the winter, with the intention of eventually giving up their apartment in Queens and making Florida their permanent home. Since they valued both Sylvan's and my opinion, and I was not working and thus more available, they asked me to help in selecting a place. I spent several days with them, eventually joined by Sylvan for a weekend. The apartment we decided on was lovely, with a large terrace facing the ocean and the Port Everglades inlet. I subsequently made another visit to offer interior decorating suggestions—without any professional qualifications—in selecting the furnishings. When completed, the apartment was extremely attractive and comfortable.

Over the years, Sylvan and I continued to enjoy a close relationship with his parents, particularly Louis, who experienced great pleasure in seeing what Sylvan had achieved. Their apartment in Fort Lauderdale became a place to which we eagerly escaped when the weather got frigid in New York, and where we enjoyed innumerable visits with them. Often when the four of us were sitting on their terrace, having a drink as we watched the sun set, Louis would survey the scene and marvel that he was able to retire in such comfort after starting his life in poverty on New York's Lower East Side. He was a man who physically savored the pleasures of his later years—his home, and his family, particularly Ricki, whom he adored.

It was around 1970 that Arthur and Abe decided that Sylvan could be even more useful to the paper as a deputy metropolitan, or city, editor. While this relieved Sylvan of the stress of covering breaking stories, the new position brought him into an even closer working relationship with Arthur and carried additional responsibilities involving the planning, assigning, and editing of articles. Though the workday at the office ended at around 7 o'clock, Sylvan barely had time to finish dinner at home before he received a courier-delivered copy of the first edition of the next day's paper, which he had to examine carefully for any problems in stories from the metropolitan desk. Unfailingly, something required him to call, or make several calls, to the paper to discuss changes, until the problem was resolved. It was late in the evening before he could finally get to bed, hoping there wouldn't be yet another problem that would require his attention and delay his sleep. The demands were different, but no less stressful, than in his previous position.

Over time, Sylvan began to think that an assignment to an overseas bureau might be an attractive change, and he proposed this idea to Arthur and Abe. They assured him that since he was certainly qualified for such a position, they would consider him when an opening came up. However, months went by without any indication that Sylvan's proposal was getting any consideration, no doubt because Arthur was reluctant to lose Sylvan as a valued right-hand man. The situation in the newsroom continued as before, and Sylvan began to feel that the fine balance between the satisfaction of working for the *Times* and the grinding pressure of the job was tipping toward the second condition.

In 1970, we took an extended vacation to Italy, Greece, and Israel. It was a glorious trip, beginning in Rome with visits to the Roman Forum and other major historical sites, then on to Greece, where we rented a car. As we drove around the country, we were hampered only by our inability to understand the road signs, leaving us to sometimes wonder if we'd just neglected to heed a warning that a road was impassable or mistaken a sign that said "Bridge Out" for "Scenic Route." However, we managed to find the Delphic oracle, where we posed our questions but got no answers, and to enjoy the splendors of the remains of classical Greece.

We wound up our visit to Greece with a week in a tiny hotel on the seashore of Mykonos—before the island became an overcrowded tourist destination. We luxuriated in the Mediterranean sunshine, feasted on the riches of the sea, and enjoyed the warm hospitality of the people. Sylvan constantly impressed me by his ability not only to find someone who spoke English and was eager to engage in conversation, but, because of his reporting skills, to also find out more about the local customs and politics than any guidebook could tell us. This was one of the unique pleasures of traveling with Sylvan: his unquenchable thirst for learning about a new place and the lives of the people who lived there.

It was Israel, however—the final destination of our trip—that had the most far-reaching effect on both of us. We were overwhelmed by the evidence of events from biblical times, the temples, and the habitations that remained from centuries ago; and although we were secular Jews with little connection to the trappings of the religion, we could not fail to be moved by the immediacy of the traces that spoke of the long history of the Jewish culture that began on the ground where we were standing. We were equally impressed with the vibrancy of the Israeli people, who at that time still exhibited the strength of Zionism and the confidence that came from having withstood repeated military assaults. We marveled at their ability to survive and flourish, while at the same time remaining optimistic that the conflict with Arab peoples could somehow be ended without further bloodshed.

I was particularly captivated by the Hebrew language, which struck me as both melodically beautiful and ruggedly forceful. I was determined to study the language, although I didn't even know the alphabet. Back in New York, I enrolled in a Hebrew class at an Ulpan sponsored by the Jewish Agency. The Ulpan method, developed originally to provide thousands of new immigrants in Israel with a working knowledge of Hebrew, was based on the premise that only Hebrew should be spoken in classes, so that students would become familiar with the language in much the way a child would: first by learning a basic vocabulary from hearing and using a limited number of words, then, gradually, by acquiring the skills of reading and writing. The goal is to master one thousand words, to provide the student with a basic, if not elegant, means of communication. The method has been remarkably successful and is still used both in Israel and around the world. Within a few months of rigorous study, I had acquired a rudimentary ability to express myself and read simple material in Hebrew.

Back in New York, Sylvan resumed a demanding schedule at work, and still had no response to his request for an overseas assignment other than promises that it was being considered. How much these circumstances contributed to our feelings of unease over the next months is hard to measure, but, in addition to the pressure that Sylvan was feeling, we were growing increasingly dissatisfied with conditions in New York, the political climate of the country under Nixon, and the continuing disaster of the Vietnam War. From our perspective, the country seemed to be in worse shape than it had ever been as far back as we could remember.

While we were confronting these feelings, Sylvan received an invitation from a colleague to attend a reception hosted by some Israeli politicians. The colleague, who had many contacts with Israelis both living in and visiting New York, knew that Sylvan had been fascinated by the country during his recent trip there, and thought he would be interested in meeting some representatives of the government.

The reception, during which Sylvan had a lengthy conversation with an official from the foreign ministry, led to an invitation for Sylvan to explore the possibility of his working for the ministry as a consultant in press relations.

Subsequent conversations with a number of government people produced an attractive offer of a job in a department of the foreign ministry called *hasbarah*, literally "explanation or propaganda." Its purpose was to provide guidance to the government in how to present a favorable image in dealings with other countries, a skill that the Israelis were still far from mastering. The job, which would be conducted in English with the assumption that Sylvan would eventually learn Hebrew, would involve a combination of press relations, public relations, and tactful instruction of everyone from the top down.

As we considered the offer, which, once more, would require a leap into the unknown, we felt great ambivalence. On the one hand, Sylvan was feeling extreme discomfort at the *Times* and wanted to get out of an oppressive work situation. On the other, could we uproot ourselves from New York, our home for so many years? Could Sylvan leave his position at the *Times*, which he had struggled so long to attain? Could we be comfortable such a great distance from Sylvan's parents? Was it fair to Ricki, who was still a junior in college and would have to make a decision about where she would choose to live after graduating from college? The other side of the argument was heavily weighted by our attraction to Israel and the life we thought we could have there.

Trying to recapture what we were thinking at the time demands reflection on what constituted the contour of our lives from the time we met. What had compelled us to leave Juilliard to go to Paris in search of something that we could not coherently identify; to leave Berkeley and the possibilities of a comfortable academic life in search of broader horizons; to refuse to accept a job that would provide security yet be coupled with a lifetime of restraints? Yet the prestige and rewards of the position that Sylvan had struggled so long to attain were now slowly strangling us. We had always followed a trajectory that was directed by our hunger to see, to taste, and to explore as much of the world as we could. We wanted to seize the opportunities that allowed us to savor the experience of living, regardless of the risks entailed. The wonder of it was that our spirits were so much entwined that there was never an occasion when we were drawn in opposing directions.

There were always healthy amounts of dependence and interdependence in our relationship. There were also healthy amounts of love and mutual support. Whatever mistakes we made were neither irreparable nor, as far as we knew, seriously hurt anyone. Most important, we didn't regret how we had chosen to live our lives.

We spent hours contemplating every facet of the decision. We anticipated having Ricki spend part of the summer with us in Israel before starting her senior year of college, and hoped that she might be attracted enough to Israel that she would want to return after graduation. We talked about making frequent trips to visit Sophie and Louis in Fort Lauderdale to ease the separation; after all, we reasoned, we saw them now only when we visited. We looked forward to my being able to work in a psychiatric hospital or clinic when I developed greater fluency in Hebrew.

We told ourselves that we would not be making *aliyah*, permanent immigration to Israel, but rather planning an extended stay, with the length of time dependent on our reactions and the effects on the family. Even with those caveats, the decision was a formidable one, carrying stakes higher than we had ever confronted before.

In the end, our desire to make the move overcame our doubts about leaving, and we decided that Sylvan would accept the offer. It was no surprise that Arthur and Abe were shocked when he told them that he was resigning to take a job with the Israeli foreign ministry. Perhaps they saw Sylvan's decision as a temporary lapse in rational thinking from which he would eventually recover. Nonetheless, after unsuccessful attempts to get Sylvan to change his mind, they accepted his decision with equanimity, and wished him well in his new life.

Telling Ricki, Sophie, and Louis about our plans was more difficult, since the emotional repercussions for them were much more significant. We tried to present the reasons for our decision, our struggle with the pros and cons, and the efforts we had made to provide a reasonable solution for all of us. We wanted to make sure that they knew we had no intention of leaving the United States permanently, and that how long we'd stay depended on many factors. It was not easy for any of them to become comfortable with the idea, but they eventually seemed able to see the brighter aspects of it. Still feeling trepidation ourselves, we went ahead with the mind-boggling preparations to relocate.

Chapter 11

The question of where we would live in Israel was answered by assurances that we would have accommodations in Jerusalem for up to five months in a *merkaz klitah*, or absorption center, provided by the Israeli government for new immigrants, where we would attend classes in Hebrew, be introduced to Israeli history and culture, and have time to seek a more permanent residence. The center we were assigned to, in the southern section of Jerusalem, was designated specifically for professionals and academics. We learned that the apartment we would have was small and sparsely furnished, but adequate enough for a short stay by anyone willing to put up with less than luxurious conditions.

Meanwhile, we began the arduous process of obtaining visas and the other papers required for the trip, facilitated somewhat by Sylvan's employment by the foreign ministry. We decided to put our furniture in storage in New York until we knew where we would be living after our stay in the absorption center. Because we would need a car, and it would be cheaper to buy one outside Israel, we arranged to buy a Volkswagen in Munich and drive it to Genoa, where we would board a ship that would take us with the car to the port of Haifa. All of this required extended dealings with shipping companies, German auto dealerships, travel agents, and various other agencies, each one with an array of red tape.

Even as we flew to Munich, we still had conflicting feelings about the move: excitement, eager anticipation, doubts, anxiety—they were all present. And soon we were caught up in getting the car from the Volkswagen dealer, completing all the paperwork, and having a few days to explore Munich before making the drive to Genoa.

As we were checking out of the hotel, we heard a crash coming from the direction of where our car was parked. We looked out to see that another car had backed into ours, denting the front bumper. Sylvan dashed outside and approached the driver. The middle-aged man emerged from his car as Sylvan approached him, then shrugged as if to say, "Oh, well. These things happen." Reacting to the fact that our Volkswagen—barely out of the showroom—had been damaged, and with feelings that still erupted toward Germans who were of an age to have been in the army during the war, Sylvan began shouting, in English, with every obscenity he could think of. Realizing that the guy probably didn't understand a word he had said, Sylvan then called up his workable command of German to convey a rough translation. By this time a small crowd had gathered in rapt attention, whispering among themselves and waiting to see how the story would unfold. What did ensue was that the guilty driver mumbled words of apology and assured us that he would be responsible for the cost of repairs. We couldn't imagine the complexity of how this could be done in Israel, but we did exchange names, addresses, and insurance information. Sylvan's temper cooled down; and when we examined the bumper, we saw that the damage was minor enough that it could probably be easily fixed by a mechanic in Jerusalem. Thus we bade farewell to Munich and started on our way to Genoa.

We drove from Germany into Switzerland and on into Italy, making our way south to Genoa. We stayed in Genoa only overnight and then drove to the dock where we took the car aboard the ship, a midsized vessel that was plainly utilitarian, built to carry cargo and a small number of passengers in modest accommodations from Genoa to Haifa. Our shipmates included a few Europeans who were immigrating to Israel and a number of people traveling for business who had chosen to make a sea voyage rather than going more quickly by plane. The biggest attraction of making the trip this way seemed to be that it was the most convenient means of bringing a car into Israel.

After a few unremarkable days at sea, we docked in Haifa and began the arduous process of entering the country: first, the lengthy questioning by immigration officers, who had to verify our intentions and qualifications for long-term residence in Israel, with much checking of documents and repeated stamping of papers. Simply by stating that we were born of Jewish parents, most importantly of a Jewish mother, and without any need for proof, we were given Israeli citizenship, which was added to but did not replace our American citizenship. Stamp, stamp, stamp, and we became Israeli citizens.

The session with immigration officials was followed by an even longer engagement with customs people—their habit being to take a good part of the day in preparing the papers required for importing an automobile. After completing this lengthy procedure, we were informed that for us to be able to drive the car legally we would have to fill out additional registration papers within a few days at an authorized station in Jerusalem. Of course, all the forms we had to deal with were in Hebrew, which made things even more formidable and time-consuming. This was our introduction to the world of Israeli bureaucracy, which we were never able to understand completely, even after we had been in the country for months.

When we had finally completed all the papers necessary to allow us to reside in the country, we got in our car and headed down the coast to the road that led east to Jerusalem. Driving through the countryside that led up through the Judean Hills, we began to forget the discomforts we had endured that day and were overwhelmed again by the incredible beauty of the country.

We found the absorption center without difficulty and were greeted warmly by one of the directors, who showed us to our apartment. As we expected, it had a utilitarian appearance but was adequately equipped, with two small bedrooms in addition to a living room and kitchen, and simple furniture in good condition. Our apartment was in a development of two-story concrete buildings that contained residences, classrooms, and administrative offices. The whole complex housed about 150 people, mostly adults with a few children. The primary goal of the center was unmistakable: thousands and thousands of immigrants who didn't speak the language and in many cases with little knowledge of their new country had to be integrated as quickly and efficiently as possible.

When we finally lay down in bed after that long day, we were exhilarated by the thoughts of what awaited us, while at the same time more than a little anxious about how well we would cope with the challenges. We clung to each other as we fell asleep that night.

The next morning, Sylvan and I met with the director of the absorption center to be assigned to our respective Hebrew classes. I was placed in an advanced class because of my previous Ulpan study, while Sylvan went into an intermediate class based on the rudimentary knowledge of the language he had learned as a kid in Hebrew school. In both classes, each with about fifteen students, we were the only English speakers. Most of Sylvan's classmates were musicians who had played in the Moscow Philharmonic, with a sprinkling of South American lawyers and one established Russian poet. Since almost all the Russians had some knowledge of Yiddish, as did

Sylvan, they relied on it surreptitiously, breaking the rule that only Hebrew should be spoken. (Their behavior, concealed from the eyes of the teacher, reminded me of little kids hiding in the schoolyard to sneak a cigarette.) My class consisted of a mix of doctors, lawyers, and academics from France, Argentina, and Switzerland, and since we had no common language, our only way of communicating was in Hebrew.

Our instruction began in the morning and lasted for four hours every day except Saturday. Frequently we went on field trips in which we traveled in one of the center's buses, accompanied by a crew consisting of a driver, a teacher, and a husky escort armed with a rifle by his side and a handgun in his pocket. Although Israel was not at war at the time, and Arab attacks on civilians were not as common as they were later, security was always a concern, particularly in the border areas that we sometimes visited. These excursions, for which we were prepared by lectures, reading material, and printed copies of the lyrics of the songs we would sing along the way, took us to almost every section and important historical site of the country; and since all talking was conducted in Hebrew, they provided further immersion in the language as well as lessons in history and culture.

Some of the Russian musicians in Sylvan's class complained that at times they felt like they were being treated like primary school pupils, particularly during the sing-alongs on field trips. There was no question that the whole experience of becoming integrated into the society was difficult, and for many people, too humbling to tolerate. For the Russians, with music as their lingua franca, fluency in Hebrew was less essential than it was to members of other professsions. Nonetheless, I suspect that many of the Russians subsequently left Israel and emigrated to Europe or the United States, where musicians of their caliber would have had little difficulty finding employment with more lucrative salaries in major orchestras.

For most of us, learning Hebrew was crucial to our survival. We knew some new immigrants, however, for whom the difficulty of learning the language became the obstacle that destroyed their hopes of living in Israel. One fellow resident in the absorption center, a well-educated, successful lawyer from Seattle, had gone through the Ulpan course twice, then had private instruction, and was still not able to master the rudiments of Hebrew. In utter frustration, he finally abandoned the prospect of being able to practice as a lawyer in Israel and went back to Seattle with his wife and kids, who by this time were becoming totally fluent in the language.

Meanwhile, Sylvan and I had no trouble increasing our knowledge of Hebrew. We spent hours discussing the pros and cons of the center's educational/propaganda techniques, trying to maintain a nonjudgmental attitude as much as possible while absorbing the information we were offered. I confess, however, that I never could bring myself to participate in the song fests.

As we knew from past experience, unaccompanied trips that we took in our own car would be much more enjoyable and informative than tours provided by the absorption center. We wandered over every part of the country, continuing to be awed by the beauty of the landscape and the history that it held. (In contrast to the conditions that now exist, in 1972 there were few places where it was not possible to drive. This was before the walls and roadblocks dissecting the West Bank made travel unpleasant if not dangerous.) We explored the isolation of the Negev, one day coming upon a solitary ibex searching for a meal; we encountered an oasis where nomads had stopped hundreds of years ago; and we saw caves that had probably been home for countless numbers of tribes, perhaps some of whom were our ancestors. We climbed the summit of Masada, walked through the remains of what had been a vibrant community, and were overtaken by the ghosts of the martyrs who died there.

Then there was the pleasure of talking to the young hitchhikers we picked up along the road, a common practice in Israel. Sometimes it was soldiers who were making their way home on leave, youths who looked too young to be carrying the heavy gear of war; or often it was a kid who was trying to save money by reaching his destination by hitchhiking. Usually our passenger spoke some English, and Sylvan would once again demonstrate his skill in encouraging the youngster to speak so freely that the conversation became endlessly fascinating and we regretted having to say goodbye. Once, on a drive to Beersheba, we gave a ride to a young woman who was such a pleasure to talk with that we ended up going off our route to drive her home.

Setting aside the annoyances that sometimes beset us—primarily involving byzantine red tape and bureaucracy—there were many reasons we felt comfortable in Israel, not least of which was our appreciation of its social democratic values: emphasis on education and the arts; the expectation, derived from the Zionist tradition, that a citizen would contribute service for the good of the community; the health care and social support that were available to citizens regardless of their economic position. In the midst of this, of course, stood the unavoidable question of the rights and privileges of Arab Israelis, a thorny problem that has only worsened over the years. We had lengthy discussions with people whose beliefs represented the entire spectrum of opinion regarding the roots of the problem and the proposals for correction. At least there was the presence of healthy debate, albeit in the absence of solutions.

As we felt ourselves becoming increasingly familiar with Israeli society, we began to examine our Jewishness, which until then had been largely defined by what we were *not*: we did not belong to a synagogue; we did not practice Jewish rituals; we did not believe in God; we did not believe in prayer. Yet, whenever we were asked to indicate our religion, we unhesitatingly answered Jewish. We were often challenged by observant Jews who maintained that it was impossible to consider oneself Jewish with the beliefs we held, a position that we could not adequately defend. The question of who is a Jew is a topic that arouses intense passions and endless debate, never completely satisfying anyone. Thus the question inevitably leads to more questions—a most typical Jewish phenomenon. Our self-examination in Israel led us to identify with the large number of secular Jews who constituted an essential piece of the Israeli mosaic, while the thousands of years of Jewish history, culture, and philosophy became the core of our Jewishness, which we no longer felt compelled to defend. The Jerusalem we knew at that time, not yet the overwhelmingly ultra-orthodox city that it is today, allowed us to live there comfortably with our beliefs.

Soon after we arrived at the absorption center, Sylvan began spending time each day with the people at the foreign ministry. As he and the staff got to know each other, he settled comfortably into his position as consultant. Sylvan found that because of his credentials his opinions and suggestions were accepted with respect and attention, but not always acted upon as rapidly as he might have wished. Sylvan's immediate boss, Aluf Har Even, a handsome man of military bearing, had roots in Jerusalem that went back five generations. He had served as an officer in the Israeli Defense Force, in which he had seen action in several wars, and had a Ph.D. in political science from Hebrew University. His intelligence and competence were typical of many of the people who worked in the government, often at odds with an unyielding political structure.

Shortly before Passover we received an invitation from Aluf to join him, his wife, and children for Seder dinner at their home. When we arrived we were welcomed into a beautiful apartment that held a wealth of Israeli artifacts and reflected the warmth of its occupants. Since both Aluf and his wife were secular Jews, the Seder was a celebration of a historical occurrence, combining the reading of the Haggadah with a discussion of implications that the event had in the present. We were impressed that the Har Evens' young teenaged son participated in the conversation with as much enthusiasm and understanding as the adults. The younger children also offered some of their thoughts: "We're still having as much trouble with the Egyptians as we did then," one of them commented. We enjoyed a delicious Passover dinner and joined in the hearty singing of the traditional songs of the holiday. Later, when we looked back on the evening, we saw it as an illustration of the most attractive aspects of Israeli society as well as a manifestation of secular Judaism in its best sense.

As the weeks passed, we gave serious thought to the question of how long we would remain in Israel, and what our plans would be if we stayed. I knew that I wanted to get a job if we stayed. I had begun to investigate the possibility of working in a psychiatric facility, which seemed a reasonable goal once I had increased my fluency in Hebrew. Sylvan seemed satisfied with his work at the foreign ministry, although there were times he missed the challenges of a New York newspaper. We also had to consider where we would live when our time in the absorption center was over. On Sylvan's salary, which we were told was as high as that of a Cabinet minister—high by Israeli standards but certainly not what would be considered high in the United States—renting an attractive apartment would be possible. We could foresee living comfortably in this country, for which we had developed great affection.

Our plans, however, depended to a great extent on whether Ricki would see Israel as a place she would choose to live after college. We missed her greatly and felt her absence as the most significant reason for having difficulty in seeing the country as "home." With eager anticipation, we looked forward to her visit in the summer. We wondered: would she feel the same delight here that we had?

In the meantime, we found a spacious, airy apartment in a relatively new neighborhood of Jerusalem, where our terrace looked out over a spectacular view of the Knesset buildings in the valley below. The beauty of the city, the golden hue of its buildings in sunlight, the indescribable quality of the air—all of this had infiltrated our senses as much as its history and immutability. I sometimes wonder now, with sadness, how much of that beauty still exists after the disruptive transformation the city has endured.

We shipped our furniture from New York, along with our two cats, to our new home. Ricki arrived and we joyfully celebrated our reunion. She spent several weeks exploring the country, enjoying the sights and experiences, but ultimately coming to the decision that she could not consider making Israel her home.

Her choice forced us to accept the fact that if we remained in Israel our contact with her would be reduced to seeing her only when we could make the long trip to New York, or she to Israel. We doubted that even frequent trips could compensate for not living in the same country. We were facing the danger of creating irreparable ruptures in our family. And although Sylvan's salary was enough to provide us with a good living in Israel, we now saw that it could never cover unlimited plane travel. There was no way we would be able to maintain sufficient contact with Ricki and with Sophie and Louis on the income we had available. What we had foreseen as a way of living in Israel had become an impossible goal.

Ricki went back to New York to start her senior year at Stony Brook, and we struggled with coming to the only decision that was reasonable: we had to leave. We would not be able to live in Israel as we had hoped.

Once more we faced the risks of an uncertain future, as we had so many times in the past. While we knew that it would be relatively easy for me to find employment, our primary concern was where Sylvan would be able to get a suitable job. We both tried to control our anxiety as we examined our situation. Sylvan's first move, without hesitation, after reconsidering his feelings about the *Times*, was to contact Abe Rosenthal to let him know that he was available if they wanted him back. Sylvan agonized over what kind of response he might get. "What if he's so pissed he'd never consider hiring me again? What do I do then?" Abe's immediate response by cable was "Welcome Home."

Thus began the process, in reverse, of doing everything we had gone through less than a year before: packing our furniture; making the endless arrangements for it to be shipped to New York and put into storage; going through the agonizing steps of getting the cats out of Israel, which turned out to be even more difficult than bringing them in; and, most essential, finding a place to live in New York. Somehow we managed to do it all, as well as book our flights out of the country. The final question of where we would live in New York was answered when Sophie and Louis generously offered us the use of their apartment in Queens while they were in Florida.

The preparations for the move were exhausting, but not nearly as difficult as the wrenching experience of leaving Israel. We had become rooted in this place, for which we had developed a great affection, although we knew we could not continue to live there. The conflict this presented made our struggle to say goodbye as hard as separating from someone you love. I tried to console myself by thinking that we would revisit Jerusalem sometime in the future. Unfortunately, that never came to be.

Chapter 12

Back in New York, living in our borrowed apartment in Forest Hills, Queens, we quickly readapted to the pace and excitement of the city. It was a relief to have Ricki a short distance away at Stony Brook, and to recapture the familiarity of everything that had been missing from our lives while we were away. As long as Sylvan was temporarily assigned to the metropolitan desk with the renewed promise of an overseas assignment, we were hesitant to make any plans for housing more permanent than Sophie and Louis' apartment. At the same time I thought it unwise to look for a job at a time when we were unsure of how long we would be in New York.

With Sylvan again making a more-than-adequate salary, we enjoyed indulging ourselves in the many luxuries available in the city. Arthur moved Sylvan to the culture desk for a while, which provided the additional benefit of easy entrée to a wide range of events; but the assignment didn't last long, since neither Sylvan nor Arthur thought that the position made optimal use of Sylvan's abilities.

In the spring of 1972, Ricki graduated from Stony Brook University and lost no time before finding a job as an editorial assistant at Macmillan Publishing. We were impressed with how quickly she launched an editorial career—and with no assistance from Dad, unless you consider the genes she was fortunate to get from him. It was a career she would pursue for many years.

During those months when I was unemployed, I had no difficulty finding enjoyable activities by myself in addition to doing things with Sylvan when he wasn't working.

I did a lot of reading, visited art galleries, did some painting, and got up enough courage to buy a good single-lens reflex camera and get some instruction in how to use it. I had always considered myself technologically challenged when it came to doing anything that required complicated devices, so it was a great accomplishment for me when I finally overcame my fears enough to learn how to load film into the camera, and how to deal with the basics of depth of focus and light measurement. When the weather got warm, I set about practicing my skills by taking pictures of spring flowers and foliage on walks in the neighborhood, producing, to my astonishment, some decent pictures.

Spring 1973 progressed into summer, and the promise made to Sylvan of an overseas assignment had still not materialized. Finally, in October, Abe Rosenthal proposed to Sylvan that he become the Southeast Asia bureau chief in Saigon. Because peace talks had begun in Paris, heralding that "peace was at hand," Abe reasoned that Sylvan would be posted in Saigon at the historic moment when a treaty was signed, and then would be there as a peacetime correspondent during the crucial postwar recovery period. It seemed like an exciting opportunity with considerable journalistic challenge; and with peace on the horizon, Sylvan figured that the dangers and hardships of war would be only minimal. He was assured that there would be no problem in my accompanying him, which Sylvan said would be a necessary condition.

After we talked it over, considered the professional opportunities it would offer Sylvan, and agreed on our readiness to embark on another adventure, Sylvan was ready to say yes to Abe. In a letter to Ricki that Sylvan wrote sometime later from Saigon, he asked, "How could we turn down an offer of a once-in-a-lifetime experience like that?"

Arrangements quickly got under way for Sylvan to take over the position of bureau chief from Craig Whitney, who would remain in the office for a few weeks until Sylvan was fully oriented. Among the many chores we had to attend to before leaving was going to the *Times* medical department for all the necessary immunizations. The ordeal left us feeling like pincushions. Just about every communicable tropical disease was still rampant in Vietnam, most prominently malaria, for which we were given a supply of antimalarial medication to be taken regularly during our stay. Other diseases, including leprosy and polio, which had been all but eradicated in the Western world, were still endemic there. We were also warned about the dangers of drinking tap water and eating uncooked foods. In spite of the strictest adherence to this advice, most people, as we later discovered, succumbed at least once to gastrointestinal distress.

Preparing to leave New York this time was less emotionally demanding than when we went to Israel. As much as we anticipated missing Ricki, we were comfortable knowing that she had established an independent life for herself with a job and an apartment, and we could realistically afford visits to see her periodically, or she to see us. She unhesitatingly shared our enthusiasm about the move. Our stay in Vietnam also had a predictable time frame, dictated by the length of Sylvan's assignment, on which there were reasonable limitations.

We would travel, at least until we got to Vietnam, in luxurious conditions. At that time, the *Times* spared no expense in paying for the travel of its foreign correspondents and their families: first-class flights, accommodation in the best hotels, and generous expense accounts. It was expected, after all, that someone representing the august *New York Times* should present an appropriately impressive appearance.

After saying goodbye to Ricki and packing our suitcases with a good supply of warm-weather clothes, we headed off to Hawaii, where we would stay for two days. We were booked into a palatial, ocean-front suite in the Royal Hawaiian Hotel, with a lanai just steps from our own private section of beach. Sylvan was up at dawn to take a swim in the Pacific, while I was still trying to overcome the effects of a minute amount of sleep medication that I had taken the night before to help me adjust to the time difference. I discovered that day, and confirmed many times afterward, that I am particularly sensitive to sedatives. It was only after a lengthy walk along Kalakaua Avenue, a main street in Waikiki, with Sylvan struggling to maintain me in an upright position, that I became fully awake and able to enjoy the sights of the city. We had barely adjusted to the new time zone when we were off to Tokyo, our next stop.

Our two-day stay in Tokyo allowed us to have a quick look at the city and to leave us overwhelmed by its size and modernity. We later wrote to Ricki that by comparison New York looked almost like a hick town.

Then it was on to Hong Kong. Our trip was broken into segments because there were no direct flights to Asia in 1972, although it would have been possible to make fewer stops had we chosen to. The most memorable part of the flight, the last few minutes of the approach to the Hong Kong airport, was not for the faint-hearted. Because the airport was practically in the middle of the city, planes had to make sudden, stomach-dropping descents, directly over tall buildings. I'm sure it was a maneuver that even the most seasoned pilots made with clenched teeth and a prayer. But once we were on the ground, and our terror had subsided, we enjoyed our first impressions of Hong Kong's beauty, a combination of strikingly modern and old traditional buildings existing next to each other in a setting that reminded us very much of San Francisco.

Awaiting us at the airport was the Rolls-Royce chauffeur-driven limousine that the Peninsula Hotel provided its guests, ready to whisk us off to our destination, where we were escorted into our breathtakingly beautiful suite. Fresh flowers decorated the living room, and within five minutes a waiter arrived bearing a tray with a pot of jasmine tea and biscuits. Our personal "houseboy" then came to the room to ask if we wanted him to unpack our suitcases and arrange to have our clothes pressed. Never had we been exposed to such pampering! It was our introduction to the most outstanding hotel service and comfort that we would ever encounter.

Soon after our arrival, we got a call from Craig Whitney, who was in Hong Kong for a brief R&R. We met him in the hotel's main dining room and had a superb dinner in which the food, wine, ambiance, and service equaled that of any restaurant in Europe or the United States. After a brandy in the bar, we were ready for a good night's sleep in our luxurious quarters.

The following day we took care of shopping for the electronic equipment we knew we would need in Saigon: a shortwave radio, a tape-cassette player with speakers, a portable cassette recorder, and a hair dryer. Sylvan also ordered a couple of suits and some slacks from a highly recommended tailor, to which he returned in the afternoon for a fitting.

Then it was off for some serious exploration. The city was divided into two main parts: the island of Hong Kong and mainland Kowloon, with swooping hills and peaks in the distance, and a harbor bustling with small boats of every description, ferries, and larger ships. We took a ferry from our hotel, which was in Kowloon, to Hong Kong Island, where the main business and commercial center was located. The city combined the elegance and efficiency of Britain, which at that time ruled the colony, with the fascinating qualities of a Chinese city. There were modern stores and fashionable restaurants that could easily have been found on a London street; at the same time, there were shops and food stalls that looked as though they had been transported from Shanghai. Although only about one percent of Hong Kong's population was made up of English citizens, they maintained a noticeable position of prominence. The city was permeated with the air of a thriving British banking and commercial center.

After Craig Whitney returned to Saigon, we had two more days to savor the pleasures of Hong Kong before Sylvan was scheduled to begin work. During that time we were invited to dinner at the home of the *Times* Hong Kong bureau chief, Tilman Durdin, who had been a correspondent in the Far East for years. The Durdins lived in an exclusive neighborhood, in an apartment high on a hill, with a breathtaking view of the city. Our other companion at dinner was introduced to us as Sid Perelman—better known as S.J. Perelman, the humorist and writer—who regaled us with anecdotes about his misadventures during his recent visit to Australia, but no stories about what we really would have liked to hear: writing for the Marx brothers movies. Perelman's tales and the Durdins' accounts of their life in Hong King provided wonderful highlights for our farewell to the city.

The vacation part of our trip ended when we took a Cathay Pacific flight to Saigon. It was a hot evening as we landed at Tansonhut Airport, clouds of dust swirling across the tarmac and the buildings, coating everything with layers of grime. After dragging our suitcases and cartons through customs inspection, we were met by Craig, who was waiting with a car and driver from the *Times* bureau. We drove past the army checkpoint and out of the airport on poorly lit roads that seemed to have endless stretches of barbed wire. As we approached the city, we encountered our first sight of the entanglement of Honda motorbikes zigzagging crazily on the streets without any regard for traffic regulations. Our destination was the Hotel Caravelle, where we would be staying temporarily. It was a shabby French Colonial building, long past its prime and showing the effects of years of war.

Our room was quite clean, with chipped furniture in modern style, and stucco walls badly in need of paint. The bathroom had a leaky faucet and rust stains from the water. A weary air conditioner tried vainly to provide some cool air. The one bright note was a little balcony that looked out over the main streets of the city. The hotel was in jarring contrast to the one we had left in Hong Kong that morning.

After washing quickly and putting on some lighter clothes, we were ready to set off for dinner with Craig, who once again picked us up in the car provided by the bureau. We discovered that the only safe and reasonable way to travel around the city was in the bureau car, which, thankfully, was always at our disposal. That first night we were joined by some of the other bureau staff and a correspondent from the Associated Press in a private dining room of a Japanese restaurant. After a lengthy dinner consisting of a number of tasty dishes, we all went to the apartment of one of the reporters, where we finished the evening with a few more drinks. Our exhaustion from the trip, the heat, and the copious amounts of liquor left us eager to get back to our room and to sleep.

The next morning we walked the two blocks down Tu Do Street to the building housing the *Times* bureau. By 9:00 the streets were alive with people, and traffic was impossibly clogged. Pedicabs, motorbikes, jeeps, trucks, and battered little cars all vied for road space and seemed determined not to stop under any circumstances. Adding to the exhaust fumes from all the vehicles were the smells of garbage, food being cooked outdoors, and the litter from makeshift structures housing people on the street.

The bureau occupied the entire second floor of a building dating from the period of French occupation. The office was one long series of open workspaces, each with a manual typewriter and the basic accoutrements needed by a reporter, but with few amenities and without the support system of a switchboard, secretaries, or copy boys. It was a clean, air-conditioned haven in the midst of the grimy, chaotic environment of Saigon. However, in contrast to the usual American newsroom, there was an absence of any indication of how stories were to be transmitted or printed. The Saigon bureau had to use the facilities of the Reuters news office, located several blocks away, to send stories to New York and to receive responses, thus increasing the effort involved in every transmission.

On our first day we were introduced to those members of the bureau staff whom we had not met the night before. In total there were four reporters, in addition to Sylvan, who was the bureau chief. The office manager, Vo Chan, was a young university graduate who took care of the endless tasks of obtaining passes, renewing documents, applying for visas, arranging for housing and transportation, and acting as the primary translator for everyone in the office. Without Vo Chan, who was able to navigate the intricacies of the Saigon bureaucracy that required the appropriate dispensation of bribes and tips, the bureau could not have functioned. The staff photographer was Luong, another competent young Vietnamese man who also acted as an interpreter. The rest of the staff consisted of a number of Vietnamese drivers, clerks, and messengers, none of whom spoke much English. We learned over time that as pleasant and accommodating as these employees seemed, one could not safely count on their consistent allegiance to the South.

The first documents we required, which Vo Chan arranged to get for us, were press passes. Though not a member of the press, I needed one because, in addition to allowing reporters access to press conferences, the pass was the most reliable means of establishing authorization to be in Vietnam. We also needed membership cards for the Cercle Sportif. I learned that this was the exclusive club that had been established many years before by the French community to provide its members with a country club complete with tennis courts and a luxurious swimming pool in one of the better neighborhoods of the city. Like so many other buildings in Saigon, what had originally been an elegant example of French architecture had become a victim of the neglect and ravages of war. But the swimming pool, tennis courts, and the basic support services still provided one of the few places for recreation available to those who could afford it, largely the foreign press and diplomatic corps.

While Sylvan was familiarizing himself with the equipment and facilities of the office, I discovered that daily editions of the *Times* were delivered to the bureau, albeit a day late, as well as current issues of *The New Yorker, Time, Newsweek*, and a few other American publications. The office was to become my air-conditioned, quiet reading room where I could catch up on events in New York and the rest of the world. Soon it became my daily routine to spend an hour or more reading in a corner of the office before joining Sylvan for lunch, if he could get away.

Sylvan quickly settled into covering the situation in Vietnam, turning out page-one stories on the war, which, in spite of optimistic news from the Paris peace talks, was continuing. At that point the press seemed to be focusing on discussions about the size and shape of the table around which the delegates would be seated, although it was the more serious demands from both Hanoi and Saigon to change the terms of the ceasefire proposals that were creating serious obstacles. Nonetheless, the word from Paris, Washington, and Saigon was that in a few weeks the war would be over.

One of Sylvan's first observations of military operations occurred when he accompanied a group of U.S. marines to the nearby Bien Hoa air base. The base had come under rocket attack by the North Vietnamese that morning. The response was to dispatch Phantom bombers to attack the area north of Bien Hoa. Sylvan was struck by the remarks made to him by a lieutenant colonel who had just returned from one of the missions. The colonel spoke about the satisfaction he had when they could report "secondary" damage—meaning destruction of civilian property, and possibly civilian lives—near the designated targets. It typified the casual attitude expressed by the pilots toward what was for them nothing more than their daily routine.

Sylvan later told me how astonished he was that the job of going off to kill people could become as mundane as going off to a day's work in the office.

We had been in Saigon for a few days and were having a drink with an army captain in the officers' club—a full-service restaurant and bar that could have been lifted out of a first-rate hotel in any American city—talking about our first encounters in the city. After Sylvan described his initial efforts at becoming familiar with the army's operations, the captain turned to me and asked politely, "And what are *your* impressions of Saigon?"

"Well, I've been a little disconcerted by the sound of shelling that we hear every night," I responded.

The captain smiled as he took a swig of bourbon. "You don't have to worry. What you're hearing is outgoing. Nothing's coming from the enemy."

I was still puzzled. "How do you know if the shelling is outgoing or incoming?" I asked him.

The captain's smile broadened. "If it was incoming, you'd know because you'd be blown out of your seat. And that might be the last thing you'd ever know."

Sylvan and I looked at each other, silently registering our acceptance of another one of Saigon's insanities.

It was the practice in Saigon to have designated American army officers conduct press briefings every afternoon, which either Sylvan or one of the other reporters from the bureau and all the other foreign correspondents attended. These sessions were referred to as the Five O'clock Follies by the reporters, suggesting that they had serious questions about the reliability and completeness of the material. Sylvan soon got to know other members of the military, as well as members of the American and foreign embassies, who could provide more useful information; one of them was a gentleman who was associated with what was facetiously called a "Certain Important Agency."

I established something of a daily routine for myself that began with having breakfast with Sylvan before he started his workday. I went over to the bureau for an hour or more to read the *Times* and news magazines before going off on my walks, equipped with my camera, around the central parts of the city. I set off from Tu Do Street, the main commercial thoroughfare, and also the site of throngs of refugees. Trying to walk on the sidewalk meant sidestepping so as to avoid intruding into the flimsy homes of the families living there.

I was most disturbed every day by the sight of an infant, no more than six months old, lying naked in the intense heat on the bare sidewalk a few blocks from the *Times* office. Her older brother, whose duty was to beg for money, stood next to her with his palm outstretched. When I asked Vo Chan whether there was anything that could be done to remedy the situation, he told me that their mother was probably nearby, and that the authorities were unable or unwilling to take any action. It was one of the many sickening, frustrating situations that I experienced every day in Saigon. I managed to continue my explorations in spite of regularly encountering the infant and dozens of hideously deformed victims of the war, polio, and leprosy, all begging on the streets. I wandered the streets branching off from Tu Do, tightly packed with tiny shops, street vendors selling black-market cigarettes and electronic products, and open markets overflowing with fruits, vegetables, and live chickens. The crowds of shoppers suggested a thriving economy.

The women who sold goods on the street customarily squatted next to their stalls, and always wore a conical straw hat, black pajama-like pants, and white silk shirt. Although there were frequent reports of foreigners being the victims of thefts and muggings in broad daylight, I had no unfortunate encounters as I wandered the streets.

I took large numbers of photographs as I explored the city, and was able to have the *Times* photo lab develop my film and provide me with contact sheets and prints, all in black and white, since that was the only way they worked at the time. Much of the rest of my day was taken up with sketching, keeping a journal, and writing long letters describing my impressions of Saigon to Ricki, Sophie, and Louis. Ricki foresightedly kept our letters and returned them to us after we came back from Vietnam. My personal accounts were in marked contrast, of course, to the reports of the war that Sylvan was writing for the paper.

When I look back now, I see that two parallel stories played out during our time in Vietnam: one was that of our personal experiences; the other, the more complex and tumultuous one about the continuation of the war and the prospects for peace. I was to make no attempt to describe the latter, of course, which was thoroughly documented by the news reporting at the time and the innumerable histories that followed. Although both Sylvan and I knew at the time how important my presence was for Sylvan, it was not until many years later that Sylvan would look back on that period and comment that he would not have been able to survive if I hadn't been there.

Thinking I could make use of my nursing background, I looked into the possibility of doing some volunteer work at a hospital that was staffed primarily by Europeans and Americans; however, at that time, an attempt was being made to "Vietnamize" the hospital and minimize foreign involvement. I was told that it was unlikely that my services would be accepted there.

I soon learned that medical volunteers were needed at a primitive clinic of sorts for refugees at a site north of Saigon. With a driver in an open jeep, another American woman and I made a harrowing, hours-long trip to our destination: a tin-roofed hut that had no running water or electricity, a few primitive medical supplies, and several bare cots. We were told by an elderly Vietnamese man that several foreign doctors had promised to visit the "clinic" to offer their services, although neither they nor any other medical personnel were in sight while we were there. One little girl, no more than six years old, who lay unmoving on a cot, was the only patient. An elderly man, who I assumed to be her grandfather, stood next to her and seemed to be waiting. For how long? For whom? From what I gathered, the people at the settlement saw the clinic as a place of last resort to which one came only when death was approaching.

The futility of the situation convinced me that I couldn't make such a difficult, potentially risky trip with any regularity; and I wondered how much could possibly be accomplished with the pitifully meager resources available. On the trip back I decided that I should forgo the idea of attempting to volunteer there.

It was dark by the time the jeep finally reached Saigon. I hurried to the *Times* bureau, where Sylvan was waiting anxiously for me. As he hugged me in relief, he reminded me that it wasn't safe to be on the road after nightfall. I agreed that I had to be more cautious to avoid creating stress for everyone.

About two weeks after we had arrived in Saigon, Sylvan decided to travel to the northern part of South Vietnam as far as the seventeenth parallel, an area separating the North from the South, where active warfare was continuing. He assured me that he would avoid taking unnecessary risks, because, as he said, "it isn't worth getting into trouble with the war coming to an end."

This is part of Sylvan's account of his trip, which he included in an audiotape that he sent to Sophie and Louis. We found this to be a better means of communicating than letters.

"Craig and Luong and I got a ride in a military plane to the coastal town of Da Nang, where we got appraisals of the situation from the American consul and two Vietnamese colonels. Da Nang, as you know, was heavily bombed during the war, has become a refugee camp housing sixty-nine thousand people, and is still a site of active warfare. The three of us spent the following day interviewing South Vietnamese troops who were positioned at the site.

"The next morning we hired a car to drive us north to Hue. What was once a beautiful city that had long before been the capital of South Vietnam is now reduced to nothing but ruins. We spent the night there after speaking with soldiers engaged in defending the remains of the city. From Hue, we got a jeep to take us farther north on Route 1, known as the Street of Horrors, because, as you may remember, it was the site of bloody battles that had caused thousands of casualties. By then a heavy rain had started, and with the sounds of shelling getting ominously louder and louder, we made our way over bridges damaged by the bombardment and arrived finally in Quang Tri on the demarcation line.

"The fierce battles that took place there during the past year have transformed the city into a pile of rubble. Hardly a building or tree is left standing, leaving only a maze of mud pathways traversed by jeeps and trucks. South Vietnamese soldiers were hunkered down in watery dugouts and in the remnants of the citadel that had once stood there. There was no letup in the exchange of gunfire that went on between the poor bastards and the North Vietnamese who were a short distance away on the other side of the line. Craig, Luong, and I spent several grueling hours there, examining the scene and interviewing some of the soldiers, before making a hellish drive back in torrential rain to Hue and then Da Nang. We managed to eat some dinner in Da Nang, and then were able to get a jeep to drive us to the airport, where we were lucky to get seats on a military plane that took us back to Saigon."

While Sylvan was gone I was intensely aware of being alone, worrying about him, and, for the first time since arriving in Saigon, feeling acute anxiety. This was in stark contrast to what I felt when Sylvan was with me. In the evenings that Sylvan was away, I met some of the other correspondents for dinner but had little inclination to eat. Then, at last, Sylvan and Craig returned unscathed. That was not an accomplishment to be taken for granted, since aside from the dangers in the area, traveling by jeep or car was always risky because of the uncertainty of the allegiance of residents and soldiers; it was not uncommon for someone to express loyalty to the South during the day and to become an equally loyal member of the Vietcong after sunset.

When Sylvan and I went for dinner that evening, it was a great relief finally to have him back, to be in his presence, to relax with him, and to know that he would be in bed beside me that night. But Sylvan could allow himself only a short break before getting back to the typewriter to write the story for the next day's paper.

During that same period Sylvan wrote a feature story about how people in Saigon felt about the supposedly imminent ceasefire. He interviewed representatives from every walk of life, and elicited responses that expressed fear of the consequences, doubt that there would ever be peace, distrust of the representatives on both sides, and some optimism about the outcome. The most common concern was what the Vietcong would do after the U.S. troops were withdrawn, a fear that turned out to presage a disturbing reality.

When we had been in Saigon for a while, I was invited one Sunday, while Sylvan was working, to accompany three other women—a reporter for AP, a freelance photographer, and the wife of another journalist—on a trip down the Mekong River. We left Saigon by car with a driver early in the morning on a route that took us through countryside filled with rice paddies in which farmers and water buffalo were toiling side by side. Banana trees, coconut trees, and thatched huts dotted the rich, tropical landscape. After a drive of about two hours, we arrived in My Tho, a small but bustling town, and pulled up along the bank of the Mekong River. We were surrounded immediately by dozens of tattered little kids who peered through the car windows, staring at us in wonder, and frantically competing with each other to rent us a boat.

We selected two little boys, no more than seven years old, who agreed to take us by motorboat to the island of the Coconut Monk, a figure well known to journalists in Saigon as the eccentric leader of a small Buddhist sect. We boarded a small, flat-bottomed boat, accompanied by a little girl who we assumed was the younger sister of one of our "boatmen." A beautiful, sad-faced child, she had silky black bangs fringing her forehead, and her eyes searched us inquisitively during the entire trip. I wanted so much to talk to her, but in the absence of a common language, our communication was limited to smiles.

The riverbanks, with dense tropical vegetation, were lined with thatched huts supported by stilts leaning precariously into the water. Although it was hard to imagine how these fragile structures could house a family, the domestic paraphernalia heaped on the open porches suggested they did. We saw many other small motorboats, most of them carrying women, shielded by their conical hats from the sun and accompanied by their children. A ferry that looked almost like a Mississippi River boat passed us as we made the short trip downstream.

When we docked at the island where the monk and his followers lived, we encountered a garish expanse of brightly colored ceramic decorations, statues, altars, and pennants more reminiscent of Disneyland than of a religious shrine. Crowds of Vietnamese families were enjoying their Sunday outing while the brown-robed monks circulated among the visitors with welcoming smiles. They lived in the delta in little huts built on stilts, connected by wooden walkways that served as sidewalks. In the visitors' dining room, the monks served us a tasty vegetarian meal, which we paid for by making a contribution to the community.

We finally got to see the Coconut Monk himself, who was seated in royal splendor on an elaborate throne in a canopied, temple-like setting, facing his disciples who sat in pews of wooden chairs in front of him. A wizened little old man with a head shaved except for one spot from which a waist-length pigtail grew, he sat in silence, smiling benignly and waggling a finger at his disciples. He was more than willing to pose for photographs from every angle. Since no rituals were conducted in the presence of visitors, it was hard to get a sense of the nature of their sect, and I never did find out the significance of his name.

We returned by boat to My Tho, where our car and driver were waiting to take us back to Saigon. The photographer in our group wanted to make a stop to take some pictures at the local hospital, where, to my surprise, we gained entry without being questioned. It was a hellish place occupied by patients with amputated limbs and festering wounds lying on bare cots. I was sickened by the conditions and thought that taking pictures was an unconscionable violation of the privacy of these unfortunate people. Even though I voiced my opinion, it did not dissuade the photographer. Only when she had finished did we resume our trip back to Saigon.

Meanwhile, the war went on, with the peace talks making no progress, and Sylvan was working seven days a week with little rest. Our living conditions were greatly improved, however, when we found a furnished apartment on Tu Do Street, a short distance from the *Times* office.

Our apartment was in an old French building with a creaking, open, wrought-iron elevator, and consisted of a living room, dining room, kitchen, bedroom, and huge, screened-in terrace with potted tropical plants and lounge furniture that served as another living/ dining area. In the style typical of these buildings, the floors were of tile; the walls, stucco. Instead of windows separating the main rooms from the terrace, there were shutters that extended from the floor to the high ceiling. The only room with a window and air conditioning was the bedroom. Our furniture consisted mostly of rattan and black lacquered pieces. Our resident pet was a lively, green gecko that patrolled the walls of the apartment in constant search of the insects that constituted his meals.

When the *Times,* through the services of Vo Chan, rented the apartment for us, it hired a local housekeeper, a woman named Hon, who was from the Hmong tribe, which had been displaced from the countryside north of Saigon. Hon was a shy young woman with a soft, pretty face who spoke a few words of French and almost no English. Using scraps of French and a lot of sign language, I was able to convey the most important messages of the day, which were to tell her whether we planned to be at home for lunch and dinner, and how many guests we were expecting. She was with us six days a week. The morning started with her preparing and serving us breakfast, usually consisting of fresh croissants, some French preserves, and a pot of very strong coffee. She then thoroughly scrubbed down the entire apartment and laundered whatever linens had been used and the clothing we had worn. Shopping for the food supplies and preparing our meals took up a good part of the rest of her day. With a long break in the afternoon, her day didn't end until she had served us dinner.

I discovered several weeks after we had moved in that she and a young son, maybe three years old, and a female relative shared a tiny apartment on the top floor above us. It was customary during the French colonial period and then the American occupation to provide domestic employees with living quarters in what was the attic of the building, presumably for the convenience of the workers.

Hon was an outstanding cook who enlisted the help of one or two of her friends when we had a particularly large group for dinner. I was taken aback when I first encountered three of them, squatting on the floor, busily preparing the ingredients for the evening's feast. This was the traditional method of preparing food, on an immaculately scrubbed floor, at least among Hmong women. As much as I would have liked to accompany Hon on shopping trips, she insisted that she go alone to the open markets where she purchased most of the ingredients for our meals. Her reasoning seemed to be that it would not be safe for me to wander around the stalls even if she accompanied me. I suspected too that she might have thought the vendors would have raised their prices if she was accompanied by a foreigner.

The markets had an abundance of fresh produce, meat, poultry, and fish; and a few stores sold some European-style groceries, mostly canned goods that stood forlornly on almost-bare shelves. Bakeries left behind by the French still turned out excellent croissants, brioches, and baguettes. I learned that Hon became uncomfortable if I watched her preparing meals, so I gave up trying to learn her techniques.

Since we often entertained guests for dinner, it was a great benefit to have the services of an excellent cook. Hon and her sous-chefs amazed us—and our guests—with the elaborate banquets they prepared, which were at least as good as what were served in local restaurants: incredible dumplings prepared to resemble little packages, soups whose fragrant aromas suggested a complexity of ingredients that could never be identified, succulent dishes of chicken in amazing sauces, fish and crustaceans embellished with beautifully prepared vegetables. We were constantly amazed by the culinary talents of Hon and her assistants.

As bureau chief, Sylvan had to play host to just about everyone visiting the Saigon office. Our guest list included at various times the Israeli ambassador assigned to Bangkok; an ambassador from Phnom Penh; several executives from the *Times* headquarters, including Arthur Sulzberger, the publisher; and the author James Jones, who was researching a magazine piece about Saigon. No matter how interesting the conversation, however, the eleven o'clock curfew promptly brought an end to social gatherings. Jones, for some reason, had a terrible time understanding the time differences between Saigon and New York. Sylvan spent hours showing him how to make the conversions, with no success. The only solution was for Sylvan to construct a chart indicating every hour of the day and the corresponding times in the two cities. Jones was very appreciative.

Our primary source of recreation when we were alone in the evening was to tune in to short-wave radio broadcasts from U.S. army stations and the BBC. It was a formidable task that required a lot of dial twisting and adjustments to get through the forest of static to an audible station—if we were lucky—that provided some news from around the world. Our little tape player and the classical music tapes that we brought from Hong Kong provided some music. Being able to hear a few minutes of a Brahms symphony, even on our primitive equipment, was as satisfying to us as having food on the table.

We grew accustomed to going to sleep with the nightly lullaby of outgoing shelling in the outskirts of the city, tolling the ten o'clock hour and lasting until early morning. The shelling, usually not aimed at any particular target, was the way U.S. troops deterred the Vietcong from venturing too close. The explosions caused all the doors in the apartment to rattle noisily, another disconcerting sound that became all too familiar.

Occasionally the Vietcong managed to get close enough to the city to make retaliatory forays. One morning we were shaken awake by a huge blast that rocked the building, followed by more rumblings as explosions went off in an ammunitions depot that had been hit by bombs. The rumblings continued throughout the morning and finally culminated in a tremendous, roaring boom. At that moment Sylvan was in the office of our landlord, settling some details of the rental, when the windows came crashing in, sending a torrent of shattered glass around them but, fortunately, injuring neither of them. At that same moment I was at the Cercle Sportif, preparing to put on my bathing suit for a swim. As I closed the door to the little changing cabin, the huge explosion occurred. For a moment, in my shock, I wondered what I had done to set off this cataclysm. After checking to make sure that I and everything else appeared undamaged, I went for a brief swim and then returned to the changing room. Again I heard a roaring boom as I closed the door. That was the final boom of the morning, after which I lost no time in cautiously putting on my clothes and leaving.

By mid-December the peace talks seemed to be collapsing. On December 18 the "Christmas bombing" of the North began, presumably to pressure Hanoi into accepting the terms of the peace agreement. The air attacks would continue for eleven days. On December 19 there was the depressing announcement that the United States had bombed Hanoi and Haiphong, resulting in horrific destruction in the two cities, and that two American B52s and an F11 had been shot down. On the third day, Hanoi's defenders shot down another six bombers, resulting in a large number of pilots being killed or captured. The United States ended the attacks only when the North agreed to return to the peace table. The events of those eleven days cast a pall over everyone as the prospect of peace seemed to evaporate. The war rather than the peace talks was the story that demanded attention.

The entire *Times* staff worked nonstop to cover the mass of often contradictory reports of what was going on. Sylvan had the additional task of ferreting out reliable information from people who, because of their positions, would reveal information only without attribution. There was a world composed of representatives of every country, occupying such positions as agricultural consultant, commercial representative, or embassy aide, whose titles did not encompass their covert activities. And then there were the employees of USAID, the American embassy, and the army, whose work included duties beyond their official job descriptions. Cultivating these sources required meetings that often extended well into the evening. The foreign desk in New York and the bureaus in Washington and Paris were also flooding the Saigon bureau with reports that were often at odds with what was being learned in Saigon. The process of filtering and checking the veracity of all this information before writing a story lengthened everyone's workday. I was concerned that Sylvan's long hours of rigorous work without a day off were taking a toll on him, as evidenced by his progressive loss of weight. We looked forward to getting away for a period of R&R before too long and talked about going to Singapore and Bali in January.

Before that, however, Sylvan had to visit the bureau's outposts in Phnom Penh and Bangkok. I was able to accompany him on the trip. We took an Air Vietnam flight from Saigon to Phnom Penh, where we stayed in a faded hotel of the colonial period, another aging dowager trying to maintain a semblance of her previous beauty. We were the only patrons in the dining room, which was elegantly decorated and all its twenty or more empty tables set with fine linen and silverware. It was an eerie scene frozen in the past. In silence, uniformed waiters served us a passable Cambodian version of continental cuisine.

With its lush tropical vegetation and sprawling French Colonial buildings on broad avenues, Phnom Penh had a deceptively peaceful air about it. Sylvan held discussions with the *Times* reporter based there, U.S. and Cambodian officials, and ambassadors from other countries to get their perceptions of how the war was progressing. His work left us little time for more than a visit to one of the temples and some of its monumental statues; we saw almost nothing else during our brief stay.

Our next stop was Bangkok, where we arrived a couple of days before Christmas. I have never felt so overcome by heat and air pollution; it was so thick that it was almost impossible to breathe or see across the street. After checking into our hotel, we immediately wanted to take care of getting the new visas we would need to return to Vietnam. (Vietnamese officials delighted in making it as difficult as possible for foreigners to gain access to or exit the country.) We found a cab, and although we gave the driver a note with the name and address of the embassy, he took us on an unwanted tour of the city in a car without air conditioning, eventually arriving at the embassy of some other country, from which we had to make a new start on another extended drive that finally brought us to our destination where we got our visas. What we saw as we drove around the city were masses of newly constructed, unattractive, garish buildings that bore little evidence of Thai culture. Perhaps the heat, pollution, and our annoyance with the driver contributed to our unfavorable impressions. But at least we were staying in a modern, comfortable hotel with excellent, efficient service; Bangkok had already cultivated a considerable tourist business.

Sylvan contacted Syd Schanberg, who was the *Times* man posted in Bangkok, and set up a meeting with him in which Schanberg was able to share his extensive knowledge of the situation in the area and his take on the worsening situation in Vietnam. When they had completed their discussions, the three of us took advantage of the free time to hire a guide, in an air-conditioned car, to see some of the historical sights of Bangkok.

As it was the day before Christmas, our guide, a young college-educated Thai woman who was Buddhist, asked us whether we were planning on going to church on the holiday. When we answered that we didn't observe Christmas because we were Jewish, she looked puzzled and asked, "What's that?" It was something of a shock to encounter someone who had never heard of Judaism, but we did our best to enlighten her with a somewhat abbreviated explanation. During our tour we did manage to see some beautiful traditional

Thai architecture and a Buddhist temple, but we never did develop a fondness for Bangkok.

For Sylvan, returning to Saigon meant more twelve-hour workdays, covering the continuing outbreaks of warfare, the disruptive speeches of President Thieu, and the confusing reports from Paris about the peace talks.

At last, in the beginning of January, Sylvan was able to get away on R&R and we flew to Singapore. Leaving the country on R&R was always referred to as returning to civilization. We became aware of the level of tension and stress we had been enduring only when we escaped from it. Suddenly we were free of the sounds of shelling and bombing, of being surrounded by the evidence of material and human destruction, of the chaotic activity that seemed directed by insane forces, and of the constant sense of imminent danger. We were free to enjoy the unimpeded closeness of each other.

In the tropical beauty of Singapore, we saw the results that tight regulations on public behavior produced: an incredibly clean, safe, tightly structured but also restrictive environment where one could receive a heavy fine for chewing gum in public. For us, however, it was a welcome contrast to what we had left in Saigon. We luxuriated in our beautiful, air-conditioned room in a splendid hotel that had every luxury we dreamed of, and then went for a drink at the legendary Raffles Bar, made famous by Somerset Maugham and other novelists. Singapore offered an incredible selection of international cuisine that included Scottish smoked salmon, New Zealand roast beef, Australian oysters, Russian caviar, and every style of Chinese food, all of which we enjoyed in one beautiful restaurant after another.

One morning we took a long walk through Singapore's extensive botanic garden, marveling at the array of tropical plants and flowers that we had never encountered before. We wandered the streets and noted that even in the older, crowded sections of the city where street vendors competed with small shops there was not a speck of dirt or litter. We engaged in the usual tourist activities, including going to one of the city's many amusement parks, where we watched the performances of snake charmers, one of whom provided some unplanned drama when he was seriously bitten by one of his charges. We also took an all-day trip to Johore Barou, the main town of one of the states of Malaysia. Our tour included a visit to the palace of the Sultan of Johore and to one of the mosques in the predominantly Muslim country. We never got to Bali because a mix-up in hotel reservations made it impossible to get a room, so we enjoyed the entire vacation in Singapore, where Sylvan was able to get the rest and relaxation he so much needed.

Then it was back to Vietnam, where Sylvan worked long days covering the attacks that continued between the two sides. The peace settlement, finally signed by Kissinger and Le Duc Tho in Paris, produced the ceasefire that took effect on January 27. The agreement left Thieu in power and 150,000 North Vietnamese troops remaining in the South, terms that did not completely satisfy either side and created serious questions about the ultimate results.

Sporadic fighting continued all over the country, although Saigon was relatively quiet. The mood of the people whom Sylvan interviewed in Saigon was predominantly one of fear, mainly of the unknown future. It was not reassuring to know that dozens of Viet Cong were arriving at Tansonhut Airport for meetings with the South Vietnamese. Sylvan expressed this sense of pessimism in a piece for the *Times* Week in Review in which he reflected on the potentially risky terms of the peace agreement. This view was held by many other correspondents.

During the next several weeks, all four members of the bureau filed daily stories about the negotiations in Paris and the outbursts of fighting throughout Vietnam, Cambodia, and Laos. Their work was made more difficult by stubborn interference from the South Vietnamese army, which took great pleasure in attempting to block the movements of reporters by engaging in outrageous acts such as slashing the tires of their vehicles. It was another combat story that had to be written.

With the announcement from Paris that the last prisoners of war would be released by the North and the remaining American military personnel would leave Vietnam on March 29, there seemed to be some evidence that the war was finally ending, at least for the United States.

In mid-March, Sylvan was scheduled for another R&R. We flew to Hong Kong, where once more we basked in the comforts of civilization and some much-needed quiet time together. After a few days, I left to fly to the United States to visit Ricki, Sophie, and Louis, who was about to turn seventy, leaving Sylvan to spend the remainder of his leave in Hong Kong.

I took a flight with a brief stopover in Tokyo and then flew on to New York. What a pleasure it was to see Ricki, to spend five days together, enjoying each other's company and catching up on everything that we wanted to tell each other. Then I was off to Fort Lauderdale to visit with Sophie and Louis and to be with them for a celebration of Louis's landmark birthday. They were most appreciative that I made the exhausting trip for the occasion and that I was able to give them firsthand information about our lives in Saigon.

But as much as I enjoyed the week I spent with Ricki, Sophie, and Louis, I was acutely aware of the discomfort of being half a world away from Sylvan, the first time that we had been separated by such a distance. I couldn't wait to leave the comfort of Fort Lauderdale to get back to the chaos of Saigon, a trip that took me thirty-seven hours with the stops along the way. When I got home—imagine calling Saigon home—Sylvan and I vowed that we would never again experience the pain of being away from each other for so long.

The withdrawal of U.S. troops from Vietnam left only about fifty American military advisors in the country. The conflict was now being played out by North and South Vietnam, in ongoing disputes about the structure of the government and the territory that each side had the right to control. Fighting continued, especially on the borders of Laos and Cambodia. Without the presence of American forces, it was extremely difficult and risky for the *Times* staff to report on the situation. However, the editors in New York obstinately insisted that reporters should be sent to cover the fighting, regardless of the danger. At one point the foreign desk claimed that it had received information indicating that Vietnam was planning covert incursions into Cambodia; Sylvan could not substantiate the rumor, however, and adamantly refused to endanger himself or other reporters by investigating what appeared to be nothing more than flimsy tips. Ongoing hostilities throughout the country had become the focus of the situation "postwar."

As the weeks went by, Sylvan continued to lose weight and be increasingly fatigued, causing us both growing concern. We wondered whether he had contracted one of the innumerable tropical diseases that flourished in the country and decided that he needed to be checked out. We were able to make an appointment quickly with a highly recommended British doctor in Hong Kong.

A courtly gentleman in his late fifties, with steely-gray hair and a firm handshake that immediately conveyed his serious intentions, he spent ample time taking a complete history and performing an impeccable physical exam, after which he scheduled all the requisite lab tests. We were impressed as much by his caring manner as his thorough knowledge of tropical diseases.

When he had reviewed all his findings, he told us that Sylvan's symptoms, rather than being caused by physical illness, were the result of extreme overwork and stress. As he concluded his diagnosis, his exact words to Sylvan were: "You're killing yourself. Get the hell out of Saigon."

We returned to Saigon relieved that Sylvan wasn't suffering from a serious organic illness but still needing to face the doctor's sobering piece of advice. That evening, as we sat having a drink in the apartment, Sylvan began by asking, "So, what do you think?"

"I don't think he could have given you a clearer message. But the question is: How do you get out?" I answered.

"The damn trouble is that the foreign desk doesn't let up with their unreasonable demands from halfway around the world, and it's getting harder each day to cover what is unquestionably a war story. These minor skirmishes are developing into full-blown warfare between the North and the South, and it's become riskier for us now that the American troops have left."

"This sure as hell isn't the peacetime assignment they promised you."

We couldn't miss the ironic humor: it hadn't been that long ago that the top editors at the *Times* had enthusiastically described to Sylvan the opportunities that would be available as the bureau chief in Vietnam "when peace broke out."

Sylvan continued, "Okay, so what happens if I manage to get replaced in Saigon? It's back to a position on one of the other desks at the *Times.*"

"And back to a position where you'll be confronted with the same problems that you previously struggled to be free of."

"There's no limit to what's expected of you from the goddamn *New York Times*!" Sylvan sputtered in frustration. He paused for a minute while taking a sip of his drink and letting his thoughts wash over him before he continued.

"I want to find something that will not suck the blood out of me and will give me the kind of pleasure again that I used to get from writing, even if it means a lower salary. Who cares if I make less money, as long as I can get out of this impossible situation?"

We agreed that whatever Sylvan chose to do would require his leaving the *Times.*

Following our discussion, Sylvan wrote to the foreign editor, describing his growing dissatisfaction and his belief that he could no longer continue as an employee of the *Times.* After offering an account of the recommendation he had received from the doctor in Hong Kong, and his own reaction to it, he asked to be relieved of his position. His letter was answered with a suggestion that he take some time off to rest and rethink his decision while giving some thought to a position on another desk in New York. It took repeated communications between Sylvan and the foreign desk and the executive editor before they finally accepted that Sylvan was determined to leave.

During our last weeks in Vietnam, we considered many of the attractive options that Sylvan had open to him: a teaching position; a job on another paper, not necessarily in New York; work in one of the fields related to journalism. Before we could come to a decision, however, we needed time to think things over and allow Sylvan to rest. Convinced we were making the right move, Sylvan submitted his second and final resignation to the *Times* and we left Saigon.

Chapter 13

As we were planning our return to the States, Sophie and Louis, who were staying temporarily in their Forest Hills apartment, offered us their place in Fort Lauderdale. This was yet another demonstration of their unwavering generosity, for which we were deeply grateful; they made an apartment available to us until we were able to set up a home of our own.

By mid-May, we were back in the United States, with hardly more than our summer clothes, the only things that weren't with our other belongings in storage. For a couple of weeks, we did little but lie in the sun, enjoying the undemanding activities of South Florida without considering the future. Sylvan ultimately decided that he wanted to stay in the newspaper business, so, having made that decision, he got in touch with an old colleague, Dave Laventhol, who had been at the *New York Herald Tribune* when Sylvan was at the *World-Telegram* and was now the editor of *Newsday*, on Long Island.

Within a short time, Sylvan was invited to Garden City, where *Newsday* was then located, to meet with the publisher and the executive editor and subsequently was offered a job as the Queens-Nassau editor. The attractions were many: *Newsday* was growing in circulation and influence; the job presented many opportunities for professional development; and the atmosphere at the paper contrasted markedly with the pressure cauldron of the *Times*. Sylvan enthusiastically accepted the offer, and I, in turn, looked forward to getting back to work in psychiatric nursing.

Once again, we faced the question of where to live. I flew to Long Island to meet with realtors. I explained that we didn't need a sprawling, suburban house for just the two of us, especially since both of us would be working, yet every real estate agent I contacted seemed to think that a three-bedroom house was "small" and insisted on showing me examples of what they thought was the minimum space needed by two people but was much more than we wanted. Someone finally suggested that I check out some of the condos that were being built in the area. The one we decided on was within manageable commuting distance from *Newsday*, in the small, working-class town of Copiague, in Suffolk County. The apartments, in a cluster of buildings bordering a creek coming off the Great South Bay, were two-bedroom duplexes, each with a little patio facing the water. Since this was our first experience with suburbia and home ownership, and Sylvan was facing the uncertainties of a new job, we thought it wise to buy a modest apartment requiring minimal investment, with the expectation that this might be only a temporary home.

While I was negotiating the purchase of the condo, Sylvan shopped for a car in Florida. He ended up getting an excellent deal on a manual-drive bare-bones Ford Pinto. As soon as I got back to Fort Lauderdale, we packed our few belongings in the car and made a leisurely drive from Florida to our new home in Copiague. Shortly after we arrived, our furniture and other possessions, showing the effects of the wear and tear of moving and storage, joined us.

Before I could begin to look for a job, we had to shop for a second car, since Long Island has virtually no public transportation. We made a tour of all the Ford dealers, looking to buy another Pinto at the same price Sylvan had paid for the first one. With his excellent bargaining skills, we finally ended up with the same model—in a different color—for precisely the same cost. Our transformation into a suburban couple was complete: we had a mortgage on a home and two cars. But in contrast to the route taken by most people, we arrived at this point as middle-aged adults who were long done with childrearing and launching our careers.

I started my search for a job knowing that I'd need time to get back up to speed after not having worked for so long. With no difficulty, however, I found a position as a staff nurse in a small, proprietary psychiatric hospital close to Copiague. In addition to introducing me to the demands of commuting by car to work, the job enabled me to readjust to full-time employment while maintaining a household.

Sylvan quickly settled in to his position at *Newsday*. His expertise and experience were acknowledged in an atmosphere free of the debilitating tension he had endured at the *Times*. This was due in great part to the collegial relationship he had established with the executive and managing editors.

As I anticipated, after a few months at my reentry job, I felt ready to move on to something more challenging. I applied for a position as nursing care coordinator of the adolescent unit at Hillside Hospital, the psychiatric division of Long Island Jewish Hospital. Although my lengthy absence from the workforce raised questions of whether I was prepared to handle the responsibilities, I made a favorable enough impression during my interview to be hired. I was happy to be working again at a hospital with an outstanding reputation.

Established in 1927, Hillside was known for its pioneering work in diagnosis, treatment, and research, and for many years provided long-term treatment of carefully screened patients. By the 1970s, however, short-term hospitalization had become the rule. The hospital, on a tree-shaded campus in eastern Queens, included a number of cottages, each with about twenty patients who lived there. Additional buildings housed locked units, as well as research, administrative, and educational facilities, outpatient services, and accredited elementary and high schools. The adolescent unit, where I would be working, was for patients between the ages of twelve and seventeen.

Nurses at Hillside occupied a critical position in the therapeutic team and had ample opportunities for learning and advancement. My position entailed managing the nursing staff and coordinating our activities with other members of the team—primarily psychiatrists, psychologists, and social workers. From the beginning, I developed an easy working relationship with Mary, the psychiatrist in charge. As a former nurse herself, she was extremely supportive of the nursing staff and an approachable colleague. She and I had much in common in our philosophy of treating patients, and we shared a sense of humor that got us through many difficult days. The work was challenging but satisfying, with barely a moment to eat a quick sandwich in the nursing station before patients knocked impatiently, looking for someone to attend immediately to their needs. But I enjoyed the demands of the job, and after the long drive home, I was eager to sit down and relax with Sylvan and talk about our day.

Looking back, I think it was the first time in many years—probably since his early years at the *World-Telegram*—that Sylvan was having fun at work. He enjoyed greater independence in making decisions, and his performance was rewarded with praise and appreciation. He took particular pleasure in providing instruction to the younger members of the staff, always with a touch of his inimitable humor, as, for example, when he said to a less-than-attentive novice reporter: "You are like the son I'm glad I never had." He was free of the constant tension he had known at the *Times*, and welcomed this newfound freedom. His reputation was as a tough, fair-minded editor who demanded the highest standards of journalism from his staff, who soon learned that there were few acceptable excuses for screwing up a story.

During his early years at *Newsday*, Sylvan wrote a series of pieces about the social and economic conditions of Panama and Cuba and spent a short time in each country. His stay in Cuba, at a time when few journalists were allowed there and which required conducting circuitous negotiations to obtain a visa in Mexico, was supposed to include an interview with Fidel Castro. But like many of the assurances of the Cuban government, the offer was rescinded for no rational reason. However, Sylvan did spend about a week there gathering material for several long articles.

He was taken to most of the places he wanted to visit in a car driven by a government-approved driver and accompanied by a government-approved translator/guide. His guide, Hilda, a young woman from a prestigious Havana family, was, not surprisingly as a qualification of her job, thoroughly indoctrinated in the tenets of Castro's Cuba. Sylvan enjoyed challenging the validity of many of her firmly held beliefs and teaching her about the American way of life. By the end of his stay in Cuba, Sylvan had so impressed Hilda with his good-humored instruction that they were on the best of terms when he left.

His examination of Cuba and Panama culminated in a lengthy series of articles that were highly praised by the managing and executive editors at *Newsday*. Those about Cuba were probably the more fascinating because they revealed much about a society still concealed in secrecy.

***

In our new environment on Long Island, we discovered a wealth of experiences that had previously been unknown to us, starting with the simple pleasure of watching the water fowl that inhabited the creek a few yards from the sliding-glass doors of our living room. We became intimately familiar with the phrase "ducks in a row" as we got to know the family of ducks whose life cycle was paraded before us; and we marveled at the swans in their graceful performances. We looked out across the creek at an old shingled boathouse belonging to the family who owned the house behind it. In good weather, a pair of robust young men would set forth on the creek in a dilapidated motorboat to catch eels, which they speared expertly with what appeared to be tridents. Circling slowly around the creek, they spotted the eels, and with swift, stabbing motions, captured one after another. Within an hour or so, their catch was plentiful enough to make a hefty meal—which I assumed was the goal of their venture.

The creek was also home to blue crabs, which the men caught by casting traps to capture the tasty critters. We were inspired by their activity to do a little investigation at the local bait and tackle shop, where we bought a few traps and were given simple instructions in how to use them. There was nothing more relaxing on a warm afternoon than to sit on our patio, cold drinks in hand, and wait patiently—very patiently—for our crab traps to yield some bounty. Since the crabs were incredibly small, it took many castings of traps, and thus many refills of drinks, to get enough of them to feed two people. I'm not sure what we enjoyed more, catching or eating them.

The seashore and parks of Long Island became a great source of pleasure to us on the drives we took to become familiar with the area. One of our favorites was Sunken Meadow State Park, where we spent hours walking on the boardwalk along the ocean shore, talking not just about our current activities but where we thought the trajectory of our lives had taken us and might take us in the future. Our shared wish to be open to new experiences and free of restrictive limits was a theme we repeatedly returned to during our long conversations. I still marvel that this theme and its variations remained a constant throughout our lives.

As we saw more of the north shore of Long Island, and the hundreds of boats docked in the harbors on the Sound, we became intrigued with learning how to sail. Our interest led us to sign up for weekly sailing lessons that took us out from Huntington with an instructor on a thirty-three-foot sloop. As consummate landlubbers, we had, not surprisingly, a great deal to learn, including, at least for this member of the crew, overcoming a fear of capsizing and drowning. This was in contrast to Sylvan's fearless approach, which of course was supported by his superior athletic ability. Nonetheless, we learned to become novice sailors, and after a few weeks, we were both thoroughly enchanted by the indescribable exhilaration of being transported over the waves by the wind and by being able to control the sails to direct this miracle. Part of our instruction involved learning the basics of navigation and the arcane rules governing a boat's operation on the sea, which required spending hours poring over this essential material. As a result of our diligent practice and study, we eventually were able to handle a thirty-three-foot sloop on our own. How sad that the skill, like so many others, was lost to disuse over the years.

When Ricki came out to Long Island on weekends, she occasionally joined us in our sailing adventures. Although she enjoyed the outings, I think she was more comfortable engaging in activities with us on land.

Being settled once more in the New York area, we were able to spend more time with Ricki, who was living in Brooklyn, with my brother Bob, and with friends whom we had seen infrequently. Now that Sylvan was not under constant pressure at work, it was easier for him to direct his energy into social activities. Our relationship with Bob had become closer and more relaxed over the years. He had become a faculty member and eventually chair of the sociology department of Adelphi University, was divorced, had two young daughters, and had settled into an apartment on the Upper West Side, which remained his home for the rest of his life. He and I could now relate to each other comfortably as adults, while he and Sylvan had become fast friends who could enjoy animated discussions that challenged the other's beliefs, always with respect for the quirks and idiosyncrasies of the other. Many hours were spent over dinner, discussing politics, the presidency, the social problems of the country, what was wrong with the educational system, and on and on and on, usually with strong disagreements that never reached any resolution and had to be resumed at the next meeting. We all had great affection for Bob, who had a brilliant mind but often had difficulty handling the more mundane details of daily life, which led us to the inescapable conclusion that he was the epitome of the absent-minded professor.

In contrast to our frequent contact with Bob, we saw my brother Don only rarely. Our paths crossed infrequently as our lives took us in different directions. Physical and emotional distance existed for too many years; the unfortunate consequence was that we drifted away from each other while barely being aware of it.

To our surprise, as we settled into life on Long Island, we could see Copiague as being more than just a short-term interlude. It was a period different from others in our life, but one with its own distinct satisfactions. We had moved so many times, lived in so many temporary residences, that it was hard to imagine being permanently attached to a place. Thus, it was only after living in Copiague for almost two years that we could finally affix our name plate to our front door and think of it as home.

At about this time, we realized that we had reached an age when we should start thinking more seriously about planning for retirement. Until then, we had given little thought to significant savings or financial investments, but now we became convinced of the need to assign a substantial portion of our income each month to retirement savings.

Our first step in this process was to scrap the idea of buying a sailboat, something that we had been considering since our seagoing experiences. It was out of the question if we were going to be more frugal. The next step was to find a reputable investment counselor. Aided by recommendations from friends, and some careful investigation, we found a broker with whom we established a long, trusting association. We took great pleasure in spending only a fraction of what our income would have allowed us to spend, and, as a result, saw our assets growing steadily. Our initial selection of a home with low mortgage payments and low upkeep was, in retrospect, a wise decision that made it easier to follow our plan.

It was not long before Sylvan's success at *Newsday* was acknowledged by his being assigned the additional task of establishing the paper's New York City bureau, as part of its plan to extend its influence beyond Long Island. Sylvan's scope of authority enlarged to include a wide range of administrative and editorial responsibilities, which, in spite of the additional workload, he found satisfying and rewarding. In contrast to what he had felt at the *Times*, he was enjoying the heavy demands of his job as well as the valued position he had attained.

I too was meeting with success at work: after spending about two years as nursing care coordinator on the adolescent unit at Hillside, I was offered a position as an instructor in the In-service Education Department. The offer was attractive since it allowed me to have contact with patients of a wider range of ages and diagnoses, and to resume working in an educational capacity with nursing staff. I was delighted to make the move. Before long, I had established a close friendship with the woman who was the director of the department—a friendship that extended beyond our professional positions and lasted for many years after we had both left the hospital. Sylvan and I spent many enjoyable hours with Pat and her husband, Fred, who was the superintendent of one of the large state parks on Long Island. Fred was the first person we had ever met whose life was centered on the protection and care of undeveloped land, and whose daily life was usually involved more with wildlife than people. We developed a close relationship with them as we all learned to appreciate the differences and common elements of our lives. However, as is so often the case, when we all retired and moved to different locations, it became difficult to maintain our friendship.

One of the ongoing activities of the In-service Education Department was orientation of new staff, which involved teaching, testing, and supervising newly hired nurses over a period of several weeks. The major part of our work, however, and certainly the most interesting, consisted of conducting regular meetings with nurses to discuss the plan of care for a particular patient, or a broader problem affecting the entire unit. Planning and conducting these meetings required becoming familiar with the patient who was the subject of the discussion, an endeavor that was always extremely challenging and rewarding. I found myself learning continuously as a result of being involved in the care of a large number of patients, each with a different diagnosis and treatment plan. My learning was further enhanced by working with professional nurses, in contrast to my previous experience with students.

At some point in this position I decided that it was important for me to complete my master's degree, which I had abandoned earlier. I enrolled at Adelphi University, which offered evening classes, and, after a lot of hard work, was finally able to add M.A. after my name.

Both Sylvan and I were astonished at how thoroughly entrenched we had become in our way of life on Long Island. Our life was completely different from what it had been in the past: different pleasures, different habits, and a different cast of people with whom we spent time. As the old Russian saying goes: "Different places, different songs." It was a period during which we both enjoyed our success at work and, most of all, the luxury of having time to relax, be with each other, and enjoy the simple pleasures of a less stressful life. Ironically, while we were no longer struggling to reach elusive pinnacles of achievement, we found ourselves accomplishing at least as much as we ever had before.

Another significant development in Sylvan's career at *Newsday* occurred when he was asked to become the editor of the paper's editorial pages. In this new role, he shared authority with the publisher and executive editor for establishing the paper's positions and opinions on the major issues of the day. Among his responsibilities was the selection of topics to be covered by editorial comment and either selecting a staff member to write the piece or, in many instances, writing the editorials that he deemed to be of greatest significance. Without the deadline of covering breaking stories, he had more time to consider the meaning and implications of events, more time to cultivate relationships with figures who wielded power on the local and national scene, and more time to examine the moral underpinnings of decisions made by these figures. This was an ideal way for him to use the knowledge and experience he had acquired during his years in the newspaper business. Further, he concluded, his undergraduate degree in philosophy was invaluable preparation for the job. He often quipped, "The answer to the question of 'What does a degree in philosophy prepare you for?' is 'Being an editorial page editor.'" The highly developed analytical skills that he had demonstrated throughout his career were put to even greater use in this position. It would turn out to be the longest held and the last full-time position that he occupied.

My own career was also marked by a measure of success. When the director of in-service education left Hillside, I was promoted into the job. I enjoyed the additional scope of my work but decided that I would never want to expand my administrative responsibilities. It was one of the reasons that the higher-paying positions in clinical supervision never appealed to me; I knew I lacked the necessary competitive drive to reach for greater authority.

The other change in the family occurred when Ricki left New York to move to Los Angeles to be with Frank, who would later become her husband. While they were there, Ricki became an editor with the Los Angeles Times Syndicate and Frank completed his coursework for a Ph.D. in film studies at UCLA, so the move resulted in much success and pleasure. We made a delightful visit with Sophie and Louis to see them during this period. Ricki had a chance to show us around her new home, and we all shared in her and Frank's achievements. Sylvan and I often talked about how grateful we were for the wonderful joy Ricki had given us. Considering how young we were when she was born, and the unorthodox paths we took in our life, we considered ourselves blessed when we saw the person she had become.

During our sightseeing trips around Los Angeles, we had time to engage in the lively conversations we all enjoyed. One afternoon, as we were driving back from a visit to the Norton Simon Museum in Pasadena, and, as usual, absorbed in a discussion of some major topic, we had to stop along the way for gas. I took the opportunity to use the restroom while the gas tank was being filled. A few minutes later, when I came out, the car was nowhere in sight. In my bewilderment, I tried to imagine how the car could have disappeared and wondered what my next move should be.

I learned later that during my brief absence Sylvan had become so involved in the conversation that he didn't notice I wasn't there as he started the car and got under way. Sophie, Louis, Ricki, and Frank, wondering how long it would be before Sylvan realized I was missing, had a hard time controlling their laughter as they watched Sylvan animatedly making a point in the conversation, and driving off, oblivious to my absence. Finally, Louis could contain himself no longer and said, "Aren't we missing someone?" After a quick turnaround, Sylvan sped back to recover me, sputtering his apologies as he whisked me back into the car. Only someone who knew Sylvan as well as I did could understand how he could have become so involved in conversation that he didn't notice he'd left his wife behind at a gas station. The incident never ceased to be a source of amusement for all of us.

I recall many visits we made at that time, many with Ricki, to Sophie and Louis's apartment in Fort Lauderdale, and they provided some of the happiest moments of our being together as a family. Louis, more than Sophie, basked in his retirement in Florida. Beaming as he sat on the terrace of his apartment, a Scotch in hand, and looking out over the waters of Port Everglades, he'd marvel that he had been able to arrive at this comfortable position after having started out from such humble beginnings.

Both he and Sophie were proud of Sylvan's accomplishments, but it was Louis and Sylvan who developed an extremely close relationship of mutual respect and the special love that can accompany maturity. Louis got particular enjoyment from being able to turn to Sylvan for an opinion or a piece of advice about any number of things he thought Sylvan had greater knowledge about. I think he sometimes searched for a question to pose to Sylvan simply to uncover some new aspect of his store of knowledge. And it was to Sylvan that Louis often confided his frustration with Sophie's complaints of dissatisfaction, the roots of which we could never really understand.

My affection for Louis had grown over the years as we developed a closeness that far surpassed what I had experienced with my own father. What incredible changes had occurred from the time when, as the strange Canadian, I first entered the Fox household and encountered the uncomfortable wariness that I feared would always confront me. Louis soon accepted me for who I was, and then welcomed me as a member of the family and as a daughter, more than I ever could have imagined.

Sophie, by contrast, always maintained a certain distance not just from me but also from Sylvan. We were both amused and sad to see the verbal circumlocutions she used to avoid calling Sylvan by his proper name or the nickname Louis used—Bill. She referred to him as "my son," or simply by the pronouns "he" and "him." The reason for this was another mystery we were never able to solve. The closest we could come to an explanation was that Sylvan always addressed his mother and father by their given names, never Mother or Mom, Father or Dad. He started doing it when he was a young child. When I asked him why, he answered, "It seemed reasonable, since that's what everyone else called them." As simple as that, it continued throughout his life.

It didn't seem to bother his father, but I think his mother saw it as some kind of rejection of her motherhood, and perhaps in reaction, she never called him by his name. In spite of this, our relationship with her was free of any major problems until the final months of her life.

Both Sophie and Louis enjoyed endless delight in being with Ricki, the granddaughter they adored from the time she was born and who reciprocated equally in her love for them. The moments in the Fort Lauderdale apartment embodied the best of what we shared as a family in our adult years, but they were accompanied by a sense of their fragility and impermanence. Louis began to experience increasing signs of health problems that he had had for several years; and even though he was only in his seventies, we could see that he no longer showed the vigor that had always been his hallmark.

After living in Copiague for more than five years, we realized with astonishment that we had lived there longer than anywhere else. We had become as accustomed to the traffic snarls of Long Island, and the predictable storms that marked the seasons, as we were to the satisfaction that we both got from our work, and the availability of leisure time.

Sylvan assumed an increasingly critical role in the operation of *Newsday*, maintaining relationships with major figures in government—mayors, governors, senators, presidential candidates—who sought access to the editorial pages, which they knew had significant impact on the course of their careers. As his stature was enhanced by these associations, Sylvan found himself, in conjunction with the publisher and executive editor of the paper, wielding significant influence over the choices readers of *Newsday* made in presidential, state, and local elections.

Sylvan developed a close relationship with Mario Cuomo, who was governor of New York at the time. In particular, they greatly appreciated each other's intellect.

Sylvan always said that Cuomo was one of the smartest men he had ever met, as well as the most honorable. The governor often called Sylvan directly—greeting him with "Hi, this is Mario"—about some problem affecting the state, about which an extensive conversation ensued.

Once, we were invited to dinner with a few other guests at the governor's mansion in Albany, where I had the honor of being seated next to Mario and being totally taken by his erudition and charm. It was a delightful evening capped by a tour given by Matilda Cuomo, Mario's wife, of the mansion—not the most beautiful building of its kind, but steeped in the history and grandeur of the state.

Sylvan was also in regular contact with Ed Koch, New York's inimitable mayor. He was a frequent visitor to *Newsday*, where he expressed his views and opinions vociferously to the paper's editorial board, and where Sylvan provided equally strong responses. He and Sylvan continued to stay in touch after Sylvan retired. When they met, Koch would inevitably challenge Sylvan about why he wasn't engaged in some kind of work, as he was. "Why are you not writing something?" was his usual question, to which Sylvan would respond by explaining that he was busy enjoying the leisure available to him now that he wasn't working at a newspaper full time. In spite of their distinct differences about the meaning of retirement, they had an amicable relationship.

Our pride in Sylvan's accomplishments was always accompanied by the awareness of the good fortune that had marked our lives. We had traveled a great distance—in every respect—from the uncertainty we experienced following our departure from Berkeley to where we were now. Part of that good fortune undoubtedly was due to being mutually instrumental in how we became the people we were. I became who I was because of Sylvan, and he became who he was in large part because of me. The quality of interdependence that was so critical in our marriage is difficult to describe, and has always been difficult for other people to comprehend. We knew that we had given each other our lives, an act that we saw as the ultimate expression of love.

One evening in late May 1980, a few days before a trip we were planning to Fort Lauderdale to celebrate Sylvan's birthday, we received a call from Sophie telling us in an eerily calm voice that Louis had suddenly passed away. He had been sitting on the couch in the living room after dinner when she found him, lifeless, apparently having had a massive heart attack. The shock of the news, and our overwhelming grief, was only mitigated by our belief that if one could choose the most peaceful way to die, this would be it.

The loss was profound: Louis had been the stalwart patriarch whose presence had touched everyone around him. Because he was always there when someone needed him, it was hard to imagine the family without him. As we tried to absorb the meaning of his death, our own mortality loomed larger. We would have to assume the responsibility of caring for Sophie, who we knew would need a great deal of support. In the hours immediately after Louis's death, our first concern, of course, was arranging the details of the funeral, and of gathering family and friends to pay tribute to a man who had so thoroughly enjoyed his own life and brought so much joy to others. As we gathered in Sophie and Louis's apartment in Fort Lauderdale after the funeral, the occasion was as much a celebration of Louis's life as it was a time for mourning. Only when that was complete did we start to think of the work we faced in providing support for Sophie.

Additional changes in the family occurred about a year later when Ricki and Frank got married, after Frank was offered a teaching position at Ithaca College, in northern New York. They settled into a comfortable house in the quintessential college town, where Ricki got a job as an editor at Cornell University. Visiting them was much easier now that they were in upstate New York rather than in California. Our trips were always a great joy, and certainly the landscape of Cayuga County provided an impressive backdrop for our visits. Sunshine was always in short supply, however, and my memories of Ithaca, as enjoyable as our visits were, are always sepia-toned, regardless of the season.

When Sylvan and I realized the amount of attention that Sophie would need from us, now that Louis was gone, I thought it best to leave my job at Hillside so that I could spend sufficient time with her. Even with that arrangement, there was still more than enough for Sylvan to take care of as well. As the executor of Louis's estate, he was confronted with many time-consuming financial and legal matters to attend to, some that took months to resolve.

The most immediate problem, however, was that, like so many people in South Florida, Sophie and Louis had used a car to go shopping, to the doctor, and so on. No longer able to drive, Sophie now had to rely on expensive taxis. While she agreed that the only reasonable solution was to sell the apartment and find one in a building with bus service, taking any action on her own at that point was difficult. I spent time with her during the week scouting housing possibilities in nearby communities, and Sylvan joined us on weekends. We finally settled on an apartment in an attractive complex in North Miami Beach that offered not only bus service, a pool, and other outdoor facilities, but also a varied program of activities in the building. We hoped that, in addition to providing access to transportation, the new place would enable Sophie to make friends or at least acquaintances. When we inspected the apartment and toured the building with her, she showed limited enthusiasm—not unusual for Sophie—but acceded to our recommendation that she take it. I was glad that I had the time to help her with the sorting, shedding, packing, and arrangements for moving that she could not have done on her own.

Once settled into her new apartment, she immediately began finding fault with the other residents of the building; her major complaint was that the women were in cliques that excluded newcomers, thus making her feel that she wasn't welcome to join any activities. She refused to see that the invitations she received from her neighbors, her "so-called friends," as she referred to them, were expressions of hospitality; and she ultimately proclaimed one day that Jews could be more cruelly exclusionary than any other ethnic group. As a result, she was minimally involved in any activities that were available to her.

As the months passed, Sophie's way of expressing her grief remained unchanged: she was adamant in voicing her anger toward Louis, whose death she described as "leaving her." It was almost as though she imagined him off somewhere having a great time without her. Our attempts to get her to see the situation in a different light met with no success. To say that we felt frustrated by our inability to bring about any positive change is a great understatement.

Once we saw that Sophie had settled into a routine in which she was nominally self-sufficient except for managing her financial matters, which Sylvan took care of, we continued to call her regularly and visit her periodically. She never completely found the arrangement to her liking, but it was the best we could devise; and now that Sophie didn't need constant attention, Sylvan and I agreed that it was possible for me to go back to work.

Rather than returning to Hillside, I decided to investigate jobs outside the clinical setting, where I might find new challenges. I learned of an opening in the test-construction department of the National League for Nursing whose purpose was to develop standardized achievement tests for students, as well as national exams for licensing professional and vocational nurses. The position called for a nurse with clinical and teaching experience in psychiatric nursing, which seemed a good fit for my background. I submitted my application, was quickly scheduled to be interviewed by senior consultants and the director of the department, and, having made a satisfactory impression, was hired.

The NLN was located at that time in Columbus Circle, in Manhattan. My commute now involved driving to the Long Island Railroad station in Copiague, making a one-hour train trip to Penn Station, and then taking the subway to Columbus Circle. The round trip added three hours to my workday. I became accustomed to reading on the inbound trip and napping on the way home, but it was an exhausting commute. However, the work was totally absorbing since it demanded new ways of thinking about the knowledge required for competent nursing practice, and the means to assess the level of this knowledge. I was introduced to the basics of test construction, a subject that I discovered was more complex than I ever imagined. It was exciting to develop competence in this arcane occupation that seemed to require, in addition to nursing expertise, the imagination of a fiction writer, the obsessiveness of a proofreader, and a talent for crossword puzzles. It presented an opportunity to explore new ways to exercise my mind in a supportive environment with collegial co-workers. I remained at the NLN for several years, until 1985, when I resigned.

The years that followed continued to give us pleasure in our precious free time: a Thanksgiving dinner that Sylvan and my brother Bob and I enjoyed with Ricki and Frank in Ithaca; celebrations of holidays with Ricki and Frank; visits to Sylvan's cousin Sidney and his wife, Ruthie, in Gloversville, New York, where we always resumed conversations we had interrupted at the end of our last visit; and casual get-togethers with friends. Our greatest enjoyment, however, continued to be our closeness and the wonder of being together.

With the leisure that I now had because I wasn't working every day, I was able to resume sketching and painting, which I hadn't done much for years and was a source of immeasurable pleasure. As my interest increased and I felt more eager to improve my work, I looked for a place where I could receive constructive criticism and possibly have contact with other painters. Fortunately, I learned of Paul Wood, a painter who brought together art students a few times a week at his Port Washington, Long Island, studio. In addition to a large working space and a model for those who wanted one, he offered critiques and suggestions when requested. He was accepting of whatever style students were working in, while using a critical eye to help us see elements of a painting that required further development. I went to his studio as frequently as I could, as I found the sessions extremely helpful; and when I was not at his studio, I did a lot of painting at home. I think I showed more development during that period than at any other, and I'm proud of several of the paintings I did then.

The counterpoint to our comfortable lives during this period was the growing difficulty we were having in meeting our obligations to Sophie. On one occasion, when she was unable to reach us by phone for a couple of hours, she became so distressed that she called the police, local hospitals, and relatives in various cities in an attempt to locate us. When she finally reached us, she berated us angrily by demanding, "How could you do this to me?" All of this occurred, of course, before the advent of cell phones, which I suspect, had they been available, would have made our situation even more difficult. We were, unfortunately, the prime target of her dependent and controlling behavior.

Sophie's decline, which extended for eleven years after Louis's death, began as Sylvan and I were thinking about our plans for re tirement. I had switched to part-time work so that I'd have more time to attend to Sophie and soon stopped working completely. Sylvan had set a tentative goal to retire by the time he was sixty; he felt that he had poured enough of his life into the newspaper business, racing from one crisis to another, writing at a furious pace to meet deadlines, and dealing with the unrealistic demands of autocratic editors. And although his position at *Newsday* gave him the chance to work in a more contemplative mode, he wanted to retire while he was still physically and mentally able to enjoy it. After weighing the benefits of early retirement against the option of working for a few more years, we concluded that we could manage financially if Sylvan retired before sixty. We decided that was what we wanted to do.

The question then was where we would go. With the whole world available to us, we could consider living in any one of the attractive places we knew, or one we had only dreamed about. We spent hours letting our fantasies take us everywhere. We knew we didn't want to stay on Long Island, and eliminated the idea of living in a foreign country; we were too rooted in the United States to become permanent expats. In the end, we narrowed our choices down to the New York area. But where? With the hope of finding a house in the country with a little bit of land, close enough to New York so that we could easily get into the city, we began exploring the counties of New York and Connecticut north of the city. Weekends were taken up with drives to view the environs, investigate real estate prices, and look at available properties. Each house seemed appealing in its own way: one had great views; one had a lovely stone fireplace; one was nestled in a grove of towering trees; one had a spectacular kitchen. Would we ever be able to pick the one we wanted?

As we were anticipating retiring and moving from Long Island, Sophie was becoming less attentive to her own needs, wasn't eating adequately, and, as a result, became increasingly frail. To add to her physical problems, she was diagnosed with breast cancer, which necessitated a total mastectomy. She accepted my staying with her during her treatment and recovery with resignation and what could almost be described as relief. She politely ignored the recommendations offered by the visiting nurses, who tried to make her convalescence more comfortable, and she brushed aside my suggestions, of course, with even less attention. Sylvan and I could only sigh in frustration, and say, "That's Sophie." As time went on, when it became apparent that she could no longer manage her apartment on her own, we arranged for her to move to an assisted-living facility where she'd have support services but her own living space.

Sylvan and I visited her frequently, and on one occasion Ricki and I went to see her together. We were sitting outside with her in the building's comfortable garden, having a quiet conversation, when Sophie turned to Ricki and said abruptly, "You know, your mother is a cold fish."

Ricki and I could do no more than stare at each other in disbelief, wondering what precipitated this remark. I was hurt more than I could admit at the time. I tried to attribute the statement to her dwindling control of social behavior, but there had to be real feelings underlying the comment, and this is what disturbed me most. From her point of view, what I had done to try to help her, to take care of her, had apparently meant nothing.

Sophie became increasingly more dissatisfied with her surroundings, and less willing to do anything for herself. We had no choice but to transfer her to a nursing home where she could get full-time care. With that move, she seemed to lose all desire to continue living, and refused to eat altogether. For us, the conflict was between our wanting to keep her alive and acknowledging her loss of a will to live. She developed pneumonia and organ failures, which led to her being hospitalized in an ICU. For two excruciating months, Sylvan and I took turns spending time in Florida so that we could visit her while she lingered on. Then one night we received a call from her family physician informing us that she had passed away.

Both Sylvan and I felt strong, emotionally mixed reactions to her death. As difficult and inscrutable as she could be, she was, after all, Sylvan's mother, and she occupied that critical position that could only belong to her. And although Louis's personality was always the stronger, Sophie was part of the parental fabric that made up Sylvan's early life. As adults, Sylvan and I loved her in our own special ways, and never gave up trying to understand her, even as we succumbed inevitably to frustration. Because Sophie's last days were so difficult, we felt a great relief when they were over and she was at peace.

There is a chilling finality to losing one's second parent. We can never again allow ourselves the fleeting thought of being someone's child. We find ourselves now in the position of having no barrier between us and oblivion.

Chapter 14

Our search for a place to retire ended in Kent, Connecticut. After touring the counties within a hundred-mile radius north of New York, we found ourselves returning repeatedly to Litchfield County, which we found particularly attractive. A real estate agent told us about a contractor who was building two houses in Kent. The village is about ninety miles north of New York, on the Appalachian Trail, with the Housatonic River running through the middle of it. It has the charm of a New England village, and boasts two covered bridges, a few antique shops, a couple of bookstores, some decent country inns, a private boarding school, and an Indian reservation just outside town.

When we met with the contractor, we discovered that one of the houses he was building was within two or three months of completion, which allowed us time to make modifications in the construction if we chose to. We were captivated by the thickly wooded site the house occupied on the side of a hill that led up to the border of New York State, and by the little brook that ran through the property. With no neighboring houses in sight, and a long driveway down to the road, we would be assured of privacy. We lost little time in negotiating a deal with the builder—and no time in imagining a house with a large music room where we could install a new grand piano.

The months of late summer and early fall were taken up with plans for Sylvan's retirement and repeated trips to Kent to monitor work on our house. At one point I had some moments of anxiety about its size—we had never before lived in a place with more than two bedrooms. But Sylvan assured me that it would be great for him to have a separate room to use as an office, and we were excited about having a music room lined with bookshelves. And we certainly wanted a spare bedroom for guests.

On each visit, we were excited to see the house taking shape: here was the stone fireplace in the living room; here were the soaring windows looking out over the foothills of the Berkshires; here were the window seats in the music room where we would be able to play the piano at any hour; here was the kitchen, for which we had painstakingly selected cabinets, floor covering, drawer pulls, and more fixtures than I had ever heard of.

I have not yet mentioned the furniture. Planning, selecting, and arranging for the delivery of what seemed like an endless array of new furniture was a full-time occupation that was new to me. I spent weeks in preparatory study, poring over decorating magazines, roaming furniture stores, until Sylvan could join me in the final decisions about purchasing all the things we would need in a large house. As exhausting as these efforts were, it was fun to put together the pieces of what would become the comfortable home we envisaged.

By the late fall of 1987, arrangements had been completed for Sylvan to turn over the reins of *Newsday*'s editorial pages to his successor. Sylvan was appropriately honored at a farewell celebration, where we toasted his past accomplishments and the beginning of this new phase in our life. We marveled that we had lived for fourteen years on Long Island—the longest time we had ever lived in one place: fourteen good years, productive years filled with many happy memories. Yet it was time to move on. After selling our condominium in Copiague at a nice profit, and packing up our belongings, we were off to Kent.

The house was beautiful. Like any newly built house, it had minor problems that appeared almost every day: a door didn't hang correctly, a floor tile was less than perfect, and something was out of line in the mantelpiece. And while the house still had to get into the rhythm of being a living, breathing organism occupied by people, we were delighted by how comfortable and attractive it was.

There were a couple of unexpected surprises: we discovered that to get television reception, we would have to install a satellite dish. Until that rather expensive undertaking was completed, we had no TV. We also discovered that there was no delivery of the *New York Times* to where we lived, which meant that we had to drive to town every day to get the paper. We learned too that we would have to employ an arborist—a very well-paid member of an occupation we had never heard of—to cut down or trim some trees that were dangerously close to falling on the house.

The family of deer that frolicked on the lawn made a charming sight, but we were told they would consume everything we planted unless we got rid of them. Likewise, the family of beavers that built their dams in our little stream seemed innocent enough until one day we lost television reception because they had chewed through the cable that ran from the satellite dish across the stream to our house. As bizarre as it seemed to us, it was not the first time that the repairman had encountered the problem.

None of this interfered with our enjoyment of our new life, the greatest enjoyment coming from playing our new Yamaha grand in the music room—at any hour of the day or night, without worrying about disturbing the neighbors. With the unlimited time we could spend at the piano, not only were we individually getting back to the level at which we had once played—probably higher—but we had resumed playing four-hand music with more enthusiasm and musicianship than ever. Before long, we were impressed with how we sounded after so many years of not playing together. "We're pretty damn good," we said on at least one occasion. A couple of times, we even gave some well-received performances for friends.

Some of the most memorable hours of our time in Kent were spent working on the more demanding pieces in the piano four-hand repertoire, followed by a rewarding drink in front of the fireplace. Playing four-hand music—if it's with someone you love—the sensitive listening, attuning one's rhythm to that of the other, matching sound to sound, and the profound joy of creating a beautiful piece of music is an experience unlike any other except perhaps that of an ideal sexual encounter. It is difficult for me to hear any of the music we played without recalling those blissful moments.

We had ample opportunity to take long drives to become familiar with the beautiful countryside of Litchfield County and the neighboring counties of New York State. Before long, we knew our way around the back roads that wound through farmland, charming villages with steepled churches, historic houses, perfect village greens, and the expansive estates that nestled in the hillsides. We found places to buy artisanal cheese and homegrown produce; quiet inns where we could enjoy simple dinners; and little stores selling everything from hammers to snow shovels that were still able to survive in small towns despite the encroachment of massive malls.

Before the winter set in, we had a number of visitors who happily accepted invitations to enjoy some time in the country. Bob came with a friend for Thanksgiving weekend, an eccentric woman who was a colleague of his at Adelphi; on another occasion, Sidney and Ruthie came to stay for a few days; Ricki and Frank came from

Ithaca; and other guests made visits for varying lengths of time. There was no question that it was a house that accommodated guests comfortably, and we enjoyed our newfound opportunity for entertaining. There were times, though, when we had back-to-back weekend visitors, that I admit I began to feel as though we were running a B&B.

While the weather was good we were able to get to New York in about an hour and a half, a manageable length of time to get to the theater or a concert, which we did frequently. However, as snow began to make its appearance, we noticed that we always had a much larger accumulation in Kent than in New York City. We soon found that we had to have our driveway ploughed regularly, and once we got to the nearest road, driving was slow even when the plows had come through. There was no doubt that we were in a snow belt. The trip to the city became considerably longer and more difficult; and on more than one occasion, when we were ready to go out for the evening, the rapidly accumulating snow made it impossible to get the car out of the garage, resulting in our canceling our plans for the evening.

We encountered additional transportation problems because our driveway was on the steep incline of a hill. The driveway accumulated all the runoff when any melting occurred; and then, when the temperature dropped, it acquired a surface of sheer ice. This became evident to us one snowy night when the car could not make it even halfway up the driveway. We were forced to get out of the car and inch our way cautiously on foot to the house. It was disconcerting to wonder what we would do in an emergency if an ambulance or fire truck had to reach us. From then on, the driveway loomed as a problem that had to be solved.

Fortunately, the discomfort of winter was relieved by our getting away on two occasions, the first to Baylor University in Waco, Texas, when an old friend of Sylvan's, who was the chair of the journalism department, invited him to conduct a one-month graduate seminar there. Sylvan had spent some short periods of time teaching undergraduates at Baylor when he'd been at *Newsday*. He had enjoyed the experience, having found the students bright and well motivated, and he looked forward to doing another stint.

We flew to Dallas, where we picked up a rental car, drove to Waco, which is about halfway between Dallas and Austin, and settled into the small, furnished apartment close to the campus that the university provided for us.

Spending a month at Baylor was like visiting a time capsule from the 1950s. A Baptist school whose influence was evident in the manners, dress, and outlook of its students, it presented a fascinating contrast to the atmosphere of most universities of the time. When I wandered around the campus—a large, beautiful expanse of traditional academic buildings set on manicured lawns—I felt like an anthropologist observing the interesting behaviors of an alien culture. The female students all wore skirts, the men wore neatly pressed trousers and had neatly trimmed hair, and they always greeted me with a smiling hello or good morning. Sylvan, meanwhile, as he had in past sessions, told the students not to address him as "professor" and assured them that not only did they not have to always agree with him, but that they could challenge him if they felt so inclined. As had happened on previous occasions, they responded. Within a few days, they were engaging in active, heated discussions of a variety of topics.

In the evening we were always eager to venture out for dinner to one of the dimly lit, smoky steakhouses along the banks of the Brazos River for good Texas cooking, country music, accompanied by the drawls of Texas voices in the background, and the atmosphere that could only be felt in a Texas town like Waco.

As foreign as the environment seemed to us, we in turn were certainly looked upon as foreigners, clearly "not from these parts." (Our lack of cowboy boots and Stetsons was a dead giveaway.) After showing up a few times at the same restaurant, we would inevitably be approached by a waiter or a patron whose curiosity would lead him to ask us where we were from and "What brings you to Waco?" On many occasions, after answering the inquiries, Sylvan would draw the person into a description of what his life was like and, over the course of an hour or more, acquire a wealth of information that we would otherwise not have had. Sylvan's journalistic instincts never failed him. It was one of our few opportunities to hear the unhesitating expression of solidly right-wing views on integration, the rights of immigrants, abortion, the value of gun ownership, and every other provocative subject. It convinced us that the cowboy past was alive and well in Waco.

When Sylvan's friend Loyal and his wife, Ilga, invited us over for the evening, we had an opportunity to meet with some of the intellectual residents of Waco, whose thinking contrasted with that of most of the locals we had met in town. The rabbi of the local congregation, several ministers of different faiths, and faculty members of the university made lively dinner companions with whom we spent hours exchanging ideas and developing an appreciation of the diversity of the community.

In our free time on the weekends, we managed to take drives to Dallas, Austin, and San Antonio, each day trip offering us a snapshot view of the city. One weekend we wandered the hill country made famous by Lyndon Johnson. Our explorations, though brief, gave us a fascinating view of a part of the country with which we had been totally unfamiliar. As incredible as it seemed to friends when we later described our visit, we had a most enjoyable time in Waco.

When it was time to leave, Sylvan received enthusiastic expressions of appreciation from his students, and he could look back on his time with them as totally rewarding.

Back in Kent, we were faced again with the snow and frigid weather, and with the isolation imposed by the location of our house; unfortunately, its many comforts did not alleviate our distress.

Before long, we were thinking of getting away again to someplace warm. We decided to rent a condominium for a few weeks in Boca Raton, Florida, where we spent most of our time happily taking long walks in the sun. But that was a temporary respite before having to face the return to Kent. We were developing a sense of disquiet about the house that was disconcerting to both of us.

With the spring thaw came a new problem: melting snow and rainwater had transformed the driveway into a veritable muddy river that ran down to the road, making access to the house increasingly difficult and unpleasant. When we consulted an engineer about how to solve the problem, we were told that the correction would involve extensive reconstruction, which of course would be very expensive. The alternative, which we opted for, was to put up with the situation for the time being and wait for the warm weather to do its job. It was not a solution we were happy with, since we knew that the driveway had become a permanent problem we could not escape.

It's hard to remember exactly when we started to think of selling the house. There were so many things about it that we liked, but there were more and more things that were interfering with our leading the kind of enjoyable life we had looked forward to. Our sense of isolation, emphasized by the problems related to driving, had become major sources of discomfort. Unlike many of the people with houses in Kent, including our nearest neighbors, we didn't have an apartment in the city. We had hoped that being reasonably close to New York would allow us to have the best of both city and country; when we realized that was impossible, that we were missing too many things that were important to us, we decided that it was time to move back to New York.

We put the house up for sale. Unlike what we had encountered when we had sold our condominium in Copiague in a matter of days, we faced a tough situation, as real estate in the entire region was in a slump. A slow trickle of real estate agents escorted potential buyers, each of whom found something unacceptable about the house. Anyone who has been in this position is familiar with the chorus of criticisms emanating from potential buyers: too many rooms; not enough rooms; kitchen too small; windows too tall; missing a pool. Yet with all the complaints, no one seemed bothered by the driveway. Weeks and then months went by as the shoppers, almost all from the city and looking for a second home, found one reason or another why the house wasn't for them. Totally discouraged, we began to think that we would never be able to get out of Kent.

As the old saying goes, "It takes only one buyer." Our buyer turned out to be not someone looking for a second home but a family from Kent wanting to move to a larger house. Our elation was indescribable. We lost no time in planning how to make the move back to New York. Since we had to get out of Kent, and wanted adequate time to search for a co-op or condominium, we decided to rent a house temporarily on Long Island that could accommodate our furniture while we conducted our search. Eventually, we had to sell some of the furniture because there wouldn't be room for all of it in a New York apartment. The most difficult part of this was selling the piano; in no way would its physical size or the volume of its sound fit into what would be our new home. It was a painful but unavoidable decision.

We began to consider what we wanted and absolutely had to have in an apartment: we needed the security and convenience of a full-service building; we refused to consider any apartment that required turning on a light for illumination in the middle of the day; we wanted to have windows that looked out on something other than a blank wall; and we didn't want the noise of heavy street traffic directly below us.

Those were the basics. We didn't care if a building was prewar or postwar as long as it was in good condition, and although we were most interested in the West Village and the Upper East Side, where we had lived before, we were open to other neighborhoods. The most critical factor, of course, was price; and being familiar enough with the New York real estate market, we knew our limitations. Our days were filled with expeditions into Manhattan to meet with realtors with whom we trekked from one two-bedroom apartment to another, checking out floor plans and closet space, while examining the condition of the unit, the building, and the immediate surroundings; it was Sylvan's idea to include checking out the crime statistics of the neighborhood at the local precinct. Now that we were on the other side of the real estate equation, we were confronted with many apartments with unacceptable problems.

I couldn't believe how many otherwise attractive co-ops had views of dingy alleys; one place seemed quite acceptable except that the floors sloped at such an angle that it would be a considerable challenge to anchor the furniture; and I lost track of the number of apartments that never saw sunlight, and of kitchens too small to turn around in.

"Why worry? Nobody cooks in Manhattan," one real estate agent informed us. Her pronouncement didn't convince me.

Finally we found the place we wanted, in the sixties, east of Second Avenue, which put it in an affordable price range compared to places west of Second; the apartment was on the eleventh floor of a sixteen-story building, with good-sized rooms, a dining area, a spacious foyer, ample closet space, and—most important—plenty of light, and it looked south over skyscrapers, the Queensboro Bridge, and the Chrysler building. It needed only painting and some minor repairs to bring it into good condition; and since we were satisfied enough with the appearance of the bathrooms and the kitchen to put off any plans to renovate, no major work needed to be done.

There followed the arduous process of providing the co-op board with more information about our personal and financial lives than we knew even existed and the dreaded interview with the admissions committee, which turned out to be an amiable chat that ended in our being warmly welcomed.

Chapter 15

We were home!

Never had we felt so strongly that we were back where we were supposed to be. We couldn't wait to start roaming the city, getting reacquainted with old, familiar places, and discovering all the changes that had occurred since we had lived here many years before. It was like a recapitulation of what we had done when we were kids in Juilliard: the two of us together, finding wonder in the spectacular and commonplace facets of New York. We planned "outings": a ride on the 59th Street tram to explore Roosevelt Island; taking the Staten Island ferry to see the historic treasures of the harbor; wandering through the Wall Street area and visiting the World Trade Center to have a drink on the uppermost level; touring the Lower East Side to find that amid all the changes the venerable appetizing store Russ and Daughters—where years ago Sylvan had told me you could get the best smoked salmon and sturgeon—was still there. It was time to renew our addiction to their incomparable smoked fish and other delicacies.

Most important was our rediscovery of Central Park. The park was not only our favorite destination, but also the source of boundless pleasure as we walked its pathways in the changing colors of the seasons, or sat and watched the endlessly interesting parade of passersby. It was always a favorite game of ours to observe people, who were sometimes alone but more often with a companion, and speculate about who they were, their histories, what language they were speaking, and what they were saying. Our subjects would never know the intricate stories we imagined about them, or how much fun we had constructing them.

When we made periodic visits to the little boat pond in the park, we became familiar with the serious bird watchers who sat armed with long-range binoculars, and who, like us, had come to follow the gestation and birth of the offspring of the red-tailed hawks in residence on a balcony high in a luxurious Fifth Avenue building. It was always easy to become engaged in conversation with the bird watchers, who were eager to share information with us about the habits of the red-tailed hawks, and who generously invited us to take a peek at the nest through their binoculars. We had many such comfortable encounters with fellow New Yorkers.

One of my fondest memories is of a walk we took that led unexpectedly to the lovely carousel in the park. It was a glorious sight: its gilded horses gleaming in the sun, its calliope playing merrily. I commented to Sylvan how much I had always loved carousels. I couldn't remember the last time I had been on one and doubted I ever would be again. After all, you were supposed to be accompanied by a child on a carousel, weren't you? Without hesitating a minute, Sylvan bought a ticket and urged me to climb aboard. In the end, I abandoned all fears of looking ridiculous, became a child again, and mounted a handsome steed for the carousel ride to end all carousel rides. I don't know who enjoyed it more—me or Sylvan as he watched me.

Our long walks often ended with a Scotch at the Oak Room of the Plaza Hotel, or at one of the many other watering holes in the city. As unremarkable as it is to observe the flow of urban life in a beautiful New York bar, it became a treasured experience for us because we were doing it together. Again I see the parallel between what we were experiencing when we were in our sixties and seventies and the original experiences we had when we first met: what we were doing was far less important than the fact that we were doing it together. When I think of the eighteen years we shared in our Manhattan apartment, memories of the daily, unremarkable events are the most vivid and long-lasting.

One evening when we were relaxing at home after dinner, the phone rang and Sylvan answered. He heard a female voice with a Spanish accent on the other end asking, "Is this Sylvan Fox who used to work at *Newsday*?" Sylvan assured her it was. "Do you remember your guide in Havana? Hilda?" It took Sylvan a moment before he could make the connection and answer, "Yes, of course. Where are you?" Over the next few minutes, Hilda described how she had come to be living in Miami, after fleeing from Cuba illegally. Before the conversation ended, we told her that she would be welcome to spend a few days with us in New York and began to make plans for her visit.

During her stay, her first time in New York and an eye-opening experience for her, she told us the lengthy story of what her life had been like in Cuba. For several years, she had been the host of a respected television program. Gradually, however, government superiors had begun to exert control over the content and character of her program. At the same time, she was undergoing a change in her thinking, moving from unquestioningly supporting the government's policies as doctrine to seeing the flaws and untruths.

As she said, "I became aware of the dishonesty, the deception, the hypocrisy I couldn't see before." Eventually she found it intolerable to remain in Cuba. She arranged a trip to Mexico, presumably to work on a segment for her television program, and then, abandoning everything she had in Cuba—her home, belongings, family, and professional reputation—she sought asylum in Miami with an uncle.

Hilda's initial visit to New York was the beginning of a long-standing, warm friendship, which included many subsequent visits and her introduction to Ricki and Frank. We all spent a few enjoyable days together in Atlanta, where Hilda was a guest in their home. As Hilda tried to find a way to resume her television career in the United States, we gave her support and advice, but unfortunately her efforts met with limited success.

When we had been back in New York for some time, Sylvan was invited by the head of the journalism department at New York University to teach a reporting course for senior-year journalism majors. Since he had previously enjoyed working with students, Sylvan accepted the offer.

Once again in the academic setting, he became happily involved with the classes, in spite of the nuisance of the usual nonteaching activities. His students were a more heterogeneous, and in many ways more interesting, group than in Waco: there was a wider demographic spread, and more differences in age, educational background, and ability. The time with them in the classroom was stimulating and satisfying. However, since the students were required to submit reporting assignments, Sylvan had to spend several hours each week reading and critiquing the students' writing. That, and assigning grades at the end of the semester, took a considerable bite into his leisure time, which he didn't appreciate.

When he was asked to return the following semester to teach a graduate class, he deliberated for some time before agreeing to take it on, albeit with some reservations. During that semester he had many of the same negative responses. Sylvan's experience at NYU confirmed for him that he had made the right decision years before when he chose not to make a life in academia; as much as he enjoyed the teaching role, he could not tolerate the restrictions and demands that accompanied it.

When the graduate course was finished, Sylvan announced that this marked the end of his teaching career, at least for the foreseeable future. As he said, "This part-time work has become too much of a full-time job."

During those wonderful years of having nothing to tie us down, and of still being in reasonably good health, we indulged ourselves in taking some of the trips we had often talked about. We returned to France and spent a leisurely time in Paris, the city we loved so much, revisiting familiar haunts and discovering the additions that had arisen since we were last there.

Another year, we went to Vienna and feasted on the wonders that were so much a part of our cultural heritage—the music, the art, the architecture, and the history—to say nothing of the city's gastronomic wonders. Sylvan's knowledge of German gave him the advantage of being able to converse with people and, as usual, to use his consummate skill in engaging them in conversation. We paid due homage to the founder of psychoanalysis by visiting Freud's residence, and we were fascinated by a visit to a historic orthodox synagogue, where we stayed for part of the Friday-night service. We visited palaces and beer gardens and as much of the city as we could see using the city's excellent transportation system. There was more than we could possibly absorb in one stay; we vowed that we would return.

On that same trip, we traveled to Prague, whose beauty impressed us but left us with unpleasant memories as I had my wallet snatched trying to exit a train. Two burly thugs had their act down pat: one stood firmly planted in the doorway, while the other slipped the wallet out of my bag as I was trying frantically to get off the metro. When we discovered the theft, Sylvan was determined to report it to the authorities. We asked directions to the nearest police station and made our way to a dark, ancient building. Once inside, we found ourselves in a tiny, dank anteroom reeking of disinfectant. The room was empty except for a window well below eye level that opened into the interior of the station. It required bending down uncomfortably at the hips to attract the attention of one of the two officers ensconced in an office behind the glass. Several taps on the window finally convinced one of them to appear and face us. Sylvan asked him if he spoke English, to which he answered with a vacant shake of the head. He responded in the same way when asked if he spoke French or German. In total frustration, we returned to our hotel, where the concierge told us that we should return to the police station after four o'clock, when someone who spoke English would be there. We were furious when yet another sullen officer who could speak only Czech was the only officer available when we returned at 4:30. Could something so Kafkaesque occur anywhere but in Prague? When we expressed our outrage to the concierge at our hotel, and asked if we would be faced with the same response if we were reporting an armed robbery or a serious assault, he shrugged and proffered that it was difficult to get competent municipal employees because the pay was so low. We couldn't decide which was worse: the crime or our treatment when we tried to report it.

Sylvan refused to passively accept the way we had been treated. His response to the incident, when we returned home, was to write a letter to the *Prague Post,* an English-language newspaper, in which he described eloquently, in great detail, what had occurred, and posed the question of whether the city wanted this callous lack of concern about safety to become known to future visitors. The paper published Sylvan's response not as a letter but as a feature story, giving it a position of prominence it would not have had as a letter to the editor. He received a copy of the paper, as well as a check as payment for his writing, which he never cashed because of the difficulties of exchanging the money into U.S. dollars.

From Prague, we traveled to Hungary, where our experience was totally delightful. We spent most of our visit having a glorious time in Budapest, which we found to be one of the friendliest cities we had ever visited. We heard wonderful music, not just in concert halls but in restaurants and little cafés, where the folk music enchanted us and had us saying to each other: "Of course, here are the roots of Bartok!" In one restaurant, a musician who was playing a cimbalom, a traditional Hungarian stringed instrument, came to our table during a break and asked me if I'd like to try to play it. A few feeble attempts convinced me I should stick to the piano.

We saw some of the beautiful countryside and historic sites of the region when we took a day tour of the Danube Bend. We left Hungary with the hope that we would return someday.

When we got back to New York, one of the editors at *Newsday* asked Sylvan if he'd like to do a column aimed at mature and armchair travelers. "The Golden Globetrotter," as it was called, was planned as a biweekly column, which Sylvan could write at home and which would not require him to do any additional travel unless he chose to. Sylvan warmed to the idea, produced many entertaining columns, and had fun writing them for about a year, until he saw it as yet another job that was becoming too demanding of his free time. "The Golden Globetrotter" was retired.

In 1995, I sustained a stroke. I awoke one night with the classic signs of double vision and weakness and paralysis on one side of my body. I knew immediately what was happening, was able to speak, and woke Sylvan to tell him that we had to get to the hospital immediately. Fortunately, the worst of my symptoms were brought under control during a week in the hospital. I regained function of my left arm and leg, though I was left with paresthesias on my left side that remained for several years. And it was months before I was free of the fear that a similar or worse occurrence would befall me, in spite of the modifications made to my medical regime. It was the old "When is the other shoe going to fall?" syndrome.

Our lives eventually returned to our normal enjoyments. We made more wonderful trips: one in which we took an extended drive, starting in Portland, Oregon, through the Pacific Northwest and into British Columbia. Vancouver captivated us with its beauty and its Asian-influenced cosmopolitan character; and we were particularly awed by the magnificent grandeur of the totem poles displayed in the Museum of Anthropology, where we returned for repeat visits. We took the boat over to Vancouver Island and enjoyed the charm of Victoria for a couple of days before proceeding by ferry to Port Angeles, Washington, and then back down the coast.

One of my most treasured memories of that trip was a visit we made to a wolf preserve in Washington State, where we were in close proximity to the animals. Wolves have always been among my favorite creatures, and it was a delight to howl with them and get a chorus of responses from everywhere in the compound. I don't know how I developed such a fondness for these creatures, but being so close to them in their habitat and joining them in a chorus of howls was a thrilling experience.

On another trip we spent several weeks in California, revisiting Berkeley and then driving down to the Monterey Peninsula, where we stayed in a marvelous hotel looking out over the Pacific. Most of all, we treasured the good fortune that had allowed us to reach a point in our lives where we were able to enjoy the experiences of our retirement years together.

Things began to change sometime around 2004. Sylvan started noticing a weakness in his legs and unsteadiness in his gait. We got the name of a good neurologist who, after examining him, was not able to make an immediate diagnosis but suggested following him carefully over the next few months. Sylvan's symptoms subsequently worsened, to where he was having difficulty controlling forward movement when walking. This propulsive gait, as it was called, which was not always apparent, was suggestive of Parkinson's disease, as were some of the other symptoms he was showing, although he didn't have the tremors that usually characterize the disease.

By this time, Sylvan had been referred to the Neurologic Institute of Columbia Presbyterian Hospital, where he became a patient of a neurologist in the Department of Movement Disorders. An extensive series of tests ruled out Parkinson's as well as a number of other diagnoses.

It became more and more difficult for Sylvan to move about, and he also had greater difficulty with short-term memory and concentration. All any of the doctors could say was that he was suffering from a progressive neurological disorder for which there was neither effective treatment nor a definitive diagnosis. With each trip that we made to the Neurologic Institute, we became more discouraged. On several occasions, Sylvan said, "What difference does it make which name we attach to this illness if there's no treatment for it?"

His ability to move independently became so impaired that he needed assistance to move from the bed to a chair; and his poor balance led to a number of frightening falls, both inside and outside the apartment. Even with the assistance of a cane, and leaning heavily on me, it was impossible for him to walk more than a short distance. He was slowing down in every way: in his thinking, his comprehension, his communication, and his ability to carry out basic daily activities. It was painful to see him struggling to have a conversation with me, and to say to me more than once, "I'm sorry I'm such a burden on you."

I was torn apart seeing what he was losing and by being unable to stop the horrible sequence of events. I tried to be with him every minute, thinking that somehow my constant presence would deter the progression of his illness. I foolishly resisted the idea of having someone come to the apartment to help me. It was important to me that I do everything for him myself, even though I was becoming progressively worn down by the effort. There were times when we were able to go out for dinner and have a conversation almost like we used to. On days like these, my magical thinking allowed me to imagine that somehow he would recover and be his old self again. At other times, I was convinced that I was witnessing an inexorable route to death, and that I was losing him minute by minute.

We both suffered terribly through this period: loss and the anticipation of greater loss. There was less and less spoken communication. Once, when we were sitting quietly, our hands clasped together, Sylvan turned to me and said, "We must remember every word." I knew that he meant the myriad words that we had spoken to each other in the past and the precious words that were left to us now.

On a Monday in December 2007, Sylvan became acutely ill with a gastrointestinal infection that led to his becoming totally dehydrated and fainting. On the advice of our internist, we went to the emergency room of NYU Hospital, where Sylvan was admitted. Intravenous feeding was started, but almost immediately he showed signs of pneumonia, for which he was treated with IV antibiotics. Our internist assured us that the pneumonia would be easily resolved and that with good hydration Sylvan would be ready for discharge in a day or two.

But Sylvan did not respond well to treatment, contrary to the doctor's prognosis. I could see that he was becoming increasingly disengaged from what was occurring around him, and his responses were growing more and more limited. While he didn't want to talk, he continued to be concerned about the effect that his hospitalization was having on me. He repeatedly insisted that I go home because I looked tired after spending hours by his bedside. He seemed to be having difficulty swallowing, causing him to eat very little, but he offered the explanation that he had no appetite, especially for the hospital food. A gastroenterologist performed tests on his esophagus and upper GI tract that revealed no abnormalities. At the same time, a pulmonologist was consulted because his breathing seemed labored, although the pneumonia had been resolved. The examinations revealed nothing to account for his failure to show improvement. What I was seeing—his diminished response, his withdrawal, his continued physical decline—I could only interpret as evidence that he was giving up and losing the will to live.

Contrary to what I was witnessing, when the internist visited Sylvan late Friday afternoon, he was optimistic that if Sylvan started eating a little more he could go home in a couple of days. He suggested that I bring in some home-cooked food, to which Sylvan nodded agreement.

I was torn between what the doctor was saying and my own concerns about Sylvan's condition. After staying with him for some time, I kissed him good night and told him I would be back early tomorrow.

I had dinner with Ricki and we talked about Sylvan's condition and the doctor's prognosis, after which I began planning what I should prepare to take to Sylvan the following day. I went to sleep with that in mind: cook something that he likes, that he will eat, and it will make him feel better. How much of this was my magical thinking, and how much was the confidence that I had placed, mistakenly, in the doctor's evaluation?

Early the next morning, the phone rang as I was getting dressed to leave for the hospital. A male who identified himself as a doctor at the hospital said, "Mrs. Fox, I have some terrible news. Your husband passed away a few minutes ago." I screamed, "What are you saying? What are you telling me?" The doctor's words made no sense: "A nurse found Mr. Fox not breathing. We tried to resuscitate him but were not successful. You should come to the hospital as quickly as possible." I tried to comprehend what was happening as my chest began pounding and I was overcome by the sense that the whole world had disintegrated. I managed to call Ricki to tell her what had happened. I don't remember what I said, other than to tell her to pick me up in a cab.

When we got to his room, Sylvan looked as though he was peacefully asleep. I kissed his eyes and his face, still warm. I sat next to the bed and lay my head on his shoulder, feeling the familiar contours of his body. I could not grasp that the world had been transformed, that this was no longer Sylvan. Someone came into the room and asked if we wanted to request an autopsy. No. Someone else came in and told us that we had to pack up his belongings and leave; the staff had to do what must be done after a death, of course. No one came in to offer a word of condolence or any further explanation of what had happened. Ricki and I left and went back to the apartment.

We had to make calls, to inform people. We had to select a funeral director. Ricki got the name of someone from a friend. We made an appointment for the following day. I was numb, unable to feel anything as I tried to move through a fog of unreality.

We met with the funeral director and made the necessary decisions, completed the paperwork, selected a casket, planned for the service, and arranged for the burial in a plot on Long Island that Louis had acquired years before. I would not have been able to manage this without Ricki, who had the strength to support me through the entire process. The funeral was scheduled for Monday.

I consented to having a rabbi conduct the service because I thought Sylvan would have wanted that. It was a brief, traditional service followed by a eulogy by one of Sylvan's colleagues.

Then, as the rabbi was about to conclude, I said that I wanted to speak, although I hadn't prepared anything. I talked about what a remarkable man Sylvan was, the many passions he had—for literature, for writing, for music, for living—and his love for Ricki and me. I talked about the importance of music in our life, of the joy of playing four-hand pieces together, and of how that experience was analogous to the progression of a marriage. I was determined to say these things without tears. Ricki followed with remembrances of Sylvan as a father, which I'm sure would have pleased Sylvan very much.

During the trip to the cemetery, I was still encased in unyielding numbness. I looked out the car window to see we were driving past *Newsday*, along the very road Sylvan took to work each day. And, ironically, the cemetery was less than a mile from his office.

We arrived at the cemetery and made our way to the gravesite, which was sheltered by the bare trees of winter. As I went through the ritual of laying soil on the grave, I still could not believe that it was Sylvan whose body was in the casket. Surely I was witnessing some dreamlike event that would soon be over.

After the burial, a few friends returned with us to the apartment, where we laid out some food for the guests. Some people had Scotch, and I kept thinking that I would have to be sure to replenish the stock, because it was Sylvan's favorite drink.

The visitors eventually left and Ricki went home. It was only after I was alone that the reality—that Sylvan was gone—began to sink in. Overwhelmed with pain, I finally succumbed to the tears I had not allowed until then.

Our story ends here. Only the beautiful memories remain.

Chapter 16

I am living two concurrent lives. The inner one, accessible only to me, is a welter of thoughts and emotions, and of dreams that seem real and in which reality seems like a dream. My exterior life is an attempt to find some way to function again in the world—a world that I see as irrevocably changed. Like two courses of a stream, the two lives diverge and merge, seemingly at random.

Sylvan is no longer with me. I can feel only the terrible sense of being alone and the pain of emptiness. I died too; but somehow I am still here, enduring the passage of empty days and interminable nights. I am cold, a constant cold of fear and dread and loneliness that makes me tremble, and that nothing can dispel. The realization that I am alone is accompanied by the impossible simultaneous presence and absence of Sylvan: at the same moment that I feel the overwhelming pain of his absence, I have the strong sense that he is here.

I sit down to have breakfast and look at his empty chair. I wait for him to begin a conversation and there is silence. No more talking about the little things that will fill the day. No more discussing stories in the *Times*: politics, cultural events, baseball, obits, everything. No more sharing thoughts and ideas, jokes, worries, doubts, questions. Only the agonizing silence as I wait to hear his response to my question: what do you think?

I go into the living room and wonder why he is not in his favorite place on the sofa. He's not in the room, yet he is everywhere. I see him coming into the kitchen to find out what I'll be making for dinner. Sometimes he comes up behind me and strokes the back of my head, my hair still damp from a shower; I tell him he's patting me like a cat. I see him in the bedroom, pulling on a shirt and slacks. His clothes hang in the closet and fill the dresser drawers, waiting for him. They can't be moved.

When I return to the apartment after being out for a while, I listen for his unmistakable "hello," which always greeted me when I opened the door; now, silence is my only greeting. Yet I hear his voice.

Sylvan appears almost nightly in my dreams: he is returning from some distant reporting assignment; he is standing, half obscured, in the doorway of a public building; he is waiting for me as I frantically search dark, unfamiliar streets to find him. He comes back to the apartment, exhausted from work, needing to take a rest; he suddenly appears in the bedroom looking for a fresh change of clothes. He kisses me, he hugs me, and I am happy, until I am wrenched back to being awake, in tears, feeling empty and alone, experiencing the loss again as though for the first time.

My lawyer calls to tell me that he wants to meet with me to go over details of the will. As he describes the legal minutiae of what remains to be done, I try to focus on what he is saying. I answer him, "Yes, certainly. I'll be there tomorrow."

I have to go to the Social Security office to fill out endless forms. I diligently follow instructions and it's done.

Credit companies and a dozen other agencies have to be notified. More forms to fill out. I lose track of the sheets of paper accumulating on the desk, but I check off more tasks on the list of things to do.

Ricki is on the phone and I answer her questions. "Yes, I'm taking care of everything that has to be done. Yes, let's have dinner on Friday." (See how organized I am.)

"Ricki, maybe you can come up with the names of some therapists. I think I should see somebody. I've lost touch with everybody I knew in the mental health field. No, I don't want a group. I know it wouldn't be good for me. I need to talk to someone privately." She gives me the names of several therapists with their qualifications. I select one, Brian, and make an appointment.

I remind myself that I existed as a person before I met Sylvan, and I existed as a person in my relationship with him. There must be a way for me to exist now, though I haven't found it yet. I'm no longer the frightened little girl who came to New York in 1947, but who am I now? I have no idea. How can I establish an identity from all the remnants of the past and the fragile shreds of the present? I doubt I can do it. I don't want to continue existing this way, surviving days filled with tears.

I reject thinking of myself as a "widow," a term that doesn't seem to fit; after sixty years, there's no question that I am still married to Sylvan. I realize I should make an effort to build friendships; I should try to become more sociable. I must extend myself, although I have little desire to do so. It was only when I met Sylvan that I no longer felt like an isolated alien. The acceptance and love he gave me sustained me throughout my life. Only with Sylvan could I feel the total joy of being safe and loved, and now that no longer exists.

The relationship that Sylvan and I had with each other was so essential to our lives that the friendships we had with other people, while enjoyable and rewarding, in no way attained similar importance. I miss the few close friends I had; in recent years I have lost so many of them because they either moved away or passed away.

When I first meet with Brian, I anticipate being able to outline in a clear, straightforward, professional way why I think I should be in therapy, expecting it to be short term. I say that my main goal is to find relief from my intense pain.

But then, suddenly, I break down into uncontrollable crying as I try to describe the circumstances of Sylvan's death. No more am I the stoic thinker. For the first time since losing Sylvan, I am allowing myself to express what I am feeling, and, most important, it feels safe to do so. I set up regular meetings.

In my attempt to establish some kind of routine, I return to my weekly Hebrew class. We are a small group that has been together for years, of mixed ages and backgrounds, but joined in our love of the language and our determination to become more fluent in it. Everyone offers condolences and is extremely patient as I try to find the right Hebrew words for what I want to say. Although I try to concentrate, my mind keeps wandering off to the thought of going home when the class is over. In the past, I eagerly anticipated going home for dinner and a relaxing evening with Sylvan. Now, in the empty apartment, I want only to retreat to bed.

I see Ricki for dinner when she is free. She is the only person with whom I feel any emotional attachment, yet I am reluctant to reveal to her the depth of my depression because I don't want her to be contaminated by my feelings. She encourages me to get together with people I know, to develop more social contacts, to get out and do things. I promise I will.

My friend Elaine, who was a colleague at the National League for Nursing, asks if I would be interested in joining her in doing some part-time work for an organization that does test construction, which is what I was doing when I last worked. She has already talked with the woman who owns the organization, whom I also used to work with, and they think it would be beneficial for everyone involved. They need another nurse and suggest I might enjoy working again. Since I haven't worked in a long time, I wonder if I can still be productive, but I tell them that it sounds interesting and I'm willing to give it a try. Work will become part of my identity.

I venture out to see a movie by myself, and another day I go to the Museum of Modern Art. My reactions are tempered by wondering what Sylvan's responses would be. I'm making an effort to find constructive ways to fill the hours; more accurately, it feels like killing time.

Listening to music, which was always one of the most joyful components of our lives, has become cruelly transformed by the associations I have with every piece of music. There is nothing I can hear that is not connected to the experience of listening to it with Sylvan. What contributed so much to our intense pleasure was knowing, without having to put it into words, that we were sharing common responses and enjoyment. We first heard this together; we discussed the structure of this together; we played a four-hand version; we compared the different recordings and the different interpretations. Now, I listen to music that I love and am overcome with tears. The first few measures of the *Ravel Piano Concerto* are unbearable. I hear the beginning of a Brahms symphony and I cry uncontrollably. Yet I cannot give up one of the few enjoyable parts of my life.

I don't know who I am anymore, and I don't want to go on like this. I wish I didn't have to continue living, but I could never do anything to end my life. My meetings with Brian give me the faint hope that I will not always be in such pain. Being able to express these feelings to someone who can accept them is a relief.

Although I don't know why, I begin to keep a diary. Is it possible to translate tears into words?

Ricki and I go out to dinner on Sylvan's birthday. I think of last year, the last birthday Sylvan had, how on that evening he was able to enjoy a good dinner at one of our favorite restaurants and was feeling well enough to keep up an active conversation almost like his old self.

Ricki and I toast Sylvan with a glass of champagne and I keep from crying until I get home.

I talk to my strong, stable, solidly Canadian brother, Don. Over the years we haven't seen each other much as our lives went in separate directions. He and his wife, Joan, continued to live in Sudbury until his retirement, when they moved eventually to Burlington, in southern Ontario. Although we got together only infrequently, we had good times that always included Don and Sylvan spending long hours exchanging views on Canadian and American politics.

After not seeing Don for some time, I'm surprised by how easy it is to talk to him, how comfortable it feels to have this connection with my last remaining brother. His intelligence and reasoned thinking impress me, and I recognize in his reserved manner a part of my own personality. Besides our blue eyes, I think we do share some familial characteristics.

Don has had some serious medical problems, and Joan is deteriorating physically and mentally. She has required several hospitalizations, which have been difficult for him to bear. Since it is impossible for them to visit me, I am determined to get to Burlington to see them.

At some time during the summer, I develop an excruciatingly painful cellulitis in my lower right leg, for no known reason; it's serious enough that I have to be admitted to the hospital. After a week of treatment, I go home, in constant pain. The condition worsens and I'm readmitted to the hospital. I'm not satisfied with the treatment I'm receiving, particularly the nursing care, and I'm discouraged by the persistence of the infection, despite being given powerful IV drugs. After another week, my doctor reluctantly discharges me with a prescription for oral antibiotics. At home, lying with my leg elevated, still in pain, I'm unable to do much more than hobble to the bathroom.

The prospect of being in a permanent state of dependence is more frightening than anything I can imagine. Death, which has already extended its hand in invitation, seems even more attractive.

As summer slips by, my physical condition improves, but there is no end to my loneliness and the hopelessness I feel about the future. I am not a whole person. It's eight months since Sylvan died.

I see Brian each week and gain enough support from him to be able to survive until the next meeting. He is a lifeline that I cling to, although I am still not sure where that lifeline leads. It's hard to describe why I feel better after seeing him: he coaches me in how to use meditation, which I find beneficial when I am most depressed; he suggests that I assess my level of emotional distress on a scale of one to ten; most of the time I'm stuck at the higher numbers. But these interventions, while important, don't begin to encompass the most essential part of treatment, that ineffable effect achieved by communicating with someone who understands what you're saying. I am grateful for it even as I can't define it.

Once a week I work at my job in test construction. It's satisfying to discover that I still have the skills to perform adequately as a professional. Yet it's difficult for me to feel comfortable meeting and working with new people; and I sometimes wonder, as I try to recognize myself: who is this person who is appearing in the office each week?

I want to introduce Sylvan to the people I'm meeting so that he will know them too. I have to hear what he thinks of them.

Alan, a colleague of Sylvan's, and his wife invite me to a party at their home. Alan likes to host gatherings of his friends who represent all of the arts and a number of professions. He is an accomplished amateur violinist and music lover, and often provides musical entertainment for his guests. Sylvan and I always enjoyed these occasions, where we could engage in interesting conversation with people we knew or just met. Now I hesitate to attend on my own, since I don't feel like a whole person and wonder how I will present myself. I vacillate for hours and finally decide to go to one of his gatherings. I manage to be a pleasant guest, although I keep looking for Sylvan to come up beside me. Fortunately, I recognize a few people and, in spite of the distance I feel from what's going on around me, I engage in conversation.

On our sixtieth anniversary, I feel Sylvan's presence intensely, an experience that is at the same time comforting yet painful. I recall how much we had looked forward to this day. I try to console myself with the thought that his spirit is free of the physical anguish he endured in the last year of his life; his presence is more real now than what surrounds me in the supposedly real world.

Each event that occurs as the year passes—my birthday, the running of the New York City Marathon, Election Day, Thanksgiving—is another milestone that I mark with tears. When I contemplate the anniversary of Sylvan's death, I decide that I'd like to visit the cemetery before the cold of December sets in.

Ricki, Frank, and I drive out to Long Island to the cemetery. While it was clear earlier, the day has turned rainy and cold. At the cemetery office, we're given a map showing the general location of the grave. We drive down the road we were told to take, but there are no numbers to indicate the location of the plots or other landmarks to help us. By the time we get out of the car, hoping to find something to give us a clue, it's raining heavily and the earth has become sodden. I am in a nightmare in which my only thought is that we will plod in endless circles in the rain without ever finding the grave.

We return to the office to ask for more directions, but the clerk can only tell us the section we need to go to. Again, we trudge between graves, on ground that has now been turned to mud. By some miracle, Frank spots the site. As I approach, I am jolted when, for the first time since the funeral, I see the grave, now marked with the memorial stones. The large one at the head carries only the name Fox, marking the family plot; the smaller one at the foot bears the inscriptions about Sylvan. Neat shrubs have been planted around the gravesite, but the trees are stripped bare. Following the tradition of marking our visit, we each place the small stones we have brought with us on Sylvan's gravestone. As I stand looking at where Sylvan is buried, transfixed by the sight of his name etched in Hebrew and English and the dates of his birth and death, I am consumed with tears. At the same time, I feel Sylvan standing beside me, telling me that this is only the place where our bones will rest together; our spirits will be free to fly far beyond the cemetery walls. For a few minutes, Ricki and Frank and I stand close together in the rain, and then we leave.

In the days leading up to the anniversary of Sylvan's death, I can't help reviewing again, probably for the hundredth time, the events of his last week, and wondering whether I could have done something that would have helped him, something that would have prevented his death—thoughts that are ultimately irrational but continue nonetheless. Should I have allowed him to be admitted to the hospital? Should I have spent more time with him there? Should I have not left on Friday evening? What was he thinking on Saturday morning before he stopped breathing? How could I not have been with him to say goodbye? And then I keep hearing the phone ringing and the ghastly voice of that doctor who called me. All of it keeps coming back.

On December 22, I search the drawers of a filing cabinet and find copies of the travel pieces that Sylvan wrote for *Newsday.* As I read through them, I hear his voice describing the trips we made, the places we visited, and how much fun we had together, and I am desolate knowing that nothing like that will ever exist for me again. I am with Sylvan all day, looking at photographs of our sixty years together, thinking about the wondrous life we shared, and then ending the day by having a drink with him and telling him how much I love him.

I spend New Year's Eve alone but feel Sylvan's presence. I remember the many years when just the two of us, happy to look forward to the future, celebrated the stroke of midnight with champagne, followed by our ritual of eating herring as the first food of the year. Now, in my loneliness, I dread the thought of facing 2009.

With the beginning of the new year, I am still suffering from guilt about what I think I should have done for Sylvan, augmented now by guilt that has surfaced as I think of events of my childhood: being told that I was the one responsible for my mother's illness, an outrageous accusation, delivered with absolute cruelty, and yet that I accepted as the only explanation for things that were incomprehensible to my ten-year-old self. My guilt is often followed by periods of intense anxiety, reminiscent of what I felt in Levack: abandoned, alone, and helpless. How can those feelings have acquired such strength to haunt me now?

With Brian's help, I manage to survive these episodes, struggling to gain some insight into the significance of events from seventy years ago; but doing so requires the painful debridement of layers of traumatic recollections.

You think that you have shut the door
To keep them from your life. Unwanted ghosts.
You have constructed "no trespassing" signs,
And walls around the house to prevent their intrusion.
Somehow, they enter through invisible cracks

And now sit, confronting you,
Waiting to be acknowledged.

The months of January and February are so filled with doctors' appointments and diagnostic tests that I have little time or energy for anything else. Even with all the information that these examinations provide, my internist seems unable to find a way to relieve me of the debilitating effects of increasingly frequent episodes of atrial fibrillation, uncontrolled hypertension, and the worsening symptoms of my heart's inefficient functioning.

I'm dissatisfied with the attention I'm receiving from my internist, and although I hate the idea of having to start seeing someone new, I decide it's time to find another doctor. Ricki puts me in touch with a highly recommended cardiologist at New York Hospital with whom I make an appointment. After a couple of visits, during which he starts me on a new treatment program, I'm encouraged by his more concerned and confident approach. I'm sure that I was correct in finding a new doctor, and I allow myself to feel some hope that there may be some improvement in my physical health.

With Brian's encouragement, I try to find activities I might find enjoyable. When I hear that the Metropolitan Museum is accepting applications for volunteers, I decide that it might be worth applying. After completing a lengthy questionnaire, then meeting with the director of volunteer services, I'm invited to work at the visitors' information desk on the lower level of the museum on Saturday afternoons. A series of orientation sessions for me and another new volunteer is conducted by our "boss" in volunteer services, whose imperious manner I find particularly annoying.

We're introduced first to the areas and contents of the museum open to the public, which we're advised to commit to memory; and then to fascinating departments, not available to the public, housed in a maze of rooms in the bowels of the basement. The rooms are filled with craftspeople restoring every kind of artwork—paintings on canvas, paintings on wood, works on paper, tapestries, textiles, furnishings from everywhere and every period, ceramics, sculpture in every medium, and on and on. Our tour through this part of the museum, which I find at least as interesting as what's upstairs, is too brief and hurried to satisfy my curiosity. However, what is most essential to us, in our position at the information desk, is knowing how to process the membership cards that visitors present, entitling them to their little metal buttons—a different color every day—that allow them museum entry; and to be able to answer questions from visitors. I will work with a partner at the desk, so that we can assist each other when one of us seems better able to answer a question.

My most enjoyable moments come from my contact with the young children, many of them visiting the museum for the first time, whose parents ask for our advice on what they should take their children to see. The reaction of most of the youngsters when they first come in is to gaze in wide-eyed wonder at the immense, impressive building, amazed when they're told about the treasures they can discover there. Yet, as one might expect in New York, occasionally a six-year-old who is a sophisticated, veteran visitor turns to his father and asks, "Can we please not see any more Monets today?" For the time being, my volunteer work fills Saturday afternoons.

Although I tell myself that being in contact with other people can be beneficial, and Brian has said that pursuing activities can help give me some sense of who I now am, I have to arm myself to withstand the anxiety of presenting myself to others. Sometimes I see myself as a turtle retreating under the protection of a carapace.

I have to accept that I will always feel the loss of Sylvan even as I try to construct a new life. Not so easy to do. Feeling so desolate and hopeless, I have to struggle to go on; I wish I could go to sleep and not wake up.

Grief is an uninvited guest that never leaves me.
It wakes me in the morning,
Then watches silently as I move
From one empty room to another.
It presents itself everywhere,
Taking a place with me at dinner
And tucking me into bed at night.
Good night, grief.
I'll see you in the morning.

If suicide is acceptable for people who are terminally ill and in intractable pain, shouldn't it also be acceptable for people who are in intractable psychological pain? I discuss this at length with Brian, and what is most important to me is that he understands what I am saying, even though the problem may have no satisfactory resolution. "But what if you felt different in a year from now?" he asks. My response is, "But what if I felt even worse?"

More dreams in which I am trying to find Sylvan; but I'm lost and I don't know where to look, and I become frantic when I can't find him. I wake up, depressed and unable to shake the feeling.

I go to visit Mary, my oldest friend, whom I first met when we were students at Juilliard, both of us immigrants, I from Canada and she from what was then Palestine. She is the last person I know with whom I can have serious discussions about music. Mary, alone since her husband, Ed, who was also a musician, died of pancreatic cancer several years ago, is enduring the last stages of metastasizing ovarian cancer. Ironically, Ed and Mary were the most health-conscious people we knew, always adhering to a healthful diet, exercising regularly, and avoiding all known risks to their health. We maintained a close relationship with them over the years in spite of sometimes living great distances apart. It was a friendship in which we could always pick up where we'd left off, fill each other in about the happenings in our lives, and resume the conversation that had been interrupted a few years earlier.

I am the only person left who is close to Mary. When I visit her at her apartment, I am struck by how gaunt she has become from the ravages of the disease and the repeated courses of chemotherapy; but she still has enough energy to spend time at the piano, and tells me with much enthusiasm about discovering new aspects of the Beethoven Hammerklavier Sonata, *which she has played for over sixty years. It is a wonder to see how music remains such a sustaining force in her life. While we are having lunch at a nearby restaurant, I can't dispel the thought that this may be the last time we will have such conversations.*

One day I hear Sylvan saying to me: "Of course, things are not the same as they used to be; you can't do things the way we used to do them together, but you are able to continue leading a life that can bring you pleasure even though I am not there physically with you. Think of how you can spend time with Ricki, how fortunate we are to have her as our daughter. I want you to find some enjoyment in your life."

I ask him, "How?"

"You have to figure that out for yourself." So far, I've had a hard time doing so.

I am trying to construct a person out of transparent bits of colored paper that go flying into the wind as fast as I assemble them.

I've started to do some sketching and watercolor painting again. This is something that still gives me pleasure—another solitary activity that I find comforting. Some of the little paintings are quite good, I think, although I haven't shown them to anyone who can give them an honest critique. They are added to the collection of all the others I've done, filling a large part of a closet, to be taken out occasionally for my review.

I enroll in a sketching class for a few weeks at the Metropolitan Museum that takes me back to the exercise of drawing from statuary, and which I find moderately useful. I consider taking some advanced painting courses somewhere, but I can't bring myself to committing to the discipline it would require.

Brian asks me what I could imagine doing if I thought I had a limited time to live. After much deliberation, I come up with a list that includes walking on the beach in Montauk, seeing the Pacific Ocean from a place like Carmel, visiting the wolf preserve in Washington State, hearing the complete works of Bach, spending some time in a town on the Italian coast, and, of course, spending time in Paris. Everything is something that I would like to do with Sylvan—something that I have done with Sylvan. I think of what Count Basie, the iconic jazz musician, said when he finished one of his most breathtakingly exciting performances: "One more time."

I learn that Sidney, Sylvan's cousin, has died. He was eleven years older than Sylvan, widowed for several years, and had been living in Gaithersburg, Maryland, to be near his daughter Lisa. I accept Lisa's invitation to say a few words at the memorial service to be held in a few weeks. When Ricki and I get together and talk about Sidney—his life, his place in our lives, his death—I am aware that I am the last survivor of Sidney's generation. It's the end of an era in the extended family that spanned from Sophie and Louis to Ricki and her cousins and their offspring.

Being the last survivor is a position I would gladly give up. I have moments when I despair of ever seeing any relief from the pain of loss, which leads me to seeing little attraction in continuing to live; yet intermingled with the pain is the joy of being with Ricki, and of engaging in activities that still excite me: painting, reading, spending time at the piano, listening to music. And I'm still struggling with finding a way to be in the presence of Sylvan while at the same time maintaining an "exterior" life.

I am discouraged that the efforts of my new cardiologist have not brought much success.

I've had atrial fibrillation lasting for days, leaving me weak and unable to function normally. My doctor sends me into the hospital to have a cardioversion, a short procedure under anesthesia that brings about the miracle of getting my heart back into normal rhythm. Unfortunately, my relief lasts only two days before the fibrillation resumes. Now we will try some new medications and consider the possibility of a pacemaker.

Ricki and I attend the memorial service for Sidney in Gaithersburg, where Lisa is hosting the gathering of the clan, assembled for the occasion.

When it is my turn to offer remarks at the service, I talk about the early days when Sidney and Sylvan lived together in the house in East Flatbush, the continuing friendship they maintained throughout their lives, and how they loved to argue and sharpen their debating skills with each other to the very end—and perhaps beyond. Because bringing up those memories is another powerful reminder of loss, I find myself choking on my words. The kindly rabbi, sitting next to the lectern, whispers to me: "Take deep breaths." I follow his advice, regain my composure, and continue.

We return to Lisa's house, where we see relatives we haven't seen in years, little kids grown into big adults, some of them with their own little kids. We are surrounded by Sidney's family and friends, spilling over from one room to the next, in what seems like hours of sharing food and drinks and stories and amusements. I'm impressed by this warm gathering of people who loved Sidney, yet I feel like a bystander, looking on at a celebration in which I can no longer take part, knowing it's time for me to move on.

There are endless days when all I want is to find a way to kill time, kill the pain that never leaves me, and escape from the dreams in which I am still lost somewhere, searching for Sylvan. So I carry out my routine of going to work, volunteering at the museum, seeing a friend occasionally, and seeing Ricki, the only person I really enjoy being with.

I learn that Mary has suffered a massive stroke that rendered her unconscious, and that she fell and landed against a hot radiator, where she remained for hours until her aide arrived in the apartment. In critical condition, she is taken to the burn unit of New York Hospital. According to her written directive, she is not receiving any treatment other than pain medication. When I go to see her, she is barely conscious, immobile, unable to speak, but seemingly able to recognize me. I sit with her and try to assure her of my presence.

I ask the attending doctor how long he thinks Mary is likely to survive in this condition. He tells me that because she is receiving no treatment for her burns that she probably won't last much more than a week. I leave, thinking how cruel life can be in subjecting someone to such a painful death.

During the next week I make almost daily visits to the hospital. The doctor's prognosis seems to be correct. Mary is now in a deep coma, barely clinging to life. On one day, I sit next to her bed, watching her chest slowly rising and falling, broken by long pauses between labored breaths. I hold her hand for the last time and watch as the movement of her chest stops at that impenetrable moment that marks the passage from being to nonbeing. I mourn the loss of Mary, my oldest friend.

If only we could choose the way we die, quickly, peacefully, I would shut my eyes, go to sleep, and go somewhere or nowhere, and return to nothingness. At the same time, I cling with almost a religious conviction to the belief that I will be united with Sylvan.

I have a dream in which some unidentified person approaches me and lays a hand on my shoulder, causing me to shatter into a thousand little pieces of glass on the ground.

How do I reassemble all these pieces into a person? Who would that person be? The theme that occurs in most of my dreams is repeated in endless variations: I do not know where I am, who I am, or where I belong. The anxiety that I am lost in some dark, unknown place spills over into my waking moments, blurring the boundaries between terrifying dreams and hopeless reality.

As a new year begins, I try to find activities that will bring me into contact with other people. Elaine asks me if I would like to join her and some of her friends in getting a subscription to productions at an off-Broadway theater. Since it seems like a reasonable way to ensure my getting out of the house, I accept her invitation, albeit with little enthusiasm.

At about the same time, during a conversation over dinner with Ruth, a woman I've known for a number of years, we both express a wish to find people with whom we can discuss our thoughts about books we are reading. For my part, I know I am reflecting the intense loss of no longer having Sylvan as my constant companion in exploring ideas. Although that can never be replaced, the idea of getting together to share thoughts with compatible people is attractive.

Ruth quickly begins to formulate a plan to get together with a small group of friends with whom we can have serious discussions about works of nonfiction. With Ruth's broad range of contacts, it's not long before we are ready to launch our book group. Our first selection is an autobiography by a woman who is a friend of Ruth's, and who graciously agrees to join us for what turns into a lively, enjoyable discussion.

When I first meet the other women, each one professionally successful, intelligent, articulate, and outgoing, I sense that these are people I would like to associate with. At the same time, I question what I will be able to contribute to the group; my old self-doubts resurface and I wonder if there is anything left of me to be an intelligent participant. To my relief, over time, I gradually acquire a measure of self-confidence and find that the group meeting is a stimulating social activity that I enjoy. Yet, even in this setting, there is a barrier that prevents me from revealing myself as a person—whoever that person may be.

More physical problems: my cardiologist recommends that I get a pacemaker, which, he thinks, when combined with additional medication should correct my atrial fibrillation. I have conflicting feelings about doing this. On the one hand, I don't want to prolong my life; on the other, I don't want to become incapacitated from neglecting my health. I decide to go along with the doctor's recommendation.

I'm admitted to New York Hospital to install the pacemaker—an extremely uncomfortable four-hour procedure under conscious anesthesia. I stay overnight, Ricki picks me up, and I'm home anticipating the next necessary treatments.

My loneliness continues in spite of trying to be engaged in doing things with other people. When I am alone at home, I am torn between simultaneously feeling Sylvan's presence everywhere and the acute pain of feeling his absence. Everything I do is still permeated with the associations I have of doing them with Sylvan. Listening to music is still a crushing experience that brings me to tears, since everything I hear is so closely connected to having heard it with Sylvan. As an experiment, I try not listening to music for periods of time; but rather than preventing tears, it only deprives me of one of my most treasured experiences.

I am taken with the idea of writing the story of the life that Sylvan and I shared together, beginning with our meeting at Juilliard. After starting with that premise, I realize that the story will only make sense if I go back to the beginning of my life, to my childhood and everything that occurred that shaped the person I was when I met Sylvan. As overwhelming as the project seems, and as presumptuous as I am in thinking that I could successfully complete such an undertaking, I am drawn to the idea of preserving the footprints that we left; and as I begin to write I am more and more lured by the challenge.

I decide to make the trip to Burlington, Ontario, to see Don. Ricki and I fly to Toronto for an overnight stay. The city has layers of memories going back to my childhood—many of them distressing to recollect—and continuing through the happier times when Sylvan and I spent time there over the years. Ricki and I drive from Toronto to Burlington and spend a couple of days visiting with Don, Joan, and their son, Tom, and daughter-in-law, Marian. Joan's condition has worsened; in addition to needing constant physical assistance, she is showing obvious signs of psychological problems. I enjoy seeing Don and finding how comfortable I am talking with him, but I am saddened by knowing that it will not be easy to plan future visits.

Days turn into weeks colored with the monotony of depression, broken occasionally by the activities that can still bring me pleasure, the greatest of which are those I do with Ricki and Frank: having brunch, going on an outing somewhere, seeing an exhibit at a gallery. I treasure my time with them and the affection they show me.

I continue to wonder how I can create a life for myself, and, more important, how I can create an identity. There are moments when I feel totally dissociated from the world around me; there is no me, I do not exist, and there is only nothingness around me. It's a strange experience that catches me unawares, that has neither a positive nor a negative emotional tone, and that disappears as mysteriously as it comes. I wonder if this sense of nonbeing is akin to the approach of death.

I think about the word *silence* and its possible meanings. There should be separate expressions to convey all its nuances, in the same way that the Inuit have many ways to refer to snow. These are some of the silences I've thought about:

The silence of an empty room.
The silence of fear.
The imposed silence of a library.
The pregnant silence of waiting.
The silence of a frozen lake.
Silence measured by a ticking clock.
Silence burdened by unspoken thoughts.
The truce of silence after angry words.
The relieved silence after exhalation.
The sublime silence after the last note has been played.
The peaceful silence of understanding.
The silence of remembered voices.
The unending silence of death.

My diaries from these years are filled with accounts of my dreams, of trying to find some pleasure, and of continuing to break into tears when I'm alone at home, although I feel safest there.

After a time, I decide to give up some of the activities that I originally thought would be beneficial to me: I discontinue my Hebrew class because it's become difficult to keep up with the work, and less rewarding as the conversations seem to be increasingly centered on people's trips to Israel, something I can no longer identify with. I stop volunteering at the Metropolitan Museum when I conclude that the director of volunteers is taking advantage of me, and the work is no longer enjoyable. While I continue to attend the theater with the group of women I've met, I am comfortable with acknowledging that I'm unable to develop meaningful relationships with most of them.

In contrast, I enjoy the company of the members of my book group and the discussions we have at our meetings. They provide me with intellectual stimulation, as well as the motivation to pursue some challenging reading. In addition, I continue working once a week at my job in test construction, which is a pleasant exercise for my brain muscles.

More losses: Don's wife, Joan, dies of pneumonia and complications of COPD after repeated hospitalizations. Don and I have a lengthy telephone conversation in which he expresses a mixture of feelings that include both grief and relief that she is no longer suffering. He tells me that he is grateful to be able to talk to me about the conflicting emotions that he is feeling. Again, I am amazed at the strong familial link that survives in spite of long geographic separations.

I tell Don that instead of making a brief trip to attend Joan's memorial service, I will plan a more extended visit in the summer. He agrees it would be better for me to wait. When I go to Burlington later in the year, we have long conversations and enjoy each other's company. In addition to telling me fascinating stories about Sudbury in the 1930s, for the first time Don tells me about what it was like for him during the difficult years in Sudbury and Levack, and his perceptions of the long series of painful events we were both subjected to. I am struck particularly by his description of how he saw our father: lacking the capacity to express affection and appreciation in all his family relationships, while I always thought I was the only one to feel unloved. Don's accounts provide me not only with new information about the events of that period, but also allow me to clarify many of my own memories and associations. After too short a visit, we promise that our conversations will continue.

The counterpoint between my inner and outer life continues.

I think or dream: winter. I'm waiting for Sylvan to come home. When I hear him at the door, I rush to greet him, to kiss him, his face cold from the chill outside. I take his coat from him; he announces, "Let's have a drink," then goes into the kitchen to inspect our dinner cooking on the stove, and to sniff approvingly. "I'm having Scotch. How about you?"

"Sure. It's a good night for Scotch," I answer.

He gives the mail a quick look, puts it aside, and pours our drinks. I get out some cheese and crackers. The radio is playing a section of Vivaldi's *Four Seasons—Winter*.

My moments of greatest pleasure are the ones I spend with Ricki and Frank. Ricki is unfailing in her attention to me, calling me on the phone almost every day, showing her concern about my well-being, and, along with Frank, inviting me out for dinner at a restaurant, or to spend an afternoon together. They take me to a celebratory dinner on my birthday; I enjoy Thanksgiving with them; I delight in seeing how they have decorated their new apartment.

Looking at Ricki, I recall the feeling of "us," of the three of us—Sylvan, Ricki, and me, when we were all very young; it's a lovely feeling. When I look at Ricki, I see Sylvan, although she doesn't bear that much resemblance to him. I realize how fortunate I am to have Ricki as my daughter. My love for her is what sustains me during my darkest hours, the most important part of my exterior life.

I still struggle to be more open with Ricki, to be less afraid to reveal myself to her. I hope that the memoir is an opening, but I have to do more than that.

In 2012, I am faced with one physical problem after another, each one leaving me more physically and mentally depleted and discouraged, and thinking that there is little point in trying to go on. I feel very old and wonder why I cannot join Sylvan. I persevere with writing the memoir, and even take a writing course at the 92nd Street Y to try to get some feedback on what I have put on paper. I can't help thinking how much more eloquently Sylvan would express what I am trying to say. When I tell him this, he says that although he might write it differently, I have to speak in my own words.

Working on the memoir, I'm transported back to the memories of being together with Sylvan in a past that is a more attractive place to inhabit than the present filled with pain. In my sessions with Brian, he assures me that it is possible to find a way of combining a life in the present with a continued connection to Sylvan, an idea I understand intellectually but that is difficult to grasp emotionally.

Early evening is the best time of the day, when I can sit with Sylvan, listen to music that often brings me to tears, and share a closeness that is more real than anything that pretends to be the real world. These are the moments when the poignancy of Sylvan's presence and absence is most compelling.

I look at the two tributaries of my life, the interior and the exterior, each one flowing through a different uncharted landscape that is fascinating in its own way, yet at the same time often frightening. My hope is that I can follow both tributaries until they come together in their ultimate conclusion, accompanied by a final harmonious chord.